Keeping Your Family Together When the World Is Falling Apart

Books by Dr. Kevin Leman

Making Children Mind Without Losing Yours

The Birth Order Book

Bonkers

The Pleasers: Women Who Can't Say No
and the Men Who Control Them

Measuring Up

Smart Kids, Stupid Choices

Sex Begins in the Kitchen

Unlocking the Secrets of Your Childhood Memories

Growing Up Firstborn

Were You Born for Each Other?

Parenthood Without Hassles* (*Well, Almost)

Parent Talk

DR. KEVIN LEMAN

BEST-SELLING AUTHOR OF *THE BIRTH ORDER BOOK*

Keeping Your Family Together When the World Is Falling Apart

PUBLISHING
Colorado Springs, Colorado

KEEPING YOUR FAMILY TOGETHER WHEN THE WORLD IS FALLING APART

Copyright © 1992, 1993 by Dr. Kevin Leman

Library of Congress Cataloging in Publication Data
Leman, Kevin.
Keeping your family together when the world is falling apart / Kevin Leman.
   p. cm.
Originally published: New York: Delacorte Press, ©1992
Includes bibliographical references.
ISBN 1-56179-180-6 [Formerly published by Delacorte Press under the ISBN 0440-50516-X]
1. Family—United States.   2. Marriage—United States.
3. Discipline.   I. Title.
[HQ536.L45 1993]
306.85'0973—dc20   93-5068
                                            CIP

Published by Focus on the Family Publishing, Colorado Springs, Colorado 80920. Reprinted by arrangement with Delacorte Press.

Distributed in the U.S.A. and Canada by Word Books, Dallas, Texas.

Jacket design © 1993 by Andrew Newman.
Jacket photo © Tony Stone Images.
Photo of Dr. Leman and his family by David E. Anderson, Jamestown, New York.

Printed in the United States of America

94 95 96 97/10 9 8 7 6 5 4 3 2

I affectionately dedicate this book
and the rest of my life
to my wife, Sande;
daughters Holly, Krissy, Hannah, and Lauren;
and my son, Kevin II.

Contents

PART III
LEMAN'S SECOND LAW:
TO KEEP YOUR BALANCE AS PARENTS,
ALWAYS BE READY TO PULL THE RUG OUT
FROM UNDER THEM

Prologue

A S A PERSON WHO TRAVELS THE COUNTRY REGULARLY AND ACCUMU-
lates more frequent flyer miles than I care to admit, I confess
that when I board a plane, I sometimes put on headphones just to
communicate to my seat mates, "I'm tired, and I don't want to
talk." One time, however, on a flight from Norfolk, Virginia, back
to my home city of Tucson, Arizona, I got into a conversation with
a man in his late 60s. It turned out that he was from Tucson, too.

I learned the man was from one of the pioneer families of Tucson. We chatted about the city and its history, and then he asked
what I do for a living and why I had been in Virginia. I never know
how to respond to the job question. If I tell people I'm a psychologist, I often get a response like, "Oh, are you going to psychoana-
lyze me?" If I say I'm with a ministry, they usually won't order a second light beer. Either way, things get a little awkward. So I simply
said, "I was here to do a television show."

"What do you mean 'do a television show'?" he asked. "Were
you a guest on it?"

"That's right," I said.

"What did you talk about?"

"Oh, family, marriage, kids, discipline, the sad state of families
today—things like that."

He then asked what kinds of things I had said, and I gave him
a brief description of some of the concepts you'll read in this book.

When I had finished, he replied, "Young man, those are some

wonderful ideas you've got there. How did you learn such things at your age?"

Reflexively, without any forethought, I responded, "Actually, I got them all from one book."

"Really?" he said incredulously. "One book?" He reached inside his jacket and pulled a note pad out of his pocket so he could write down the title of this amazing book. "What's the name of it?" he asked.

"Well, it's called the Bible," I said. "That's B-i-b-l-e. There's one part in particular that provides the foundation for a lot of what I have to say. It was written by the apostle Paul in Ephesians 6:1-4."

I then quoted the passage to him from *The Living Bible:*

> Children, obey your parents; this is the right thing to do because God has placed them in authority over you. Honor your father and mother. This is the first of God's Ten Commandments that ends with a promise. And this is the promise: that if you honor your father and mother, yours will be a long life, full of blessing. And now a word to you parents. Don't keep on scolding and nagging your children, making them angry and resentful. Rather, bring them up with the loving discipline the Lord himself approves, with suggestions and godly advice.

What I told the man that day was true. In recent years, I've been making a special effort to reach the vast secular audience with what I've learned about marriage and parenting, so I don't always quote Scripture as much as I could in my writing. But the principles I espouse always have been and always will be based squarely on the truth of God's Word. The passage I just quoted is the foundation for this particular book, as you'll see in the opening chapters.

When we seek God's guidance and strength for daily living, we can't help but benefit. And parents and spouses have never needed

His help more, because our modern world is anything but family friendly. For more about that, turn to the first chapter.

My hope is that as you read through the book, you'll take the time and effort to do one or more of the practical application exercises at the end of each chapter. And my prayer is that as you do, all aspects of your family life will grow healthier and happier.

Part I

Leman's Initial Observation:

The Real World Is Not Family Friendly

Chapter 1

"Can Your Family Beat the Odds?"

It's a World That Is Not Family Friendly

"The odds are definitely against the average family."
I mutter these words every day as I drive home from my office after counseling:

- a couple about to separate because she had found a very explicit letter from his "new friend";
- a sixteen-year-old who had tried to commit suicide because her parents "didn't care";
- a single mother at the end of her rope because two of her four kids (all of them under twelve) are on drugs.

And that's just a typical morning shift! As I look at my counseling caseload, I can see that the red-throated warblesnipe is not really our most endangered species. The family is. If you doubt this, all you have to do is look at what the odds keep saying:

The odds say that more than one out of two marriages will fail. If it's a remarriage, it's almost two out of three.

The odds say that the typical couple about to walk down the aisle is guaranteed a marriage that will last about seven years—less than the life of their washer, dryer, or refrigerator.

The odds say that you and your kids will be approached by drug pushers, or at least by peers who want you and your family to light up and be part of the fun.

The odds say that if you have two or three kids, at least one will be a "powerful little buzzard" whose behavioral problems may threaten to drive you crazy.

The odds say that in your family, Mom is already working or will choose to go to work in the near future. And when Mom works, she is an odds-on favorite to become stressed out while she tries to have and do it all.

THE EPIDEMIC OF DYSFUNCTIONALISM

There are many causes for the family's turmoil today. The media constantly report the tragedies of divorce, delinquency, inadequate education, and unwanted pregnancies. Crime is on the increase, often connected to alcohol and drug abuse. Clinical terms like *dysfunctional family, co-dependency, enabling, toxic parents,* and *ACOA* (Adult Children of Alcoholics) have become standard vocabulary. In fact, from the number of articles and books written on these subjects, it looks as if we have an epidemic of dysfunctionalism and co-dependency on our hands.

The best definition I have seen of *co-dependency* simply says: "An addiction to people, behaviors, or things."[1] According to the Minirth-Meier Clinic, the term *co-dependent* has been around for several decades now, originating with efforts to help alcoholics and their families. The best known of any of these organizations or movements is Alcoholics Anonymous (AA).

As AA began having some success working with problem

drinkers, it made an interesting discovery. As soon as it managed to get an alcoholic to stop drinking, his or her family would often come apart at the seams. As AA workers sought the reason, they learned that just as the alcoholic had been dependent on his alcohol, his family had been dependent on helping him with his alcoholism. They had adjusted their entire lives to dealing with the alcoholic's habits, and they didn't know how to function without this problem in their midst. In other words, they became dysfunctional (unable to function normally), caught in a vicious circle of co-dependency.[2]

I know the epidemic of dysfunctionalism is real—inside the church as well as outside—because I work constantly with families who have been infected by its deadly virus, and not all of them are involved with alcohol. A wide range of problems creates and affects dysfunctional families, including physical and emotional abuse, infidelity, eating disorders, sexual addiction, and incest.

One easily overlooked but every bit as devastating addiction that ruins many marriages is workaholism. Until recent years, husbands were the major culprits, but now more and more wives are falling into the same trap. Yes, "We've come a long way, baby," and now women are increasingly complaining of stress disorders such as ulcers, anxiety attacks, and heart problems.

The impact of "recreational drugs" alone is monumental. I regularly see the results of the use of cocaine sitting right before me in my office. These people aren't sniffling, bleary-eyed, ragged junkies, fresh out of the alleys of New York or some other asphalt jungle. They are bright, articulate community leaders, people with good jobs and responsible positions in major businesses.

I've had to restructure my vocabulary and interview techniques. Rather than ask a patient, "Have you ever taken drugs?" I now ask, "When did you start doing coke?" And then I hear the sad story again. It was supposed to be just a little recreational fun, I'm told, but now it's a major priority—in some cases, *the* major priority in that person's life. And his or her family? They come in a very distant second.

Recently, a mother of four small children sat in my office and told me what it was like to be married to a man who had become a heavy user of cocaine. She had taken a job as a waitress to help support the family while her husband, a sales representative for a major firm, had gone through "intervention treatment" twice. She described him as a "nice guy but very compulsive." Coke had taken over his life, and he was now abusing not only the drug, but her and the children as well. Theirs is only one case of the many I see that confirms that abuse of cocaine and other drugs cuts across all economic lines.

HOW DID FAMILIES GET INTO THIS MESS?

The question I am always seeking to answer is "Why? Why does a family become dysfunctional and even co-dependent?" And right along with that, "Why are a lot of other families right at the brink of having the same kinds of problems?"

All the handles or labels such as *co-dependency* and *dysfunctional* are useful in describing the problems affecting families, but I am just old-fashioned enough to reduce these problems to some pretty basic causes and effects.

At the top of my list of basic causes is what I call "perplexing priorities." One major reason the families of our nation are in trouble is that *moms and dads are not really putting each other, or the family, first.*

Oh, they like to tell me they are. I've had many husbands and fathers explain that they are out there breaking their necks, backs, and other parts of their anatomy sixty and seventy hours a week for "Marge and the kids." And I have plenty of wives tell me that, though they'd prefer to be at home with the children, "unless I work, we can't cover all the payments."

I don't doubt the sincerity of my clients for a moment. The

consumer society in which we live bombards the family twenty-four hours a day with "Buy, buy, buy, buy now! Pay later." As the 1980s opened, a beer company's catchy slogan grabbed the imagination of the entire country. "You can have it all" sounded good, but a lot of people discovered that "having it all" can be very expensive, as well as time-consuming and energy-draining. By the time the eighties ended, *Lifestyles of the Rich and Famous* was ready to be replaced by what Art Levine called *Lifestyles of the Tired and Obscure*.[3]

Now that we have moved into the nineties, many families are realizing that "having it all" was a fantasy. They are discovering that "just staying even" is a real challenge. I don't think it's any coincidence that in 1990, the rate of bankruptcies reached an all-time high.

Fighting the economic battle takes two paychecks in many families. In the majority of families I see, the "working mom" is a definite reality. Gone are Harriet Nelson and June Cleaver, the perfectly groomed mothers of 1950s TV fame. I'm not sure Harriet and June ever existed in the real world, but they do symbolize a bygone era when Mom spent her days on the home front instead of at the office.

I sympathize with working moms because I deal with so many of them. And I'm also concerned about what our present way of life in American society is doing to the family as it draws so many women into the workplace for whatever reason.

I'm not much for quoting statistics, but the numbers on working women have to leap up and hit anybody between the eyes. In the early 1930s, fewer than 20 percent of the women in the United States worked outside the home. By 1988, 57.1 percent of married women with children under the age of six were marching off every morning, briefcase in hand, to help bring home the bacon.[4] That means leaving little Kyle or Katie at home with a sitter (if they're lucky) or, more likely, at the local kiddy kennel.

Not long ago, I talked with an upwardly mobile couple whose

three-year-old son was having problems at preschool. Both parents worked in important administrative positions, and they dropped their child off at the preschool at 7:30 every morning, not picking him up until 5:45 at night. They came to see me because the little boy had begun striking out at other children, pushing them down, and, in general, causing a lot of disruption for the preschool staff.

"We are trying to work on his facial expressions," the mother started to explain.

"Excuse me," I interrupted. "What do you mean by *facial expressions?*"

"We try to help him know there are really two faces—a positive face and a sober, sad face."

"What about all the other faces and expressions we see on little children?" I asked.

They both gave me a blank look. Didn't I understand that they were trying to help their little boy accentuate the positive? they seemed to ask. These parents meant well, but they had lost touch with their child. They were making him follow every bit as tough a schedule as they did—ten hours a day, five days a week. In my opinion, a three-year-old can handle preschool two days a week, perhaps three hours a morning. Anything beyond that and I'm not surprised by acting-out behavior—hitting, pushing, or worse.

I realize that in some cases—particularly when single mothers have to work—leaving the child with extended care is the only choice. In the case of this acting-out three-year-old, however, the parents were able to make other arrangements and cut down the preschool time for their little boy. His behavior improved almost immediately.

WE HAVE LIBERATED MOM, BUT TO WHAT?

In case you think working wives and mothers are a rather recent phenomenon, you should realize that back in 1975, Dr. Urie Bronfenbrenner, a leading family authority, reported that between 1947 and 1975, the number of working wives rose from 6.5 million to 19.8 million—a 205 percent increase! Bronfenbrenner called this development "one of the most significant economic facts of our time." He also noted that this increase in working women "began before the so-called women's liberation movement and has unquestionably brought many new opportunities and greater satisfaction to numerous wives and mothers. But it has also had a major impact on American child-rearing."[5]

It's interesting to note that Dr. Bronfenbrenner made this masterful understatement *more than fifteen years ago,* before the goal of "having it all" really came into vogue. Yes, we have liberated Mom, but to what? True, she is no longer barefoot, pregnant, and chained to the kitchen. Now we might find her clad in Gucci shoes and putting off having children in order to pursue her career as she works her way up to the boardroom, then runs to catch the next shuttle to Boston. Or even more likely, she's wearing Reeboks, manning the checkout counter at K Mart, and letting shoppers know about the next "blue light special."

The census bureau reports that one-fourth of the nation's working wives now earn more than their husbands. Eight million wives are primary breadwinners today, compared with six million in 1981 and four million in 1977. Some two million earn at least twice as much as their husbands. Harvard University economist Dr. David E. Bloom has said: "It's a fact the higher the woman's earnings, the higher the chance of divorce."[6]

Statistics like these aren't conclusive proof of anything, but the evidence is there: When the woman leaves home to go to work, either out of expediency or out of a drive for a more fulfilling career, there is a price that must be paid. More to the point, there are new pressures that must be dealt with, and that is what this book attempts to do—help families deal with those pressures rather than just drift with the tide that has caught millions in its grip. Yes, two-paycheck families may be the norm because economic times are tough—but while we're busy paying the bills, what about the family itself? How can we rethink our attitudes, goals, and values to ensure the family's security and survival?

THE ROOTLESSNESS OF THE NUCLEAR FAMILY

Another major reason for our perplexing priorities that often goes unnoticed or unrecognized today is the typical rootlessness of the American family. The term *nuclear family* has been around now for a long time. It simply means a family with a nucleus consisting of Mom, Dad, and the kids who have little or no contact with their grandparents, aunts, uncles, or cousins. In many cases, all these extended family members live hundreds, if not thousands, of miles away—"back East somewhere"—from the single family unit that has established its little nuclear nest in the West.

The move from east to west is exactly what happened in my own family's case. I grew up in the small community of Williamsville, New York, not too far from Buffalo, in western New York State. My father was one of four Leman brothers—Irish immigrants who all grew up in Buffalo, dirt poor, with only an eighth-grade education. My mother, a Norwegian, came from an immigrant family of nine that had also settled in the New York area. At one time, I had thirteen aunts and uncles and 108 first and second cousins!

We didn't get together every weekend, but we got together enough to keep everyone aware that there was tremendous support, interest, and concern in the Leman clan. For Thanksgiving and Christmas, it would usually be just our immediate family, with only fourteen to sixteen people. But on a birthday or a special anniversary, there could easily be fifty to sixty people in our backyard, and on the special "family reunion" days, we topped one hundred.

Not only did I draw strength from our overloaded family photo album, but I also had the privilege of growing up in a community where people actually talked to and trusted one another. Neighbors would come over to borrow sugar, milk, or maybe just an egg. People came out at night and talked from porch to porch, or perhaps they met at the back fence to chat.

There was something about being part of all that that's difficult to explain, except perhaps with words like *stability, integrity, balance*—and *spiritual values.* I chafed under my mother's insistence that we march down to the little Covenant church every Sunday. In fact, I often sneaked out of the balcony, when she was gullible enough to let me sit there with my friends, to spend my offering on candy at the dairy bar down the block. We were always back just as the closing hymn was being sung, and Mom was none the wiser.

Despite my rebellious antics, my mother role-modeled something that became a very real part of my life. Years later, it helped steer me back to the right path after I had flunked out of just about every opportunity life had sent my way.

Perhaps some would accuse me of sentimental nostalgia, but I think there's more to my childhood memories than that. Our families today are missing the boat in so many ways. My kids don't play out in the street as I did when I was young. Kick the Can and Red Light, Green Light have been replaced by high-tech gadgetry. Nintendo is the name of the game, and millions of kids sit for hours staring at Mario as he bounces dauntlessly through all kinds of perils to his destination.

There are nine families on our street, and we have only a nodding acquaintance with three of them. You might point out that this is our fault as much as it is theirs, and I'm sure that's true. But I'm only being honest in admitting that I and my family have been sucked into the isolated life of the nuclear family, and that the huge extended family I knew as a boy is only a memory.

Nonetheless, I try to renew those memories by getting back to my roots as often as I can. My Aunt Ruthie lives in the Buffalo area, not far from Uncle Herbie, the last of the Leman brothers. Every time I go through the Buffalo airport, I try to arrange a brief layover so I can drop in on Uncle Herbie, who lives just a mile or two away. Uncle Herbie is my last link to my dad, who died in 1983. He is so much like his brother, it's almost as if I am talking to my father when we have our chats.

There usually isn't enough time to get down to see Aunt Ruthie, who lives at least thirty miles out of Buffalo, but I still try to connect with her whenever I can. A few years ago, when I surprised my mother with a trip to Norway, I included, as part of the gift, an opportunity to take her little sister Ruthie along.

What I always remember about Aunt Ruthie is the Christmas wrapping she would use on all her gifts. Every year, Aunt Ruthie's presents were covered with little snowmen, and I knew that whatever she had given me would be something I would like—not a belt or a shirt but an-honest-to-Tonka-truck toy of some kind. Aunt Ruthie had a family of her own, and she knew what boys wanted at Christmas.

I also make it a point to bring my family back to my roots every summer. We stay in a cottage on Chautauqua Lake, near Jamestown, not far from Williamsville. We spent this past Christmas there as well, and it was the first time our Arizona-raised kids had seen snow on Christmas Day.

BACK TO OUR ROOTS IN A GRAVEYARD

So intent am I to connect our children with the extended Leman family that I dream up special little field trips exactly for that purpose. One summer day a few years back, when our girls were just starting into their teens and Kevin was still a little guy, I bundled the whole family into the car and headed from Williamsville over to a little town called Gowanda, about thirty miles south of Buffalo. My destination was a cemetery, but I didn't let everyone know that at first.

As we drove along, I pointed out various landmarks:

"That's where Daddy used to go fishing." "That's where Daddy played his first Little League game."

I fully expected my kids to be all eyes and ears. Instead, I glanced in the rearview mirror and saw one of my teenage daughters with her eyes closed in obvious bliss. She was all ears, all right—bobbing her head back and forth to whatever was coming in over the headphones connected to her Walkman.

Undaunted, I drove on to the cemetery just outside Gowanda. As we pulled up to the gate and my kids realized that *this* was where I was taking them, there were cries of dismay. Dad had really lost it—probably eating too much oat bran again.

But I didn't mind. I knew my kids had never been to a cemetery, much less the cemetery that held the Leman family plot. When I told them there was a headstone in that cemetery with our family's name on it, they perked up in a hurry. "You mean it actually says *Leman?*" Krissy asked.

"Yep," I replied sagely.

"All right!" they all chorused, and then they were off like a shot as if they were looking for gold. At least twenty minutes later, I heard cries of "We found it, we found it." Sure enough, there was the Leman headstone, surrounded by many other smaller markers in the family plot. We wound up taking pictures with the kids draped all over "our" headstone.

My wife, Sande, didn't say much. She isn't keen on wandering around cemeteries; she'd much rather haunt antique shops. But she knew this cemetery expedition was important to me, so she was supportive, if not enthusiastic.

For me, it was a day I won't forget. Like my wife and children, I had never visited this cemetery before. I distinctly recall the almost eerie feeling I got as we looked at the Leman headstone and all those other grave markers that were mute testimony to how quickly life passes. There was Uncle Val, Great-Aunt Fannie, and my Great-Grandfather John Henry Leman. Oh, yes, and there, in a corner of the plot, was my grandfather's marker—Joseph Leman, who froze to death one night after collapsing drunk in a snowbank. All of them had been real people, living out their lives with their own families, and now they were gone.

I tell you this story not to indulge my own nostalgia but to remind you that your family's roots are very important, too. So many families I know are missing out on this. Do you think Alex Haley's book and the miniseries were successful simply on the strength of Haley's excellent writing? Of course not. Haley was a fine writer, but in *Roots* he struck a chord that goes much deeper. What *Roots* said to millions was: "If you don't know where you came from, you'll never get to where you want to go."

I'm afraid too many families have sacrificed something precious in the name of chasing the great American dream by pulling up stakes and heading across the country to a "can't-miss business opportunity" or a long-worked-for vice presidency in the corporation. I know economics are a very real part of life, but I still wonder if we are not sacrificing some basic things on the altar of "having it all" or at least "having our piece of the pie."

Not long ago, an editor from a magazine doing an article about the migration of families from the Northeast to the Sunbelt called me. I'm not sure why the magazine picked me. I guess the staff knew I live in Arizona, and they wanted my insight on the desirability of living in Sunbelt country.

"Well," I said to the editor, "I think that young couples today should live as close to one set of grandparents as possible."

After a long moment of silence, the voice on the other end of the line said, "I think you misunderstood my question."

"No, I think you misunderstood my answer, and I stand by that answer," I said.

Of course, all I was telling this editor was that in moving clear across the country, you can lose something, and when you lose both sets of grandparents, you have often lost an awful lot indeed.

GROWING UP ABSURD IN THE 1990s

Another question I'm often asked is, "Do you think kids have it tougher today than they did back when you were young?"

My answer is obviously yes, for many reasons, some of which I have been touching on in this chapter. Kids growing up today are living in an absurd society that puts pressures on them that were unheard of one and two generations back. I've never seen a better summary of these pressures than the following letter sent to Ann Landers:

> Dear Ann: The reader signed "Georgia," who lived through the Depression and described how hard it was to be a teenager in the '30s, said kids today have an easy time of it compared to teens in his day. You said you couldn't argue with him. Well, I can.
>
> Let me ask your generation a few questions.
>
> Are your parents divorced? Almost every one of my friends comes from a broken home.
>
> Were you thinking about suicide when you were 12?
>
> Did you have an ulcer when you were 16?
>
> Did your best friend lose her virginity to a guy she went out with twice?
>
> You may have had to worry about VD, but did you have to worry about AIDS?
>
> Did your classmates carry guns and knives?
>
> How many kids in your class came to school regularly drunk, stoned or high on drugs?
>
> Did any of your friends have their brains fried from using PCP?
>
> What percentage of your graduating class also graduated from a drug and alcohol rehabilitation center?
>
> Did your school have armed security guards in the halls?
>
> Did you ever live in a neighborhood where the sound of gunfire at night was normal?
>
> You talk a lot about being dirt poor and having no money. Since when does money mean happiness? The

kids at school who have the expensive cars and designer clothes are the most miserable.

When I am your age, Georgia, I won't do much looking back, I'll just thank God that I survived.

—OTHER SIDE OF THE STORY IN INDIANAPOLIS[7]

Other Side of the Story is obviously a member of the younger generation, which knows plenty about trying to cope in a world that is falling apart. Her letter to Ann vividly catalogs why the real world is so family unfriendly. In fact, the real world is just plain dangerous. Across the land, especially in larger cities, more and more football games are being played in the afternoon rather than at night. The reason? There is too much gang activity and violence at these games after dark.

Gang activity has become a form of warfare on our city streets, and they aren't necessarily streets in the large cities like New York and Los Angeles. According to *U.S. News & World Report*, "Disputes once settled with fists are now settled with guns. Every 100 hours, more youths die on the streets than were killed in the Persian Gulf."[8]

Protecting members of the family against violence is becoming a major concern. One set of statistics says that one out of four people will be a victim of a violent crime in his or her lifetime. Recently, I read of door locks being developed especially for the working parents of latchkey kids. When the child arrives at home and unlocks the door, his key, encoded in some way with his identity, triggers a phone call to Mom's or Dad's office, and a recorded message tells the parent that the child has arrived safely at home.[9]

We could go on wringing our hands about drugs, divorce, and dangers to latchkey kids, but it's time to ask if there is any way to beat the odds. What can we do to straighten out our perplexed priorities and get us back to basics? I don't have any instant miracle cures, but I do know of a way to beat the odds and win!

No family has to give up and resign itself to becoming dysfunctional because "that's the way things are." Your family does not have to be like everybody else's. You can change—in fact, you *must* change some basic ways of operating, or you could deteriorate or even self-destruct.

I know it can be done, because I've seen it happen in my family and in thousands of other families. People are successfully keeping their families together, and I'm not talking about idyllic households where problems never get any bigger than the ones Robert Young faced on "Father Knows Best." In the real world, families have problems—and some of them are whoppers. As Scott Peck puts it, "Life is difficult. . . . life is a series of problems."

But then Peck adds: "Do we want to moan about these problems or solve them? Do we want to teach our children to solve them?"[10]

I believe families can solve many of their problems by using the plan of action I describe in the rest of this book. It is a way of living that will make it possible to preserve your marriage and parent your kids with a minimum of hassle and heartache and a maximum of the fulfillment and joy the Creator intended when He designed the family in the first place.

What is my plan of action? I'm almost afraid to tell you, because you may dismiss it as "too simple." After all, your life has some genuinely complex problems and challenges.

I understand that. My life has a few complex challenges, too, and I'll be describing them later. I am still confident, however, that the plan of action I call Reality Discipline can make all the difference. When faithfully practiced, Reality Discipline brings all kinds of benefits to your family. For one thing, it fosters true love, mutual respect, and self-discipline on each person's part. The family using Reality Discipline *together* develops balance and coping power to handle the stress of everyday life.

What is Reality Discipline, and how does it work? I'll give you a brief survey in the next chapter.

Don't Forget . . .
- Our nation faces an epidemic of dysfunctionalism and co-dependency because too many husbands and wives, mothers and fathers, have not really been putting each other or the family first.
- Like it or not, we must admit that when Mother leaves home to go to work, a price must be paid.
- Family roots are important. They provide stability, integrity, balance, and spiritual values.
- Today's children and youth face challenges, problems, and dangers that were unheard of two or three generations ago.

And Why Not Try . . .
- Talk with your spouse, and ask yourselves, "Are we putting our family first?" List evidence for or against how much you put your family (and that includes your marriage) first—ahead of career, community, or church involvement.
- Together with your spouse, think of one thing you can do in the next week that will build closeness within your nuclear family—perhaps something as simple as playing a game of Monopoly together one night.
- If it's time your family "got back to its roots," plan a get-together with extended family members, or plan to take a trip back to where Mom and Dad grew up. If a trip is not possible soon, plan ways to reach out more often to touch other family members—by mail or by phone.

Chapter 2

What's Good for the Kids Can Be Better for the Whole Family

———————●———————

Using Reality Discipline in Any Situation

A FEW YEARS AGO, I WROTE A BOOK ABOUT CHILD REARING CALLED *Making Children Mind Without Losing Yours*. In the foreword, I coined the term *Reality Discipline* and said:

> As a psychologist and a parent with three children of my own, I am enthused about this book because I believe Reality Discipline is an idea whose time has come. What is Reality Discipline? Reality Discipline is a consistent, decisive, and respectful way for parents to love and discipline their children.[1]

In *Making Children Mind*, I tried to help parents see the difference between discipline and punishment, between loving their kids and smothering them with permissiveness. I tried to help parents answer questions like:

- How do I love my children?
- How do I respect my children?
- How do I hold my children accountable?

After years of counseling, I was sure these were questions parents wanted answered. And I was right. *Making Children Mind Without Losing Yours* became a best-seller. Typical of the letters I received about how Reality Discipline can work in a family were these:

- From a mother with three sons, ages eight down to two: "I read every book I can find about parenting, but none has helped me with my boys as much as yours. Your methods make sense, and I'm finally able to keep all three of them under control without feeling like I'm a dictator while doing it."
- From a divorced single mom with four children: "Your book must have been written just for me. My kids had me headed for the cuckoo nest, but Reality Discipline literally saved my sanity. I always knew what I wanted to do, but I had no way of pulling it off. Your book gave me step-by-step instructions."
- And a father wrote: "Your 'Reality Discipline' techniques have changed our lives. My kids, ages seven and four, are much more cooperative and respectful. My wife respects me for my new attitude and way of dealing with the children. Our family has an entirely new outlook on life!"

Letters like these would make any author feel good, especially the one from the husband, which I may have framed. Letters from men on family matters are rare; women outnumber them possibly a hundred to one, as far as my mail is concerned.

One other letter that came in is also very special because it suggested to me why the world might need another book on the family. A thirty-three-year-old mother of children ages thirteen down to three wrote this about *Making Children Mind:* "It dawned on me, after reading your book and seeing how well its ideas work with child rearing, that much of what you say also applies to adults—particularly husbands and wives. My husband and I have been through it, but we are beginning to see some positive changes by using the same techniques and applying them to our marriage."

In recent years, as the plight of the family has become even more desperate than it was when I wrote that book, I have heard other comments and testimony convincing me that Reality Discipline is an idea whose full potential has not yet been realized. As I listen to people tell me their family troubles, I continue to see that Reality Discipline not only applies to parenting children, but to the whole family as well, especially the basic husband-and-wife unit, where everything starts and around which everything and everyone must revolve. In this book, then, I want to revise my definition of Reality Discipline and put it this way:

Reality discipline is a consistent, decisive, and respectful way
for you to manage your personal life, your marriage, and your
children with love, respect, and effectiveness.

IT ALL STARTS WITH FACING THE CONSEQUENCES

You see, Reality Discipline is based on a concept that has been around for quite some time. That concept has its roots in the work of psychiatrists like Rudolph Dreikurs.[2] He believed that the best way to rear a child is to let life do the disciplining, letting children face the consequences of their own behavior. Actually, Dreikurs wasn't the first one to think of this principle. You can find the same basic idea in the biblical reminder that all of us "reap what we sow."[3]

In *Making Children Mind*, I tried to show parents how using Reality Discipline can help them avoid punishing children and concentrate on training them to be accountable and responsible. Instead of having to play the "heavy," you simply depend on reality to do the admonishing and disciplining.

For me, the apostle Paul said it best in Ephesians 6:1-4 (TLB), which I quoted earlier but which bears repeating:

> Children, obey your parents; this is the right thing to do because God has placed them in authority over you. Honor your father and mother. This is the first of God's Ten Commandments that ends with a promise. And this is the promise: that if you honor your father and mother, yours will be a long life, full of blessing. And now a word to you parents. Don't keep on scolding and nagging your children, making them angry and resentful. Rather, bring them up with the loving discipline the Lord himself approves, with suggestions and godly advice.

Paul also wrote in Colossians 3:21, "Fathers, do not embitter your children, or they will become discouraged."

The idea in those verses that Reality Discipline fits so beautifully is that we're to train our kids without nagging, without browbeating, without exasperating them. Instead of "losing it," as so often and easily happens, we're to discipline in a way that shows them loving respect yet holds them accountable for their decisions. And that's exactly what Reality Discipline does.

Reality Discipline centers on rules or agreements set up ahead of time, with the understanding that if you fail to obey those rules or meet those agreements, you will have to face certain consequences. Parents can use Reality Discipline by telling their children:

- Don't eat your dinner and it gets fed to Bowser (or the garbage disposal), and no snacks for you when the hunger pangs hit just before bedtime.

- Neglect to straighten up your room as you agreed to do by Friday, and you can't go to the big slumber party you've been anticipating all week.
- Fail to cut the lawn for the big family barbecue on Sunday, and Mom and Dad will hire your little brother to do it—paying him, of course, out of *your* allowance.
- Misbehave during piranha hour (when Mom is trying to make dinner), and go to bed with no TV, even though your favorite program is on tonight.
- If you are noisy while Mom is on the phone, she will have to put you in another room until she completes her call. (I even know of some parents who have locked their children outside until their phone calls are over, providing the weather isn't too inclement.)

But Reality Discipline doesn't have to be limited to children. Adults know all about paying the price for certain attitudes or behaviors. For example:

- Put the "pedal to the metal," and wind up doing one day's time in traffic school (as I did not long ago).
- Fail to pay your bills, and receive a less-than-friendly letter or phone call. Continue to fail to pay your bills, and find yourself without water, phone service, electricity—or even your house.
- Be continuously late for work, and get a reprimand or eventually a pink slip.

Those are just a few ideas. Just start to think about it at all, and you can see how the disciplines of reality can come to bear in all kinds of basic and simple ways. Another few obvious examples:

- Succumb to the after-dinner cup of coffee, and spend the rest of the night tossing, turning, and muttering about how you knew better, but . . .

- Stay up watching Leno and Letterman, and be mistaken for a zombie at work the next day.
- Fail to take five minutes to stop for gas, and spend two hours hoofing it back to a gas station when you run out on the freeway.

APPLYING REALITY DISCIPLINE TO "REAL ADULT LIFE"

I told you all this would probably sound too simple, but hang in there and hear me out. I was doing a radio talk show one night, and someone called in and said, "Well, I just have to comment that what I like about what I'm hearing is that you've made it simple."

"I appreciate that," I responded. "But to tell you the truth, if someone said to me, 'Your assignment is to make this complex,' I wouldn't know how to do it."

In other words, K.I.S.S. (Keep It Simple, Stupid) is much more than just a cute slogan. I am fully convinced that applying Reality Discipline to your "real adult world" can make a tremendous difference. Reality Discipline will make you aware that certain consequences are always caused by certain actions and attitudes. This awareness will help you plan and control your life much more effectively. I know that Reality Discipline takes the hassle out of parenting. But beyond that, Reality Discipline can strengthen your marriage, and it can help you manage, guide, nurture, and train the person who is your biggest problem. (No, no, not your spouse: *you!*)

In short, Reality Discipline works with and for the entire family, even people outside the family, as you keep the following principles in mind:

REALITY DISCIPLINE PRINCIPLE NO. 1:
THE WHOLE IS ALWAYS MORE IMPORTANT THAN THE PARTS.

In other words, the wishes, desires, selfishness, or greed of one person in the family can never become more important than the total family itself. This means husbands must become servants rather than autonomous providers who keep their own schedules and do pretty much as they please. It also means that wives must become aware that the total family begins with their mate, not with caring for the kids. (More on this later.) And it certainly means that the tail doesn't wag the dog. Kids are not to be in control, running the parents from pillar to post to pandemonium with their demands and antics. (There will be a lot more on this later.)

REALITY DISCIPLINE PRINCIPLE NO. 2:
HAVE VALUES, AND LIVE BY THEM.

I hear a lot of talk about the importance of "traditional" or basic values, but most of the people who come to me for counseling don't seem to have a clue about what those values might be— or they are totally disillusioned because their values have not worked. I tell them their real values are definitely at work. What they feel is *really important* are the values that are controlling their lives. They may *say* they have values like honesty, integrity, faithfulness, and love, but what they actually do with their time says something much different or they wouldn't be there paying me to listen to their problems.

When your values actually affect how you live, you operate according to "pre-made" choices. You don't make snap decisions or just follow your feelings at the moment.

When my wife, Sande, became pregnant at age forty-seven, she learned that the obstetrician who had delivered our other children had long since retired from practice. The new doctor began explaining the dangers of an over-forty pregnancy and listing options Sande might want to consider if tests showed the baby might have some "problems."

After he went on for several minutes, Sande interrupted him. "I don't understand why we have to do all these tests," she said.

Trying to look patient, the physician explained, "Well, to

repeat, at your age, the chances of giving birth to a child that is defective in some way are extremely high, and we need to take all these tests to make sure your child will be healthy."

"I still don't understand," Sande said, "because it wouldn't make any difference anyway."

The doctor's mouth dropped open just a bit, and he looked at me for some comfort as if to say, "*Now* what do I tell her?"

I just smiled sympathetically, not sure how to tell him that Sande wasn't interested in his information and options. Because she knew what her real values were and followed her convictions, her decision was simple. No matter what happened, she would have the child. (By the way, Lauren came safe, sound, and *very together.*)

REALITY DISCIPLINE PRINCIPLE NO. 3:
ALWAYS PUT YOUR SPOUSE (NOT THE KIDS) FIRST.

In almost every counseling session, I hear people describe how they make the same basic mistake: They put everything or everyone ahead of their marriage. He concentrates on his job; she concentrates on the children. Who concentrates on the marriage? The usual answer is nobody.

Reality Discipline puts the family unit first, and that means that you and your spouse—your marriage—must come first. If it does not, the reality is that your family will get frayed at the edges or even come apart at the seams because the center is not strong. To paraphrase the poet, life flies apart if the center does not hold.

Again and again, I've seen Reality Discipline inspire teamwork and communication between husbands and wives. With Reality Discipline, there can be no hiding behind silence, hurt feelings, pride, anger, or pouting. Family members must talk—and even more important, listen—to one another.

As a good friend once told me, "Never do anything of consequence before running it past Sande." We make the important—

and the seemingly not so important—decisions together, and it makes all the difference in the world.

As Reality Discipline brings a husband and wife closer together, it actually makes it possible to "affair-proof" the marriage. I'm not saying Reality Discipline can absolutely guarantee that an affair will never happen. The human heart is still far too unpredictable for that. But, as we will see in chapter 7, there are practical steps every couple can take to make an affair a very unlikely temptation.

What Reality Discipline does is help you develop "tough love" for each other and your kids. It helps you revive romance when it seems to have faded. In fact, it helps you go beyond romance to the kind of unselfish love that keeps a family together. Sande and I believe in romance, and we still do all we can to keep the sparks alive, but if you think about it, romance is based on feelings and circumstances. In other words, romance is not always reality. I'll have a lot more to say about that in part II, on using Reality Discipline in your marriage.

REALITY DISCIPLINE PRINCIPLE NO. 4:
BALANCE RESPONSIBILITY WITH FORGIVENESS AND LOVE.

In the Reality Discipline home, parents aren't drill sergeants who make their kids toe the line. Instead, parents are role models who show their kids how to be accountable and responsible by being accountable and responsible themselves.

Right along with this, Reality Discipline prepares children for the real world. As they experience the results of their decisions, they get a taste of what it will be like when they are out on their own. Let's face it—the real world *is* cold and cruel. How much better it is when children can learn something about "facing the consequences" within the loving confines of a family where forgiveness and unconditional love are always available! Reality Discipline allows for being human. There is freedom to fail, and plenty of forgiveness when someone does.

I know from experience what Reality Discipline can do when the power of forgiveness is mixed with firm reality. A few years ago, I attended a banquet given by North Park College, and as part of the evening's festivities, I was given the Distinguished Alumnus Award, as well as being called on to be the main speaker for the evening. Actually, to call me an "alum" was stretching it a bit. I had been something of a rebel growing up, and I carried my rebellious attitude all the way into college—the one hundred sixtieth college I tried to get into after compiling a grade-point average that left my high school counselor saying, "Leman, with your record, I couldn't get you into reform school."

North Park was my last hope. The only way I was given a chance to attend on probation was through an intercessory letter written by my older brother Jack, who had attended the school for two years himself. I didn't stick it out at North Park, but before leaving, I learned some valuable lessons about Reality Discipline and about allowing for people to be human.

That night at the banquet, with the Distinguished Alumnus Award in hand, I told those present the story of the only time I got drunk in my life, which was, of course, at North Park College, a highly respected, church-affiliated school.

My roommate and I decided we had had enough of studying and needed a break. We proceeded to find a cheap bottle of wine at a party and disposed of all of it before starting back for the dorm. It was a cold winter night, the sidewalks were icy, and each of us must have fallen more than a dozen times in our condition, which could have been charitably called "blind, staggering drunk."

My roomie and I tried walking up to the third floor of the dorm to our room, but we only made it to the landing, where we both decided it was time for a little nap. It was there that the man who served as head resident and dean of students came by and found us.

"Having a little problem, fellows?" he asked as he shook us awake.

"Oh, no," I mumbled. "No, just a little tired."

Somehow he got both of us the rest of the way upstairs. I had heard the expression "my head is spinning" before, but I had never fully comprehended its meaning until that night.

When we got to the door of our room, I couldn't find my key, so he reached into my pocket and found it for me. He got us into our room and "poured" us into bed.

The next morning, I couldn't remember much about what had happened, and it seems that the dean had a memory loss as well. The rules said he could have expelled us, but he never even called us in for a lecture. In a word, he gave us a break. While I was grateful, I'm afraid it didn't change my attitude or behavior a great deal.

Eventually, Reality Discipline had to click into gear. After maintaining a C average as a freshman, I started slipping badly as a sophomore and was soon flunking out. Again, there was a night when my roomie and I decided we needed to have a little fun—this time by raiding the "conscience fund box."

The conscience fund had been established after an ice cream machine had gone haywire and began giving "freebies" simply by a pull of the handle. The word had spread like wildfire, and a hungry mob of students had descended on the machine for an impromptu ice cream social. After learning that the machine had been cleaned out, the head resident of the dorm posted a sign that read:

For the information of those of you who participated in the illegal ice cream social the other evening, the dorm lost money. Please put your fair share of payment for the ice cream in this box.

The resident hoped that those students with a conscience would pop their nickels and dimes into the box and make up for the loss of all the ice cream. My roomie and I had no conscience, however, as we took every last bit of change from the box and went out to buy pizza for the entire third floor of the dorm. We thought it was great fun—a huge prank, actually—and even bragged about it around campus.

This time, the same dean called us in for a little chat. Not satisfied with my answers, he suggested that perhaps it would be best if I quietly left North Park without a lot of fanfare (or the stigma of expulsion). I decided to take the dean up on his offer. When I left North Park, I felt no rancor toward anyone—in fact, I felt only gratitude. After all, the night I had gotten drunk, I had been shown a great deal of forgiveness and unconditional love. I could have been expelled, but I wasn't. In the case of the conscience money, I had again been treated with forgiveness and love by being allowed to leave without having any black mark on my record.

The most important thing leaving North Park did for me, however, was to get my attention. Being called to account and faced with my irresponsibility helped me realize that life is full of reality, which has to kick in sooner or later. Having to leave college helped me grow up enough to realize I couldn't keep playing the clown and cut-up forever. The dean who invited me to leave was one of several people who turned me in a completely different direction. The night I received the Distinguished Alumnus Award, he was sitting in the front row, listening to me tell of my adventures at North Park and what it had done to change my life. I will never forget the look on his face and the twinkle in his eye as he remembered what had happened.

A few months after the banquet, a North Park faculty member was passing through Tucson, and as we had breakfast, I told him the entire distinguished alum story. As we chuckled together, he made an observation that has stuck in my mind ever since: "You know, Kevin, North Park is a good school for a kid to get drunk at, don't you think?"

What he was saying, of course, is that if a kid has to make a mistake, the best place to do it is within a loving family context of some kind, where his mistake will be handled with understanding and love, not punishment. It's no exaggeration to say that what I learned at North Park helped me develop my approach to rearing my own family and helping other people with their families as well.

I believe Reality Discipline fosters the correct use of parental authority. Authoritarian or permissive extremes always produce rebellion in a child, but being democratically firm strikes a healthy middle ground. I also call it "participatory democracy." Democratically firm parents invite their children's input and listen to what they have to say, but they make the final decisions for the good of the entire family. I will be discussing parenting styles and how to develop accountability and responsibility in children in part III, on using Reality Discipline in your parenting.

REALITY DISCIPLINE PRINCIPLE NO. 5:
STICK TO YOUR GUNS.

One reason my counseling calendar remains full is that so many people don't know they need to stick to their guns and be in control. They constantly bite off more than they can chew, or they refuse to use that little word *no*. Then they wonder why they wind up in my waiting room feeling burned out, fed up, and depressed. I try to tell them they must learn to "play to their strength" and be assertive but not abrasive.

I like to show people how using Reality Discipline can be a real boon in the most practical, everyday matters, when you need to be able to stick to your guns. For example, I come across a lot of clients and friends who think that buying a car is a real chore. They are never sure if they're being ripped off or given a decent deal. I show ten to twenty people per year how to use Reality Discipline when shopping for a new car. When they do, they end up in the driver's seat with a whole lot less hassle and a much better deal. Like Reality Discipline, my approach is basic and simple.

Let's say someone wants to buy a new four-door sedan. The key to buying any car is to start with the manufacturer's suggested retail price (MSRP), which is listed on the window sticker. Instead of letting this number give you "sticker shock," subtract a good 10 percent from this sticker price. You do this realizing that the dealer did not pay the manufacturer's suggested retail price for the car. The dealer paid a good 10 percent less than that price. You are simply taking advantage of knowing this.

Now you are ready to add on any profit you are willing to give the dealer to sell you the automobile. Perhaps you want to offer three hundred dollars, or if you want to be fairly certain he will make a deal on the first go-round, offer him five hundred dollars.

The key to using Reality Discipline, however, is in making a firm offer for the automobile—meaning you make *one offer and one offer only*. Here's how it works.

Suppose I pick out the car I want and the salesperson takes me into his or her office to make out a proposal sheet. We go through all the standard amenities, and the sales agent gets down my name, address, phone number, and other basic information. Then the salesperson usually turns and says, "And Mr. Leman, what will it take to get you into this car—right now—today?"

Instead of hemming and hawing around with, "Well, I'm not sure," I take out my pocket calculator, do a little number punching, and say, "Here is my offer. I'll give you this much for the car."

When the salesperson learns my "low ball" offer, his usual reaction is one of chagrin. He starts talking about how he will lose his job by even taking such a ridiculous offer to his sales manager. He then gets up to leave, to go see his sales manager. This is where the fun begins.

I stop the salesperson by saying, "Excuse me, but if you go through that door, my offer goes down two hundred dollars."

This usually makes the salesperson stop and reconsider. What he wants to do is go down the hall and come back armed with the sales manager's admonition that they can never sell the car for the price I've offered, but would I consider another—higher—price?

By using Reality Discipline, however, I never let the salesperson get control. I tell him that if he leaves the office, my offer goes down, not up.

At this point, the salesperson tells me that I might not have noticed it, but his or her name is not on the dealership—he doesn't own the place. He only works there, and he *must* talk to his manager.

I point to the telephone on the desk and say, "There's a phone. Even a prisoner gets one phone call. Go ahead and tell your sales manager my offer."

Then the salesperson has the option to call the sales manager and relay the information. But this way he can have no private conversation, and I remain in control of the deal.

After talking with the sales manager, the salesperson hangs up and tells me he will accept my offer. Or he tries to bluff and say there's no way he can take such a low figure. At that point I simply reply, "Fine. Then I'll go somewhere else."

In most cases, the phone is ringing by the time I get home. I've even had salespeople in my driveway by the time I've gotten home! You see, car salespeople don't want to miss a sale. They want to sell you a car, not have you go somewhere else. They will bend over backward to make a deal, but only if you use Reality Discipline to make them bend.

I've spent a few paragraphs on this car-buying example to illustrate one thing: Reality Discipline is based on sticking to your guns. Once you decide on what you know is right or best, do not be wishy-washy. I'm not saying you have to be bullheaded and unbending, but you must commit yourself to pursuing your convictions—and never give up.

REALITY DISCIPLINE PRINCIPLE NO. 6:
KEEP RESPONSIBILITY WHERE IT BELONGS.

Early in my career, I learned that responsibility should be kept squarely on the shoulders of the person who should be bearing it.

When people operate according to Reality Discipline, they understand that there are no excuses for irresponsible behavior. There can be forgiveness, compassion, and understanding, but no one ever ignores reality and what is really going on.

After I was invited to leave North Park College, I took a hard look at where I was headed and determined that the answer was nowhere. After working for a while as a janitor, I enrolled at the University of Arizona, where I eventually earned a degree in psychology. After graduating, I spent ten years as dean of students—actually, assistant dean in charge of discipline. During that time, I handled just about everything—murders, rapes, assaults, even the dumping of an airplane into the fountain on the mall.

With all these challenges, I still have to say that the toughest assignment I ever had was dealing with the secretarial staff in my office. We had eight secretaries in all, keeping track of a student body that numbered more than twenty-five thousand. One secretary, Mary Lou, would come in to my office, close the door behind her, and say something like, "Dean Leman, can I see you for a moment?"

Since Mary Lou was already in my office, the answer to her question was obvious. And for the next ten or fifteen minutes, I would hear all about Alice, one of the other secretaries, and everything Alice was doing wrong. In my early days, I would sit there like the village idiot and listen to all this, thinking, *My goodness, I'm helping this person. I'm listening with a third ear, showing positive regard, exemplifying everything I was taught about being a good counselor.*

When Mary Lou left, she did feel better, but I felt like a trash basket. In addition, Mary Lou's problem wasn't really solved. She still had to put up with the incompetent or inconsiderate Alice, or she was thinking that somehow I would deal with Alice and straighten everything out.

Eventually I learned to use what I later came to call Reality Discipline. One day when Mary Lou came in and told me all about

Alice, I responded, "Mary Lou, I'm glad you came in and told me this. Come with me, will you?"

Then I took her right out to Alice's desk, where I said, "Alice, Mary Lou has something to tell you."

Then I turned to Mary Lou expectantly, only to note that she had suddenly forgotten her complaint. She would say something like, "Oh, no, it wasn't anything important. I just wondered when you were going to be through with the Xerox machine. I've got a lot of work to do."

With this simple Reality Discipline approach, I kept the problems among our secretaries where they belonged—on their shoulders, not mine. If the secretary had a gripe with another secretary, it was her battle. Once the word got around the office that Dean Leman was no longer willing to be a sympathetic listener to all the backbiting and complaining, it just about stopped completely.

REALITY DISCIPLINE PRINCIPLE NO. 7:
TREAT PEOPLE LIKE PERSONS, NOT THINGS.

A family that functions with Reality Discipline is concerned first about their "interfamily relationships"—how people treat one another and why.

After I got married and became a graduate student at the University of Arizona, I took a job as head resident, which helped us pay for our housing while I got my degree. The school year was about to get under way, and I was sitting in the dean's office, getting my new assignment, and he said, "Kevin, you did such a good job last year, I'm going to move you over to be head resident in Santa Cruz/Apache Hall."

At the time, dormitories at the university were named for various counties in the state, and in this case the dean wanted to assign me to the dorm well known for housing athletes, who were not always considered the gentlest people to oversee.

"Excuse me, sir, but isn't that the athletic dorm?"

"Well, we don't exactly call it the athletic dorm, but it's true that the football team is all quartered there."

My first reaction was to submit my immediate resignation, but the dean talked me into taking the job. Later, as I was telling an older friend on the faculty about my new assignment, he gave me some good advice: "Remember, Kevin, there are 360 of them and only one of you. *Learn to win their cooperation.*"

With my heart in my throat, I prepared for my new assignment, which could easily have been described as the Bermuda Triangle for any head resident bold enough to venture therein. My first step was to meet with my student staff, who would all serve as assistant residents. In that very first meeting, one of those student assistants referred sneeringly to football players as "animals." I terminated him on the spot. That wasn't my usual style, but I wanted to make a definite point with my staff.

"If anyone ever refers to *any* of our students as an animal—and I don't care if they wear football helmets or sunglasses—he's gone. We are going to treat everybody here like people—like family. Everyone is a person, and we are going to deal with them as such, not as animals."

Following my "inaugural speech," we prepared for the arrival of the students, who were due the following week. The Santa Cruz/Apache Hall dorm had a reputation, and not much of it was good. The "inmates" had torn it to pieces the year before. Water fountains had been ripped off walls, and ceiling tiles had been burned. In general, the place had been pretty well destroyed.

Now we faced another year, with the dorm all repaired and awaiting the new onslaught.

I asked my assistant residents, "Does this hall have a constitution?"

Loud laughter greeted my inquiry. "A constitution?" somebody said. "Mr. Leman, you don't understand. There is no student government in this hall."

"George," I said, "please go get a constitution, and I don't care where you get it."

George looked at me and then said quickly, "I'll be right back."

He went down the street, "borrowed" a constitution from another dorm's bulletin board, and was back in a few minutes.

I didn't even bother to read it. If it was good enough for that dorm, it was good enough for us. After all, something is better than nothing.

"This is our constitution," I told the group. "Change the dorm name, and then I want this copied and put all over the place—on all the bulletin boards, by the front desk. These will be the rules we want everyone to live by."

School starts in Arizona the third week of August, when it's around 108 degrees. I had my staff ready to meet the students at the curb, help carry in their luggage, and in general make everyone at home. We had punch and cookies for everyone, especially parents who had brought students to school to help them get settled.

On that first day, we established a very key point. We were not the Gestapo. We were not there to police people but to treat them with respect and to serve them in any way we could.

Throughout the entire year, we had no damage to the dormitory whatsoever. At the end of the year, in fact, we were given the Student Personnel Award for doing the most for student life on campus.

I like to think that a major reason we had no trouble and even got an award for our work was what I did on the first day I met with my group of assistant residents. When I fired the guy who called football players "animals," I was taking action, not just using words. Then I followed through with a consistent game plan for how to treat everyone.

All of this paid off, especially on the night when I had what I could call "an incident" in the hallway outside Sande's and my quarters in the dorm. It was late—around 1:00 A.M.—and some loud noises woke us up. I went out in the hall to investigate and found three seedy-looking students who had a reputation for getting high on marijuana. On this particular occasion, they were very high indeed, and they seemed to take offense at my friendly question, "What's going on, guys?"

"What do you care?" they said menacingly as they started to back me up against the wall. They weren't giants, but there were three of them and only one of me, and I started feeling like Custer at the Little Bighorn. Just then, however, "the cavalry" arrived.

On the other side of the hall was the room of one of the defensive tackles on the football team—a huge fellow who stood a good six feet six and weighed at least 265 pounds, all solid muscle. We called him The Big Bear, and let me assure you it was an affectionate title—no reference to "animals" was ever intended. The Big Bear was a good student—in fact, he was on the honor roll—but he looked like a well-groomed version of Godzilla. Now his door banged open with a crash, and he came lumbering out. In one motion, he literally picked up all three of my would-be assailants and pinned them against the wall.

"I don't know what's going on here, but I want you guys to know we like Leman around here," he growled.

That was the end of it. He didn't even say anything to me. He just dropped all three of them on the floor, turned on his heel, and went back into his "den" to bed. My three "friends" decided it was time to hit the sack, and they beat a hasty retreat to their own rooms without further notice.

I relate this somewhat dramatic incident to illustrate the point that when you treat people like people and let them know they are important, it pays off. In this case, it saved me from a mugging or possibly worse, but the same principle applies in any situation where you have people who are living, working, or interacting together in any way. Reality Discipline says people are always more important than anything else, and when you treat people like persons, you will get good results.

OH YES, THERE IS A LITTLE BAD NEWS

All the above is the "good news" about Reality Discipline. But I want to be honest with you. There is some "bad news" as well. At least it may sound like bad news in a society that advocates self-fulfillment, self-aggrandizement, and unbridled narcissism. It may sound like bad news to people who have been taught: "I've got to be me. I've got to be fulfilled. What I want counts the most."

While Reality Discipline takes everyone's needs and desires into account, it allows no individual's needs and desires to control the family. Instead, Reality Discipline encourages self-discipline, self-control, and self-denial for the good of other family members.

Those may sound like ominous words. We don't hear much about self-denial and self-control anymore. When I was in elementary school, our report cards had a distinct and important category called "self-control." You can still find "self-control" on report cards today, but teachers prefer to emphasize other categories, such as "good citizenship" and "works well with others."

I suppose the enlightened generation finds something negative about terms like *self-denial* and *self-control*. We prefer to find "positive ways" of putting things and in so doing water down what a concept like self-control is really all about.

If you are sincerely interested in keeping your family together, however, there is no getting around self-discipline, self-control, and self-denial. Practically every day, people sit in my office describing situations they've gotten themselves into because they didn't want to practice these basic virtues. They thought they could burn the candle at both ends as well as in the middle, charging hell-bent for success (whatever that is), and still keep their families together. But now they're paying the price.

There are, of course, a lot of other people who think they're getting away with it. And it's possible—they may dodge the divorce bullet, and their kids may not run away and sell themselves on some big-city street corner. They may think they're coming out intact, but they aren't really in touch. They aren't really together as a family—in mind, heart, and soul.

I am fully convinced that the world is falling apart because there isn't enough interest in self-discipline, self-control, and self-denial. If you can't buy into my premise, you might as well close this book and head back down to the store to exchange it for something like *How to Have Everything You've Ever Wanted in Life Without Making Any Real Effort.* You see, I can't help you unless you are willing to face reality and cope with it in a disciplined, gutsy way. That classic oil-filter ad from a few years ago said it all: "Pay me now, or pay me later."

On the other hand, perhaps all this "bad news" doesn't scare you that much after all. You're waiting for me to come down off my soapbox and get on with showing you more about how Reality Discipline actually works. We can start by focusing on a major component of Reality Discipline—*priorities.* In many ways, priorities are the bottom line to life. Every problem that walks through my office door can be traced back to priorities or lack of same.

If you want to use Reality Discipline to keep your family together, be aware that there are no instant answers, no quick fixes or shortcuts. You must prioritize what is truly important for you and then spend your time and energy accordingly. In chapter 3 and throughout the rest of this book, I will spell out how this can be done.

TEN WAYS REALITY DISCIPLINE CAN STRENGTHEN YOUR FAMILY

1. It develops your ability to respond rather than always react.
2. It encourages reason, not force or retaliating verbally or physically.
3. It inspires (actually, it demands) action dealing with

situations instead of sulking, brooding, and playing the victim.

4. It develops consistency.
5. It emphasizes order and organization.
6. It always requires mature behavior—being accountable and responsible for your actions.
7. It fosters unconditional love.
8. It makes everyone aware of the importance of choices and the impact a certain action can have.
9. It encourages self-control of emotions, attitudes, and behavior.
10. It makes the Bible practical and effective in your family's life.

Don't Forget . . .

- Reality Discipline applies to all facets of life, not just parenting children.
- Reality Discipline helps you think about the consequences before you have to face them.
- The whole family is more important than any individual member.
- When you know what your values are, decisions are simpler to make.
- If the center (your marriage) does not hold, the rest (your family) will fly apart.
- The best place to make mistakes is in an atmosphere of understanding and love, not punishment.
- When you know what's right or what's the best thing to do, stick to your guns—don't be wishy-washy.
- Don't carry the responsibilities of others on your shoulders; keep those responsibilities where they belong—on *their* shoulders.
- Treating people like persons always pays off.

• Reality Discipline encourages self-discipline, self-control, and self-denial on the part of everyone in the family.

And Why Not Try . . .

• Memorize these seven Reality Discipline principles. (Three more will follow in part III.)
  1. The whole is always more important than the parts.
  2. Have values, and live by them.
  3. Always put your spouse (not the kids) first.
  4. Balance responsibility with forgiveness and love.
  5. Stick to your guns.
  6. Keep responsibility where it belongs.
  7. Treat people like persons, not things.
• Discuss with your spouse which of the above principles are most important to you and your family at this time.
• Ask yourself, prayerfully and as objectively as you can, whether you tend to treat anyone in your family more as a thing than as a person. If you do, what steps can you take to change the situation?
• Do you agree or disagree with me that "the world is falling apart because there isn't enough interest in self-discipline, self-control, and self-denial"? How are you and your spouse exercising these three virtues, and what could you do to improve?
• Discuss some specific ways you can put each other first during the coming week—for example, getting out on a simple date for a sandwich or a movie.

Chapter 3

Memo to Mom and Dad: The Kids and the Job Don't Come First!

---◉---

Priorities Are Crucial to Marital Success—or Failure

A S A COUNSELOR AND THERAPIST, I HAVE THE PRIVILEGE AND RESPONSI-bility of observing life behind closed doors. In any given year, I am invited into many different family circles, where people share with me their most precious possessions—their personal lives, their hopes, their fears, their problems, and their pain.

As part of my counseling, I ask a lot of questions. One of my favorite approaches is to talk to husbands and wives separately and ask, "What are your spouse's priorities?"

When I ask the wife this question, almost invariably I hear that the number-one priority in her husband's life is his job. Then she might describe his number-two priority as "the family." Not infrequently, however, she says that his golf game or some other hobby is number two and that the family comes in a distant third. Some women say, "I guess I come in around fourth or fifth."

Until recently, when I asked husbands, "What is your wife's number-one priority?" they typically said, "Oh, the children— Marge is a great mother, a great homemaker." In recent years, however, I'm hearing husbands tell me that the family isn't necessarily always number one with their wives. Now wives are being torn between the family and their careers.

When I ask a husband or wife about priorities, the answer I am hoping to hear, but seldom do, is that after God, the number-one priority for the wife is her husband and the number-one priority for the husband is his wife. When I suggest this to my clients, they look at me strangely, as if that idea were something from the distant past—back when they were dating, perhaps. Don't I realize that, once married, one's priorities have to change? Jobs and careers take precedence, and when children arrive, they *really* take precedence.

The concept of "putting each other first" is foreign to most married couples. It just isn't practical—there are too many responsibilities, too many urgent tasks that have to be done each day.

Trapped in the Tyranny of the Urgent

I counsel a lot of couples who think they are suffering from money problems, in-laws, "strong-willed" children, or "the other woman." All these symptoms may be present, but the real problem centers on what has commonly become known as "the tyranny of the urgent." I'm not sure who coined that phrase, but a man named Charles Hummel used it to title a small booklet he wrote to point out that there is a real difference between the urgent and the important.

As Hummel was talking to the manager of a cotton mill one day, the much older and experienced man said, "Your greatest danger is letting the urgent things crowd out the important."[1]

Hummel realized that the man had put the whole subject of priorities in a nutshell. *Everybody* lives somewhere between doing what is urgent and doing what is important.

In the families I come in contact with, it seems that the "urgent" things scream the loudest to be done: getting the kids up, packing their lunches, getting them to the school bus, getting down to work yourself, stopping to pick up groceries on the way home, throwing dinner together. Then, after dinner, you get to relax with a pile of monthly bills that need paying or clothes that need washing or ironing.

Unfortunately, while you're covering all these urgent bases, the important things go undone. As General—and later President—Eisenhower once said, "Urgent matters are seldom important; important matters are seldom urgent!" One problem is that the important things are seldom those that really need to be done right now, today, or even this week. You can always put off writing or phoning a friend you haven't contacted in several months of Sundays. It's always easy to find an excuse for delaying the start of your diet or your latest "I've got to get into the habit of having daily devotions" campaign.

And as I have already touched on in chapter 2, it's all too easy to put "time for each other" aside because there just doesn't seem to be any.

"DR. LEMAN, I'M GOING BONKERS!"

A harried-looking woman, dragging her leg as if she had some sort of neurological disorder, limped into my office one day. As she plopped down on the sofa, I noted that the reason for her odd gait was an eighteen-month-old child who was clinging to her skirt like a leech.

The lady's first words were, "Can you help me, Dr. Leman? *I'm going bonkers!*"

It turned out that this lady's plaintive remark eventually

inspired the title of a book I wrote to help overwhelmed women: *Bonkers: Why Women Get Stressed Out and What They Can Do About It.*[2]

The lady who admitted to going "bonkers" was a classic prototype of the stressed-out woman. She was trying hard to be a good mother to four children while balancing everything else as well: her husband, a full-time job, and three or four other assignments she had taken on from the PTA, her church, and the cerebral palsy campaign. Her story is the story of so many women who wind up in my office.

The woman who is a candidate for Bonkersville comes trudging home from her job and fixes dinner, and after hubby and the children have all eaten, she cleans up the kitchen. Then she stops to pick up the family room and living room as well.

Next, she irons something for tomorrow, packs some lunches, and finally heads for the bedroom, where she hopes to read a few pages of her mystery novel or turn on the eleven o'clock news. There she is, propped up on her pillows, reaching for her book or the *TV Guide,* and *he* walks in with a look that reminds her of Pavlov's dog and the power of operant conditioning. She spots his salivating smile and the glint in his eyes and groans, "Oh, no . . . not, not, not—no, no, no—*not one more chore!*"

Poor hubby. He doesn't realize it, but his wife has just turned on her own little neon sign that reads, *Don't Even Think of Parking Here.* Most women would rather scrub the toilet than engage in sex at 10:55 at night after working all day, cooking dinner, cleaning up, putting the kids to bed, and making sure everything is ready for tomorrow.

Our stressed-out woman doesn't realize it, but she is definitely a victim of the tyranny of the urgent. The urgent tasks of her day have crowded out the important things—including hubby and his salivating smile. Of course, since hubby hasn't done his part, all he'll get to do tonight is salivate. He could have insured himself a much warmer welcome to bed if he had helped her clean up the kitchen, pick up the house, and get the kids bathed and down for the night. But he was too busy watching the Monday night gladiators of the gridiron. After all, certain things in his life are "urgent," too.

Frankly, I talk to a lot of women who succumb to the tyranny of the urgent while their husbands succumb to selfishness or just not being aware of the situation.

If there is a message I want to communicate in this book, it is this:

Attention all husbands!

Your wife can't keep your family together all by herself.

You must play an active role in helping sort out the urgent and the important and then do your share of both.

Lately, I'm talking to more and more working wives who are rebelling against the tyranny of the urgent. They have tried to "have it all," but now they are deciding that they really prefer to give some of it back. They find themselves in the classic two-career family where both they and their husbands have stressful full-time jobs. Then these wives have to come home to "start their second job," which leaves them exhausted and depressed most of the time. Like our "going bonkers" wife described above, they wind up just "too tired" for sex or much of anything else that could remotely resemble building a strong marriage relationship.

FULL SPEED AHEAD ON THE MOMMY TRACK

There isn't any simple answer. The working-wife movement is not going away—in fact, it's proliferating. Betty Friedan has described the 1990s as a time when "women will have new economic power" because companies will have to compete to get women. Nearly 70 percent of new jobs will be filled by women and minorities.[3]

An increasing number of husbands will at least admit they should help more with the kids and the housework, but in reality, few of them follow through and do it with any regularity. Some studies claim that anywhere from 80 to 90 percent of working wives are still doing all or most of the household chores. A Gallup poll taken in 1990 puts the figure closer to 50 percent. According to Gallup:

> Men may put in longer hours at the office, but when it comes to cooking meals, doing laundry, cleaning house and taking care of the kids, women—whether they hold outside jobs or not—usually handle these tasks. Furthermore, progress toward a more even distribution of household labor may be limited by the fact that most men and women (66 percent) agree that women are more capable of handling a household than men.
>
> In the latest poll, just over half (52 percent) of all couples report that the woman does more of the household chores. . . . In two-income families, the husband's job usually has priority so the wife rearranges her work schedule when a child is sick. Nearly nine out of ten (89 percent) of working moms are responsible for their children when they get sick, compared to only one out of ten (10 percent) of working fathers.[4]

Recognizing that something has to give, employers are now offering all kinds of options to working moms, who are forced to come to grips with reality regarding the care of their families. Among these options are innovations like extended leave after having a child, flexible scheduling or flex-time, job sharing, and even telecommuting.

One other thing some working moms can consider is "sequencing"—leaving their jobs for a few years and then trying to come back and continue their careers. Some women have made this work with no apparent damage to their careers. For example, Sandra Day O'Connor, a justice of the Supreme Court, took five years off from her law career and cared for her three children. Later, she was able to return to full-time employment as Arizona's assistant attorney general, and from there she rose all the way to the highest court in the land.[5]

Bully for Justice O'Connor, but a lot of other women can tell you that sequencing has its drawbacks. They aren't able to return to their old job and continue the upward climb uninterrupted. In many cases, they lose ground on the career ladder, and sometimes it means losing a choice position and having to start over at the very bottom or in a completely new field.

I know of increasing numbers of women who are bailing out of stress-ridden executive positions in corporations and businesses and opting for the entrepreneurial route by matching up with a friend to start small businesses in their homes. It's their way of getting back their equilibrium on the balance beam of life. They keep one high heel in the business world, but they firmly plant a Reebok at home, where they are more able to spend their time according to the needs and priorities of their families.

All these options for working wives and mothers fall under a broader label called "alternative work schedules." That term was coined by Felice Schwartz, founder and president of Catalyst, a nonprofit organization devoted to advancing women's careers, in an article she wrote concerning women in management for the *Harvard Business Review*.[6] Ms. Schwartz's premise was that employers have to face reality and identify two separate groups of women employees: (1) the high-potential, "my career comes first" women, most of whom are probably childless and willing to devote unlimited time to their jobs; (2) the lower-potential, "my family is important, too" women who have children and want to spend as much time as they can in rearing and nurturing them.

Critics quickly jumped on Schwartz's concept and labeled it the "Mommy Track." They pointed out that anybody on the Mommy Track is on the "B" team down at work. Because she has made it known that she can't give it all to the corporation, she definitely can't have it all as far as advancement and rewards are concerned. Men, of course, will leave all the Mommy-Trackers in the dust as they drag their second-class status around like a millstone about their necks.

I'm sure all that is true in certain organizations, but as a psychologist who talks with burned-out superwomen all the time, I can only say that something has to give and choices have to be made. Those who criticize the so-called Mommy Track are clearly stating what they think a woman's priorities should be. Career must come first, and the fast track must be pursued right to the top. Of course, once the woman gets to the top, she may be exhausted, possibly ready for the local funny farm, and feeling so drenched in guilt about neglecting her family that she can't enjoy any of the fruits of her labor.

Or she may be so stressed out that she falls ill—sometimes very seriously ill. According to a letter written to *The New York Times* by Dr. Paul Rosch, the president of the American Institute of Stress, there is real reason to believe that the sharp increase in the death rate from breast cancer in young and middle-aged white women is traceable to the stress these women undergo on the job as they "enter a male dominated work force that fails to fulfill the promises of women's liberation efforts."

According to Dr. Rosch, "Job stress is also associated with 100 percent increase in heart attacks in certain classes of working women, especially those in occupations where one cannot express anger or that require a great deal of responsibility but little decision-making. Other illness syndromes and behavioral problems, such as smoking, alcoholism, substance abuse and obesity, appear to be consequences of increased work related stress."[7]

It is apparent that for many women, joining the work force has meant joining the rat race. They may not have wanted it to be that way, but they are trapped in the rat race, and they should never forget:

> When the rat race is over,
> you're still a rat.

In other words, if you are *willingly* sucked into the rat race and let running that race dominate your life, you have made your choice. Your priority is plain. The rat race is most important to you, and whether you like it or not, you have chosen to live life as mindlessly as a rat on a wheel, going around and around, but really not getting anywhere as far as what counts is concerned. And what counts is people. No matter how important a career might be—and I am fully aware that a career is very important to many women as well as men—a career should never come ahead of people close to you.

"THE AIR FORCE DOESN'T COME FIRST"

So far, I may sound as if I think the woman ought to do all the choosing of "alternatives," while the man can keep pouring himself into his job, Monday-night football, and getting his handicap below ten. On the contrary, I think it is the husbands of our nation who face some serious choices regarding their work and alternative life-styles. And they'd better make them fast, because for many families, time may be running out. I talk to more and more women who are considering the option of going it alone instead of carrying husbands who only add more stress to their lives. One divorcée summed it up by saying, "I used to have five children—now I only have four."

Just because I know it will get a reaction, I sometimes start a talk before a group by saying, "I'm here today to talk about submission." The women always respond with groans. I imagine they're thinking, *Here we go again. Who invited this guy?* But the verse I then quote is not Ephesians 5:22—the one they expect—but the verse that comes before it, Ephesians 5:21: "Submit to *one another* out of reverence for Christ" (emphasis added). The apostle Paul next goes on to make clear the mandate for men to keep their wives their top priority. In Ephesians 5:25, he instructed, "Husbands, love your wives, just as Christ loved the church and gave himself up for her."

In other words, husbands are to love their wives sacrificially, to put their wives' needs and best interests ahead of their own. Nowhere in Scripture are men told to give that kind of devotion to their jobs or careers. Yet many men have these priorities reversed.

I'll never forget the Air Force colonel who was in the audience when I spoke to a group of Air Force wives at the base chapel. After I concluded my talk, which featured numerous suggestions that men ought to be doing more around the house, particularly if their wives are working, I opened the session for questions. I didn't know the colonel was in the audience, but that changed when he towered to his feet and said in a loud military tone: "Doctor, could I just say one thing?"

"Of course," I invited. How could a civilian psychologist turn down a colonel who wanted the floor?

"Young man, it seems to me that you don't understand the Air Force. Because, you see, when a woman marries into the Air Force, the woman knows right off the bat, the Air Force must come first."

The colonel went on to elaborate, and I let him drone for maybe sixty to ninety seconds before interrupting him.

"Excuse me, sir, I really do believe I understand your Air Force. But the fact is, if you die tonight, your Air Force will have someone filling your shoes by 0800 tomorrow morning."

It seemed that every woman in the room rose to her feet to give me a standing ovation, while the colonel slowly sank back into his seat, shot down in the flames of his own reality. He had nicely provided a vivid illustration of the point I was trying to make: A job is *not* everything. No matter what position anyone holds, that position can be filled by somebody else. But at home, that isn't true. When you take on the commitment of marriage and parenting, *there is no one who can fill your shoes at home.* If you're off doing something else, you leave a gap that cannot be filled.

As I have worked with men in counseling situations, I have

learned that I have to convince them of their importance to their families. In addition, I always have to demonstrate what's in it for them. After all, that's how a man thinks.

So I work hard at explaining to husbands how their sex lives will improve 300 percent if they'll just take time to do the little things in life, like taking out the garbage without being asked, taking the kids to school, being more attentive to their mothers-in-law—or, possibly most important, changing their schedules.

In addition, although it's hard for them to believe it, I point out that man does not live by sex alone. Besides being males, men are *human*. When a man is on his deathbed, looking back on his corporate achievements won't bring much comfort. The human spirit has a different list of priorities. Did he take time to play with and really *know* his kids? Did he make some real friends, or did he just pick partners for racquetball or golf? Did he ever get to know his wife as his friend—the best friend he could possibly have? Did he take time to appreciate the beauty of God's handiwork? Did he take time to enjoy life, or did he just put in his time?

ALL YOU HAVE TO INVEST IS YOUR TIME

I'm not telling men anything I haven't had to learn myself—several times. It's interesting how life re-teaches you certain lessons. When our first little surprise package, Hannah, arrived a few years ago, I was forty-four and Sande was forty-two. Sande had told me she was pregnant while we were eating at a fast-food restaurant, just before Christmas. I can remember letting out a war whoop of joy, which was later countered by a few pangs of chagrin. After all, what were two people in their forties doing having another baby? We had three already; Holly, fifteen, Krissy, fourteen, and Kevin, nine. How could the champion of Reality Discipline have slipped up so badly?

Counselor, heal thyself flashed through my mind, but joy was still my predominant reaction. Maybe I was unconsciously happy about getting a second chance to try some things I hadn't done all that well with the first three.

As you would guess, Hannah's birth brought changes to the Leman household. For one thing, I had to make some changes, because I couldn't expect Sande to attend to the new baby and do everything she had been doing before. Among many other things, I altered my work schedule so I could take over driving our older kids to the school they attend, some ten miles away. That cost me some early-morning appointments at the office, and it also meant reducing income we sorely needed at the time.

I keep telling men that all any of us have is dominion over our time and how we spend it. I go to psychologists' conventions on occasion, and always, during the sessions on how to conduct a private practice, the seminar leaders keep saying one thing: "All you have to sell is your time."

That piece of wisdom doesn't just apply to running a business. It applies to being part of a marriage and a family, too. *Selling* time is only part of it. There is also the area of *investing* time, and what better investment of your time can you make than in your family?

THE CASE OF THE SEETHING SURGEON

I recall a physician—a dyed-in-his-surgeon's-gown workaholic making well over a half-million dollars a year—who came to see me because his wife had told him she was fed up with being neglected and alone all the time with the children. She was ready to walk out if something didn't change, and fast.

As this man described his schedule and daily routine, it was quickly apparent that he was married to his job, locked in to commitments, and that he was telling himself lies. One lie centered on bringing new people into his practice and supposedly making his work load go down. He had just brought in a new man, but his own practice had only gotten bigger because he was simply becoming more and more in demand for his skills.

His wife's outburst had taken him totally by surprise. She had been supermom, raising the three kids, providing a gracious home, keeping everything under control—everything but her own feelings, which had slowly deteriorated as she spent night after night eating with the children while he was still down at the office or hospital, hard at work.

In this case, the wife did not work—with an income of a half-million dollars a year, she didn't have to. And because this doctor was the sole provider of the income in his home, he could tell himself the lie that he was doing all this for his wife and children. He was beating his head against the wall for her and the kids. But now she was fed up. She wanted more than the nice home and being able to buy whatever she wanted. In short, she wanted him.

But when he did get home, he would head straight for the liquor cabinet, pour himself a drink, and try to unwind from the day. He wanted no part of the children—or of her, for that matter. He just wanted to be left in peace. He worked like this five days a week, up to sixty, seventy, and even eighty hours. He was off weekends, yes, but all he did was sit and stare at TV, trying to recharge his batteries for Monday morning.

This man was so stressed out that he paced my office like a big cat. When I asked him to take a seat on the well-worn couch where so many people sit and tell me their problems, he snatched up one of the smaller pillows and started punching it. With tears streaming down his face, he told me what it was like to be so in demand, so indispensable in the lives of so many people. He also told me he didn't necessarily like some of these people. He had to be nice, but if he had his druthers, he felt like kicking some of them right in the teeth.

This doctor was so uptight, he was starting to worry about how well he could function in the operating room, and now his wife was ready to leave him to boot. What did I suggest?

"Why don't you try using Reality Discipline on your marriage?" I suggested.

"What do you mean?" he asked.

"Well, it's obvious you have a five-day-a-week schedule that is eating you alive. Why don't you cut back to three days a week for office visits and surgery, and spend the other two with your family?"

"But I'm needed," he protested. "I don't see how I can cut back—"

"Oh, of course you can cut back. Just call your secretary and have her take the pen and cross out Mondays and Fridays. That leaves you with Tuesdays, Wednesdays, and Thursdays, unless there are real emergencies at other times."

"I'm still not sure how I can cram it all into three days," he continued to protest.

Now we were getting down to the real problem. The surgeon really didn't want to cut back on his work load. In his high-powered circles, that would be considered very poor form, and other hardworking surgeons would start to look—and wonder. In a word, his self-esteem would be on the line.

"I realize a man's self-esteem is deeply affected by his work," I told him. "We like to think we're indispensable, and we've got to do more and more to prove it. It's hard to accept the fact that no one is indispensable—at least, not on the job. What I hope I can get you to understand is that where you're really indispensable is at home, and you're not there. If you lay Reality Discipline on your situation, you will realize that there will be consequences if you don't cut back. It seems to me that your choice is rather simple. Cut back on your work, or lose your wife and your family. Do you want to pay that kind of price?"

The stressed-out surgeon looked at me for several seconds, weighing his pride against losing his family. Finally, he sat back on the couch, and I could almost see the tightly wound spring inside him start to uncoil just a little.

"Well, I guess I can give it a try. I love what I do, but I love my wife and children, too. I don't want to lose them."

It took several more sessions with the surgeon and his wife to get things squared away. But eventually he did cut back. It meant cutting his huge income, but he adjusted to that as well. And they're making it. He's becoming reacquainted with his wife and children. He has also developed a genuine friendship with another surgeon who works at the same hospital, and the families have been getting together. He takes walks whenever he can to relax between surgeries. With tiny baby steps, he's beginning to really enjoy life.

Above all, he has learned that Reality Discipline does work if you're willing to do two things: face reality, and then discipline yourself and the situation.

SOME HUSBANDS ARE TAKING THE DADDY TRACK

Obviously, the surgeon's story is not representative of the vast majority who do not make over a half-million dollars a year and who cannot afford to cut their workloads and salary by 30 or 40 percent. What the surgeon *does* illustrate, however, is an attitude that men, especially, must develop if they want to join with their wives in keeping the family intact.

This attitude goes by an old-fashioned term called *humility*. Being humble means realizing the world does not revolve around your needs and desires. Instead, being a husband and father automatically places you in a new category—that of a servant-leader who fully realizes the whole is indeed greater than any of its parts, and you must do your part to make the whole—your family—go.

Again, if the husband and wife agree that their first priority is keeping their marriage and family strong, *both* of them should be willing to bend, shift, or switch. Not to be outdone by the women on the Mommy Track, increasing numbers of men are switching to the Daddy Track as they take alternative career paths of their own in order to become more involved in their families, particularly rearing the children. I read about and talk to more and more men who are giving up promotions, forgoing pay raises, and sacrificing "status" down at work so they can take on a major share of the parenting and homemaking chores that used to be mostly their wives' domain.

In a 1988 survey conducted by the Du Pont Corporation, 33 percent of the male employees said they would like to work part-time in order to be with their families more.

In many firms, men go beyond simply wishing they could be with their families more. They take the big step and put their careers on hold.

- A lab technician refuses to work extra hours and weekends so he can spend more time with his kids, and his boss lets him know that "science can't be 9:00 to 5:00 to be significant."
- A magazine editor quits his job in order to spend more time with his disabled daughter.
- An account executive forgoes a promotion because his preschool children require more attention.
- A divorced personnel director turns down lucrative job offers that would put greater demands on his time, because his first priority is his twelve-year-old son who has lived with him since he split up with his wife.

In one way or another, all these fathers are saying, "I'm not going to do to my kids what my dad did to me. I don't want to be just a paycheck to them."[8]

There are many ways to take the Daddy Track. I recall reading about a football coach at a smaller college who was offered a choice position as head coach at a major school on the East Coast. At first he said he was interested, but when decision time came, he turned it down, saying, "My wife and I have really thought this over, and we've decided that the best thing for our family is to stay where we are."

If you know anything about football coaches, you understand

the significance of this man's remark. There is, perhaps, no more ambitious breed than the football coach, many of whom "sleep at the office" because there just isn't time to go home during the season. They're too busy watching films, holding meetings, and planning strategy. And what I especially like about this coach's remark is that he freely admitted he had consulted *with his wife* and they had made the decision together to pass up the big-time opportunity and stay in the smaller town, where their kids were firmly rooted, in order to give them the best opportunity to grow up without disruption and confusion.

In another case, I was counseling an architect who decided to put his own career on hold to allow his wife to go back to school. He was fortunate enough to be self-employed and working at home, and so he was able to cut way back on his own work to play Mr. Mom for two years while his wife finished her degree in education.

It's hard to say if the Daddy Track phenomenon will catch hold in major waves. Some critics think it's doubtful that large numbers of men will choose to break out of the more time-honored, traditional roles. One observer—a teacher of parenting courses for almost twenty years—believes that fewer men are putting their families ahead of their jobs today than they did five years ago.[9]

We could argue the pros and cons of the Daddy Track, and the Mommy Track for that matter, but what really counts is one word: *priorities.* When a husband and wife sit down and work out their priorities, they can make hard decisions about what track each of them is to follow.

DISCIPLINES FOR CHOOSING PRIORITIES

When you choose priorities, you are always dealing with at least two questions: *If* and *When.* First, you must decide *if* you want to do something at all. Once you decide that it's to be done sometime, the next question is *when.* To decide when to do various tasks, people sometimes use the A-B-C approach. To use the A-B-C system, you take your "to-do" list and rate each item as follows:

A = "must do immediately"
B = "should do very soon"
C = "could do sometime"

If you're like most people, you'll wind up with quite a few A's, several B's, and a few C's. Some people sometimes wind up with all A's, or so they want to believe. Or all their urgent tasks—the daily routine that just doesn't seem to be able to wait—wind up in the A's, and the important tasks that have a much greater long-range effect on the family wind up in the B's and even the C's.

Prioritizing your life is never simple. In *The Road Less Traveled,* Scott Peck observes that solving life's problems involves four basic disciplines:

1. delaying gratification,
2. accepting responsibility,
3. dedicating yourself to being honest and facing the truth, and
4. becoming balanced.

I couldn't agree more, because these four basic tools are Reality Discipline in a nutshell. Unfortunately, when many people choose their priorities, they often take a different route:

- Instead of delaying gratification, they want instant comfort. It's the pleasure principle revisited. The young couple buys the BMW only three years after getting out of grad school. They can't afford it yet, but all their friends are already on their second BMW, and besides, they worked hard, and they "deserve it."
- Instead of accepting responsibility, they want to avoid it. Two prime examples that come to mind are the increasing

number of divorced or estranged fathers who fail to support their children and the increasing number of college
graduates who have defaulted on their student loans. No
matter how responsible people think they are, the proof
can often be found in how they handle their finances.

- Instead of dedicating themselves to honesty, they tell
  themselves and others lies, particularly the kind that
  begin with "Someday I'll . . . ": "Someday I'll lose the
  twenty-five extra pounds." "Someday I'll quit smoking."
  "Someday I'll be able to get home earlier and spend
  more time with the family."
- Instead of becoming balanced, they overwork, overeat, or
  overuse something they shouldn't be using at all. The real
  estate broker puts in his sixty to seventy hours per week
  and takes out a membership at the health club, where he
  spends another ten to fifteen hours, turning fitness into a
  masochistic ordeal. Meanwhile, his wife is home getting
  her workouts by handling the children alone every night.

IF THE FOUNDATION ISN'T RIGHT, THE FAMILY CRUMBLES

Not long ago, we sold our home and built a new one, just a mile or
two away in the arroyos of north Tucson. The contractor who over-
saw the building of our house was without question a firstborn
child. How do I know? One major clue was his meticulous concern
over details. One morning I stopped by the job site at 5:30 A.M.
because it would be my only chance to look things over before leaving on a trip. To my surprise, there was Gary.

"I can't believe you're here at 5:30 in the morning," I said in
surprise. "The sun's not even up yet."

"Kevin," Gary replied, "it doesn't make much difference if I'm
here for a lot of the things that go into your house, but the one
thing I have learned is that this is the time I need to be on the spot.

This is the day we put in the foundation, and if the foundation isn't right, nothing else is going to be right, either."

Somehow I think there's a parable for families somewhere in Gary's statement. The foundation of every family is the husband and wife. If they don't make that foundation their first priority, everything else will receive too much, or too little, attention.

If you're really interested in keeping your family together, your first decision should not be about what to do with or for the children. Frankly, most parents are doing too much for their children already. I'll talk more about that in part III.

Your first decision must be to do something for yourselves—for Mom and Dad, the basic husband-and-wife unit of the family, around which everything must revolve. I repeat, the children are not the center of the family. *You and your spouse are the center.* And what I said in chapter 1 bears repeating, with a bit of paraphrasing:

> If the center (your marriage) doesn't hold,
> everything else (your family) is going to fly apart.

Husbands, look again at Ephesians 5:25 (as well as verses 26-33). There can be no doubt about your first priority. And wives, Ephesians 5:22-24 clearly shows that your relationship with your husband must be your greatest concern. In modern times, we are sold such a bill of goods by "experts" who tell us marriage is a 50-50 proposition. It has to be 100-100; we don't just go halfway but put our spouse's needs *ahead* of our own.

As I mentioned above, a good plan for prioritizing is to label things A—must do, B—should do, or C—can do. But over and above that, you should label your marriage AAA—must do. In other words, your marriage is the top priority of them all. In fact, your marriage is much more than a "must do." *It's do or disintegrate.*

If your marriage is coming in a distant second or third or fourth behind a lot of other "priorities," you need to grapple with reality. And reality says that if you don't start doing things differently, you have an excellent chance of becoming one more statistic, one more small part of the giant national average that says a marriage lasts some seven years and is gone.

In a word, *you must prioritize within,* and that means your spouse must come first. When your marriage comes first, everything else falls into its proper place.

I realize this may be a strange idea for many wives and husbands. The hard-driving husband who is out there "breaking his neck for his wife and the kids," working sixty or seventy hours a week, may find it just too hard to swallow. And it may seem impossible to a mom with three little ankle-biters who consume her twenty-four hours a day. Just *where* is she supposed to find all this time for her husband (assuming he's even around)?

Nonetheless, I stand by my top priority. For any couple—particularly the overly busy, hard-driving husbands and wives who are trying to juggle career and family—there is more reason than ever to seek refuge in each other, to have some time for yourselves. To keep your family together, you must start at the bottom—at the foundation of it all—your marriage relationship. Finding time for each other can be done—if you both really want to. In part II, I'll show you how.

REALITY DISCIPLINE ASKS THE HARD QUESTIONS THAT HELP YOU DEVELOP THE BEST PRIORITIES

When developing priorities, here are some questions that any family can use with profit:

- What is really important to me? to my spouse? to my children?
- What are our family's goals? What do we want to accomplish in the next ten to fifteen years? the next five years? this year? in the next few months?

- If we take a certain course of action, what will be the consequences for everyone concerned? Does it build the security of every family member, or does it leave someone feeling left out, threatened, or not as important as the others?
- Do we have time for this? If not, are we willing to give something else up in order to make time for this?
- Can we afford this? Is this the best time to buy or invest in something like this? (Possibly most important, "Is this something we *need* or *want?*")
- Is this issue or question really worth taking a stand? A key part of using Reality Discipline is to determine when it's worth slugging it out with friend, foe, relative, or family member. What principle is really involved? Am I trying to teach something? live something out that really matters?

    All these questions center on the issue of values. What is really important to your entire family? Once you identify your real values, using Reality Discipline becomes much easier. In fact, it becomes second nature.

Don't Forget . . .
- To ensure family success, put your spouse first.
- Beware of the tyranny of the urgent. Make time for the really important.
- One spouse cannot hold the family together. Both spouses must play an active and equal role.
- Husband or wife, your career should never come ahead of people close to you.
- No one can fill a parent's shoes at home.
- All you have to invest is your time. With apologies to Grantland Rice:

When the Great Scorer comes
to tally up your life,
one of His first questions:
"Was there time for kids and wife?"

- When choosing priorities, there are four basic disciplines: delaying gratification, accepting responsibility, dedicating yourself to the truth, and becoming balanced.

And Why Not Try . . .

- Sit down with your spouse and go over your priorities together. State what you believe your first four priorities are. See if your spouse agrees.
- Talk together about what is urgent and important in your lives and your marriage. Make a list of the urgent things you seem to have to always do. Then list some important things you should be doing but are letting slip by. How can you change this?
- If you are both working and your present schedule leaves little time for family life, talk together about other alternatives mentioned in this chapter: sequencing, Mommy Tracks, and Daddy Tracks. Work out a solution that leaves enough time to be parents as well as career people.
- Think of one thing you can do in the next week to encourage your spouse (a note, a back rub, twenty minutes of undivided attention, etc.). Plan a specific time to do it.
- Next time you work on the bills, discuss where you might be able to cut down on some of your debts by "delaying gratification." Decide together on specific steps to cut back or cut down.

Part II

Leman's First Law:

To Keep Your Family Together, Always Put Your Marriage First

Chapter 4

Can Two Sets of Differences Become One Healthy Marriage?

———————●———————

Yes, If You're Willing to Work at Becoming a Team

IF I HAVE BECOME CONVINCED OF ANYTHING IN MORE THAN TWENTY years of counseling married couples, it is this:

HUSBANDS AND WIVES ARE DIFFERENT.

Unless you are still fighting some of the old unisex battles, this observation may not sound too profound. But after hearing hundreds of couples "duke it out" right in my office, I'm convinced that unless a husband and wife can learn how to understand and deal with their differences, they will have little chance in a world that is not family friendly.

By "differences," I'm not primarily talking about arguments or differences of opinion. Nor am I focusing on any number of alleged male-female differences that have been identified in some interesting studies on the subject. For example, researchers have found that the emotional problems of some adolescents can be traced right back to not having a consistent mother figure in early childhood—especially the first eighteen months of the child's life. When a child doesn't bond with his or her mother, that child has great difficulty forming attachments to others later in life. If this deprivation of love continues, a child can grow up with severely inhibited emotions, incapable of feeling much joy, grief, or even remorse.[1]

I'm not sure I would agree that these research findings on bonding to mothers would hold true in all cases, but my personal experience bears out what these studies are saying. Our daughter Hannah, age three at the time, was playing around on our big four-poster bed when she suddenly took a tumble and bumped her head—hard. As she screamed in pain and came running toward me, I reached out to give her comfort, feeling very loving and fatherly. But in an instant, I was left groping like a linebacker trying to find Bo Jackson on an off-tackle play. She dodged around me and headed down the hall, covering the 110 feet to the other end of the house in 5.3 seconds to find whom? Her mother, of course.

I realize this little story, though amusing, doesn't prove much. In some homes, I'm sure a child might run right by Mom and head for Dad, but in most of the families I counsel, I'm sure it's Mom the kids want when they have a stomachache or a bad "owie"—like a bump on the head. It's my conviction that if you lined up a thousand kids with the flu and told all of them they could make one phone call, guess who they would call? Kids know instinctively, "When the chips are down, head for Mom!"

At the same time, I don't want to give the impression that just because kids may count on Mom more than Dad in moments of "crisis," dads are excused from an active role in bringing them up and caring for them. In their book *The Silent Majority,* William Westley and Nathan Epstein report their findings after studying families that produce emotionally healthy college students. Families with fathers who were strong leaders were the only type producing predominantly healthy children, while families led by strong mothers tended to have weakened qualities, such as restrained emotional ability, objectivity, and thoughtfulness.[2]

These assertions of Westley and Epstein certainly don't "prove" that men are more emotionally stable, more objective, or more thoughtful than women. But what their research does suggest is that a family begins with a man and a woman who become husband and wife. Marriage makes them a team, and they are both vitally important to the family they create.

From what I've seen, in a successful marriage, each partner has certain clearly defined roles to play. But these roles are not "predestined" or presupposed for one spouse or the other due to sex. Coming back to the team analogy for a moment, different people play different positions according to their abilities to get the job done—according to what they're suited to do best.

In a healthy marriage, the partners take stock of their differences in temperament, abilities, and interests and divide up their roles accordingly. Sometimes this can be threatening to one or both partners, because working out their roles can result in situations that are very different from what either partner grew up with.

Nonetheless, they'll do it if they truly respect each other and are sensitive to each other's feelings and needs. Their goal is to strengthen their marriage, not to have one spouse "win" over the other and force the other to take an unwanted role. They are aware of their differences in several key areas. In the rest of this chapter, I look at how differences in background and perceptions can affect any marriage. In chapter 5, we will focus on the powerful effects that personal values can have on a husband-wife relationship.

Differences in Background

Most people are familiar with the concept that different backgrounds can cause problems in marriage. But where do these backgrounds come from, and how do they develop us as individuals? In every person's background is how he or she developed a life style—that is, an individual way of looking at life. Our life style comes out of our birth order and the type of training and treatment we got from our parents.

When I suggest to a couple that we go over a few basic questions to determine their life style, they think I mean whether they are driving a BMW or an Isuzu Trooper, whether they are living in a loft in downtown Manhattan or a three-bedroom bungalow in suburbia. I try to explain that my particular training is called Adlerian, because it is based on the psychology of Alfred Adler, who pioneered in what is called *individual psychology*. Adler believed that very early in life, each of us develops a style of life or "life style." In other words, we all decide what works best for us as we try to reach our goals.

(Like all human theories, Adler's has its flaws. I've had to take from it those principles that are valid and consistent with biblical truth. One of the best is its emphasis on individual accountability for the choices we make, which is certainly scriptural.)

Even as small children, as we pursue the simplest of goals, we develop a certain perception of how we fit into the world around us. Once we have that perception, it filters everything that happens to us. As we work out who we are, we also develop what Adler called "life lines" or "lines of talk" that we feed ourselves. *Self-talk*, a term that has become popular in recent years, conveys the same idea. Throughout the day, as we experience successes and failures, we tend to tell ourselves, at the rate of some fifteen hundred words a minute, certain things that we eventually believe are true.

There are many different life styles. In fact, it would be fair to say that every person on the face of this earth has worked out his or her own unique life style. But our individual uniqueness aside, most of us fit into certain broad life-style categories. Four of the basic life styles I see in my office a great deal include controllers, pleasers, attention-getters, and martyrs.

CONTROLLERS HAVE TO BE IN CHARGE

Not surprisingly, the controller's life line says, "I only count when I'm in control, when I'm in charge of the situation." Controllers, however, are not necessarily all the same. Some are on power trips and definitely enjoy being in charge, but another kind of controller operates from a totally different motivation—fear. This person becomes a controller for defensive purposes because he fears someone else is going to take control of him.

Controllers are known for having a short fuse. They may hide their feelings for a time, but when they hit that boiling point, they explode into a temper tantrum.

Controllers have a tremendous need to be right. They are often perfectionists and can be found in precise and structured occupations, such as engineers, executive secretaries, or computer programmers.

Controllers usually keep people at arm's length. They become very skilled in avoiding intimacy and openness. In many couples I counsel, one mate controls the other by simply refusing to open up. No matter how much the other spouse might plead, cajole, or try to pry the lid off, the controlling mate simply goes deeper into his or her shell. In many cases, the husband uses this kind of controlling tactic on his wife, who then complains, "Why won't he talk to me?"

One of the most dangerous kinds of controllers is the man who is charming and glib. He has a way with words and is quite sure of himself with women. Recently I found the following personal ad in a local paper under the heading "Singles."

DYNAMITE DIVINE

Debonair, cosmopolitan, creative, sincere, Scorpio savant seeks compatible complementary companion. If you're a svelte, urbane, real woman possessing moxie, pizzazz, brains and/or beauty (prioritized); value being assertive, charming, diligent, domestic, enterprising, enquiring, neat, sensible, sexual, spiritual, thoughtful, thrifty, tolerant and trustworthy; enjoy creating culinary delights, appreciate life's paradoxical ironies, are unencumbered and fond of FUN—then I'm interested.

That "Dynamite Divine" has created a perfectionist fantasy that no mortal could fulfill is obvious, but he isn't finished. His ad goes on to say:

Vitally essential: no bimbos, blasé broads, bums, coquettes, country bumpkins, drags, drips, fools, fraidy-cats, fundamentalists, hypochondriacs, hypocrites, junkies, nags, pigs, prigs, snips, snobs, spongers, whiners or zealots. Provided you don't dwell incessantly on prattle about petty pecuniary concerns or gross gossip, want to while away your time engrossed in the babble box, or expect to be "financially secure" whatever that means in the vicissitudes of life—we might discover a DYNAMIC DIVINE DUO—and find felicity and ecstasy in the synergy of our spirits . . . LOVE. Let's communicate!

Dynamite's ad closed with an invitation to write him at a certain post office box, but I hope no woman took him up on his offer. Any duo she might create with this controller with a masterful vocabulary might be dynamic, but it definitely would not be divine. He is such a flaw-picker, a camel would have better luck getting through the eye of the needle than another human being would have trying to measure up to his expectations.

Woe unto the woman with a pleaser personality who hooks up with this kind of charming controller. I can almost guarantee that Dynamite Divine always has to be right, and what better way to ensure always being right than to put your expectations so high that no one could ever measure up to them?

PLEASERS HAVE TO BE LIKED BY EVERYONE

Pleasers are people who desperately need to be liked. Their life line reads, "I only count when I please others, when I keep everything and everyone around me smooth and happy."

Pleasers are extremely sensitive to criticism and will work hard to keep life's oceans smooth for those around them, particularly other family members. They seldom show their true feelings because they don't want to offend or be rejected. They hide their feelings behind a mask of phony smiles and acquiescence, all the while hating themselves because they don't have the courage to tell people what they really think. It is no surprise, then, that pleasers usually have low self-esteem. They don't believe they are worth much, and they constantly try to build themselves up by doing all they can to please everyone else.

I often find pleasers married to controllers, which leads to problems unless both partners are willing to change their ingrained behavior. More about that when you meet Frank and Judy in chapter 5.

ATTENTION-GETTERS HAVE TO BE NOTICED

Attention-getters are always telling themselves, "I only count when I'm noticed." Attention-getters are the carrot-seekers of life. They are always looking for rewards and praise. Because I'm the baby of my family, I confess to being an incurable attention-getter. Because

I was the lastborn, I was always trying to show my big brother and sister that "I could do it." I became the family clown, the family show-off, and it carried over into adult life. I love my vocation, which centers on helping people through counseling, but I love my avocation more—making people laugh. I do it wherever I can—speaking in workshops, seminars, and conventions or on television and radio talk shows.

Interestingly enough, attention-getters could be called first cousins to controllers. Attention-getting can be a primary cause of extramarital affairs. Because one partner doesn't get enough attention at home, he or she wanders off to find it elsewhere.

MARTYRS HAVE TO LOSE

Martyrs are people who think they never deserve to win. Their favorite life lines are "I only count when I lose," "I deserve to suffer," and "It's too much, I don't deserve it."

It's not hard to see that martyrs have a poor self-image, and maybe that's why they are so good at finding people who will walk all over them. Martyrs seem to gravitate to losers with uncanny accuracy. They may marry alcoholics, wife-beaters, or drug addicts.

BIRTH ORDER DETERMINES A LOT OF THINGS

One of the key determinants of a person's life style is birth order. Because I've covered birth order thoroughly in several other books (*The Birth Order Book, Growing Up Firstborn,* and *Were You Born for Each Other?*), I'll only touch on it here to define the term.

Birth order is simply your particular branch in the family tree—whether you arrived in your family first, somewhere in the middle, or last. Because the most intimate relationships we will ever have are with our families, and because there is no greater influence on a young child than his or her family, birth order is important. The relationships between parents and their children are both fluid and dynamic, and whenever another child is born into the family, the entire family environment changes. How parents—and other family members—interact with each child when it comes into the family circle has a lot to do with how that child develops a certain life style and a certain perception of life.

Were you the firstborn? a middle child? or the baby of the family? No matter what branch was yours, it has a lot to do with who you are today and the kind of marriage partner and parent you are.

FIRSTBORNS STRUGGLE TO MEASURE UP

Because they have only their parents for role models, firstborns are always struggling with trying to match adult standards and accomplishments. The firstborn tends to be perfectionistic, reliable, conscientious, a list-maker, well-organized, critical, serious, and scholarly.

Firstborns are also self-sacrificing, conservative, and supporters of law and order. They believe in authority and ritual. They are legalistic, going by the letter of the law rather than the spirit. They are also loyal and self-reliant, and many of them are goal-oriented achievers.

It is no accident that out of the first twenty-three astronauts the United States sent into outer space, twenty-one were firstborns or only children. All seven astronauts in the original Mercury program were firstborns. While serving as assistant dean of students at the University of Arizona, I once did a little informal research on the university faculty members. Almost every one of them was a firstborn or an only child.

Only children, by the way, can be called "firstborns in spades" or "super firstborns." Take all the characteristics mentioned above and multiply them by ten, and you have the only child, who is often an unforgiving perfectionist who is hardest of all on himself, after biting off far more than any one person could chew or achieve. Because only children never had to learn to share with siblings, they can be selfish or insensitive, often failing to understand why they are causing friction in family or group situations.

MIDDLE CHILDREN OFTEN FEEL SQUEEZED

The middle child is harder to describe than any of the others. In fact, middle children are often a bundle of contradictions. There is no telling which direction middle children might head, but you can at least be sure they will bounce off their older siblings. A lot depends on how they relate to those older brothers or sisters and the life style they develop. It's safe to say, however, that the first two children born in every family will be as different as "night and day."

By "bundle of contradictions," I mean that middle children can be quiet and shy loners, or they can bounce in the opposite direction and be sociable, outgoing, and friendly. Middle children might be impatient and easily frustrated, or they might wind up taking life in stride, being very laid back. Middle children can become very competitive or turn out to be easygoing, not competitive at all. The middle child can be the rebel and the black sheep, or he can be the peacemaker and mediator. The middle child can be aggressive, a real scrapper, or he can turn out to want to avoid conflict at any cost.

Can we say anything about middle children that sounds a bit more definite? We can say with certainty that middle children feel squeezed from above and below. They often feel they just don't get much respect or attention. I often point out in seminar workshops that the middle child appears the least in any family photo album.

Because he feels squeezed and even "unwelcome" at home, the middle child is often the first to move outside the family to make friends. He may find a group to whom he can give allegiance, such as a team, a club, or a gang of kids who hang out together. This group is his, and the family can't control or squeeze him in any way when he is in that group.

Another typical characteristic of many (but not necessarily all) middle children is their ability to mediate or negotiate, and they also can be quite manipulative. They get these skills, of course, from winding up "in the middle," where they often have to compromise and negotiate because they can't always get their own way.

Another strong characteristic of middle children is that they are the most secretive of all birth orders, and they are the last ones to seek the services of people like me. Perhaps they shun counselors and other helping professions because of another typical characteristic—they are very prone to embarrassment.

Oh, yes—one other characteristic of middle children is that they are the most monogamous of all the birth orders. Because they didn't fit in all that well while growing up in their families, they have a strong desire to make their own marriage work.

LASTBORNS SAY, "I'LL SHOW THEM!"

The lastborn or "baby" of the family often turns out to be the clown or the entertainer who keeps everyone in stitches. Lastborns seek attention because they feel so outdone and outdistanced by their older siblings.

While middle children feel rejected, lastborns often believe they are not taken seriously. As soon as they can start to figure out what's happening in life, lastborns become aware that they are inadequate. After all, they're the youngest, the smallest, the weakest, and the least equipped to cope. They are always being told, "You're not quite big enough or old enough to do that yet."

Somewhere along the line—usually early in life—lastborns say, "I'll show them!" And they do it by grabbing attention any way they can. Lastborns are very often outgoing and wind up in jobs like car salespeople and other vocations that are highly people-oriented.

OUR PARENTS LEAVE A PERMANENT MARK

We've talked about life style and birth order. Finally, we come to the third part of your background scenario: the kind of parents you had. I've saved parents to discuss last, not because they have the least influence, but because they have the most.

According to John Bradshaw (*Bradshaw On: The Family*), we have become much more aware of the impact of families on personality formation in the last thirty-five years.

Bradshaw believes we've always known the family has an influence on us, but it's only in recent years that researchers have discovered that this influence is far greater than we ever imagined. What your parents believed about life, right and wrong, and discipline (the family rules) deeply affected how they parented you and how you are parenting your children. As Bradshaw says, "Parenting forms children's core belief about themselves. Nothing could be more important. . . . All their choices depend on their view of themselves."[3]

Bradshaw is a best-selling author whose lectures have been seen widely on national television. He believes that in many families, the rules children are forced to live by are abusing and shaming because they destroy a child's inner identity. Along with shaming their children, Bradshaw says many parents "abandon" them. Sometimes they literally leave their children, or they may physically, sexually, emotionally, or mentally abuse them. There are, however, many other ways to abandon your children, even while living right in the same home with them. You can refuse to be there when they have their highs and their lows; you can be too busy to give them the time, attention, and direction they really need.

Sometimes parents use children to take care of their own (the parents') unmet needs. Parents even use children to take care of their marriages by putting them in the middle and sharing problems that are too heavy for any child to bear.

My own observations of families tell me that much of what Bradshaw says is right. Children need their parents while they are growing up, and when their parents aren't there for them, everyone pays a high price. I am confident, however, that the abandonment of children Bradshaw describes can be offset by Reality Discipline. When you use Reality Discipline with your children, you are there for them. You are interested. You aren't laying down a lot of rules that stifle their creativity and their spontaneity. You're letting them learn what life is really like by letting them experience the consequences of reality.

PARENTS SEND LIFE-MOLDING MESSAGES

We will be looking more closely at how to parent children with Reality Discipline in part III, but right now we're focusing on the kind of person you are and how that person is matching up with the kind of person your partner is to make a strong marriage. Even if your parents didn't do a perfect job, and even if they are guilty of abandoning you in one way or another, there is much you can do to offset those influences as you work with your partner to build a strong marriage team. Just being aware of how you were parented and the dynamics of the relationship between you and one or both of your parents can be a tremendous advantage. If husbands and wives want to trace some key differences in how they were parented, they need to look at four family relationships:

- how Dad treated Mom,
- how Mom treated Dad,
- how Dad treated the daughter, and
- how Mom treated the son.

When Dad treated Mom badly, the repercussions can pop up years later, when the children grow up. In one case, I was doing a radio talk show, and a woman called in to say, "I've been engaged to this wonderful guy for only two weeks. Already I'm getting cold chills. I think I want to back out. What's wrong with me?"

Deciding to give a good guess rather than a safe clinical answer, I replied, "But didn't your father leave your mother?"

I could almost hear the young woman's jaw drop over the telephone. "Why, yes—how did you know? I was fifteen and a half when Dad left. I never did understand, and nobody ever explained it to me."

"So, your perception of marriage is really that you will marry a man, pour everything into loving him and building a good marriage as your mother did, and then wind up deserted."

My caller admitted I was probably right, that she would have to think about it. I wished her well and urged her to find a counselor in her city who could help her sort out her ambivalence. Because her mother had been a good wife and her husband wound up leaving does not mean the same thing will happen to the daughter. But before this young girl marries, she must change her perceptions or she will go through married life never fully trusting her husband and always fearing the pain of desertion.

Possible scenarios and their effects on children are almost endless. Suppose a daughter watches her mother treat her dad with little respect—almost disdain. In a word, Mom dominates Dad. What kind of man do you think the daughter will find to marry? You're absolutely correct—the daughter will find someone she can push around, just as her mother pushed Daddy around. I've seen it happen again and again.

Much has been written in recent years about the effect fathers have on daughters, and I concur that their influence is tremendous. In his book *Always Daddy's Girl*, Norm Wright says:

> Like it or not, your father has made a lasting impression on you. Whether he was close or distant, present or absent, cold or warm, loving or abusive, your father has left his mark on you.
>
> And your father is still influencing your life today, probably more than you realize.[4]

There are all kinds of fathers and all kinds of relationships between dads and daughters, but one that stands out among the women I counsel is the daughter who grew up with the "dominant," authoritarian dad. He dominated his wife, and he also dominated his daughter. She learned quickly, as a very small child, that when the "big bear roared," everybody jumped. Now, at age thirty-seven or forty-four, this same woman jumps every time she hears any significant noise. And as a rule, her self-esteem is in a shambles.

In stark comparison, the father who becomes involved with his daughter in healthy, affirming, encouraging ways will give her a good self-concept—the feeling that she is worthwhile. Fortunate is the young woman who brings this sort of self-concept to a marriage, and even more fortunate is her husband.

Speaking of the husband, he, too, is a product of his parenting, and often his mother had a tremendous influence on him, for good or bad. In counseling situations, I often learn that the husband was spoiled by a mother who thought he was "so very special." Mothers often have a misconception of real love and tell dads who want to do a little disciplining to back off.

"Come on, Pete," they say. "He's only seven. Let it go."

This kind of mother treats her "little boy" like a little boy all his life, and when he grows up to be a man, he's still a little boy looking for a mom. He's still a little boy who's never been taught responsibility or how to treat a woman with respect. In fact, in some cases, he may have been allowed to get away with temper tantrums, insults, and even physically abusing his mother to some degree.

All this is very bad news—especially for the young man's marriage and the kind of relationship he will build with his own wife. Fortunate indeed is the young wife whose mother-in-law never let her son get away with anything. She taught him not to hit women, insult women, or show disrespect. And while she was at it, she taught him the fine art of picking up his socks, shorts, and other items that can get strewn from one end of the house to the other.

"Picking up after hubby" may provide all kinds of punch lines for humorous sketches on TV, but it's anything but humorous to the millions of women who have to do it day in and day out. Yes, there are some husbands who have to pick up after their wives, but I believe their number is much smaller than the number of wives who have to pick up after their husbands.

THE MASCULINE MYSTIQUE—IS IT REAL?

Out of such differences in backgrounds often come major differences in how husbands and wives perceive life and what is happening to them or around them.

At the risk of sounding sexist, I'm going to report reality as I see it in counseling sessions every week. As a general rule (and there are always exceptions to any rule), men are more external and women are more internal; men dwell on facts, while women center on feelings.

If you could eavesdrop on two men who are meeting each other for the first time, within thirty seconds you would probably hear the question, "And what do you do, John, for a living?" They both flash their vocational badge, and then, in typical male style, they'll talk about jobs, taxes, the dropping or rising price of stock or real estate, and what their favorite professional sports team is doing at the moment. They stay comfortable by keeping everything at arm's length. Later, when they arrive home, they tell their wives, "You know, honey, I met a guy today. He's all right, and next month we're hoping to get together to play some golf."

But suppose you eavesdrop on two women who have just met each other at a party. One may be an accountant, and the other has her MBA degree in finance and works for a bank. But it's doubtful that what they do for a living will come up in the conversation. If it does come up, it is usually as an appendage. It may flow right into the conversation and flow right out again—it never becomes a centerpiece. Instead, these two women will center their conversation on people—kids, men, families—and any number of other topics that will reveal who they are and how they feel.

I'm really not sure why women are so much more open and

honest, especially with one another. Some might say these characteristics are inherent in males and females. Others would claim that women learn to be more internal and feeling-centered and men more factual and guarded through the conditioning they receive as they grow up. Whatever the reason, these "stereotyped differences" between men and women are often there. The wise couple recognizes these differences, discusses them, and then tries to adjust to each other accordingly.

The goal in adjusting, of course, is to help the wife see the man's appreciation for things factual and to help the husband become willing to share his feelings. Men have made some progress in becoming more feeling-oriented in recent years, but they still have a long way to go.

I was watching an Oprah Winfrey show recently, and the subject for the day was sensitivity in men or something to that effect. Several comments had been made about how men needed to be more tender, understanding, communicative, and gentle, when a very Marlboro-looking type got up and said, "You know, all this is fine, but I think you gotta act like a man. Women may want us to say things like 'I want to share a thought with you, darling,' but the truth is, as men, we'll say it our way—'Hey, I just wanna tell ya something!'"

The young man got loud applause, the loudest I recall hearing throughout the entire show. I suppose that mostly men were claping, but nonetheless, he said something very important. No, it wasn't the part about "I just wanna tell ya something." I'm talking about the phrase "You know, you've gotta act like a man." Rightly or wrongly, this is a deep-seated male perception that isn't going to go away quickly.

The ideal goal is for a husband to "act like a man" but still treat his wife gently and tenderly. From what women tell me behind closed doors in counseling and seminar sessions, the ideal man is masculine but still treats his wife with gentle and tender respect.

The key word in recognizing each other's differences and working them out together is *respect.*

What's important to one spouse may not be equally important to the other. Nevertheless, each spouse can always respect the other's views and values. In the next chapter, I want to take a special look at values—the beliefs, convictions, and practices that are important and even vital to each partner in the marriage.

Don't Forget . . .

- There is no question that husbands and wives are different. The challenge is to put these differences together and become a team.
- When the chips are down, children will usually yell for Mom, not Dad.
- When working out differences, the goal is for neither spouse to win; the goal is to have the marriage win.
- Differences in the backgrounds of husband and wife come out of life style, birth order, and how they were parented. The wise couple is aware of these differences and makes allowances for them.
- Generally speaking, men tend to dwell on facts, women on feelings. Men are less personal and transparent, while women tend to be more open and honest. Women are emotionally closer to life; men are more comfortable at arm's length.
- The "ideal man" is masculine but still treats his wife with gentle and tender respect.

And Why Not Try . . .

- Discuss differences each of you bring to your marriage. Have you portioned out different roles according to your skills, interests, and preferences?
- Discuss your separate backgrounds. Decide who shows traits of being a controller, a pleaser, an attention-getter,

or a martyr. What significance does this have for how you treat each other? What changes could either of you make?

- Do a brief "birth order analysis" of each other. Be aware that the best birth order combinations for marriage are a firstborn and a lastborn. That doesn't mean other combinations can't get along, but they could face problems, especially two firstborns, who would tend to have very high expectations of each other. (For more on birth order and marriage, see "Worthwhile Reading" at the end of this book.)

- Discuss how you were parented. Talk about the meaning of John Bradshaw's statement on page 94: "Parenting forms children's core belief about themselves. Nothing could be more important. . . . All their choices depend on their view of themselves."

- Examine together how your personalities and the ways you were parented have shaped the way you relate to your own children. What do you see that you might want to change?

- Describe what it means to "act like a man" and "act like a woman." How can you treat each other with more gentleness, respect, and love?

Chapter 5

Why Personal Values Can Be a Minefield

———————⬤———————

And How to Deal with Their Powerful Influence

JUST AS THEY FAIL TO COMPREHEND HOW DIFFERENT THEY ARE IN background and perceptions, many couples are also in the dark about differences in their personal values. There is, however, no more powerful and pervasive force working in a home than the personal values each partner brings to the marriage.

Because values often involve strong feelings, they can cause friction in many areas. One young wife sat in my office trying to explain to me the increasing tensions in her marriage. "When we were dating, we seemed to see eye to eye on so many things. But now I can see that we are very different," she said. "For example, I can't believe Jim got so upset over something as insignificant as where to spend Mother's Day. I had no idea it meant that much to him."

The most significant words in this wife's statement were "*I had*

103

no idea it meant that much to him." But things do mean "that much" to everyone. Our values are the ideas, beliefs, and traditions that are very important to us.

What do I believe is right? What do I believe really works in life? What is worth fighting for? All these are values questions.

REALITY DISCIPLINE AND THE LEMAN CHECKBOOK

Values have always been important around the Leman house. We lean toward the old-fashioned, traditional kind. Some might say it's because we live out on the western frontier in the middle of the Arizona desert. But I think it goes back beyond any "code of the West" that we've adopted since moving to Tucson more than twenty years ago.

The values Sande and I hold dear today date clear back to the families in which we were reared. There we learned common courtesy, consideration for others, the Golden Rule, and a work ethic that assumes, "There ain't no free lunch." It may sound corny to some, but at the end of the day, we believe it's important to be able to look in the mirror and ask ourselves, "What did you do today to really help someone? Did you do a good job? Did you give it your best shot?"

Being real and genuine is also very important in our family. We aren't much for pretense or for trying to make an impression. We prefer openness, honesty, and transparency.

I was taught in my graduate school psychology courses, "Never be personal with clients." I have managed to violate this axiom consistently ever since. Why? Because I have always appreciated anyone who would take me aside and be personal with me—that is, talk from the heart. I always try to be honest with my clients. If that means expressing a "biased opinion," I go ahead and state that opinion to them, always making sure to identify it as such.

As you may have noticed in the accounts I relate about counseling clients, I often use familiar, informal language. I could be criticized in some psychological circles for doing this, but it works for me, and it seems to work for the people I counsel.

I'm sure that the major reason we practice Reality Discipline in our family and in our lives is the "traditional values" in which we believe. In a real sense, the Reality Discipline principles I have already explained to you are traditional values in themselves, such as treating people like persons, not things, sticking to your guns, and keeping responsibility where it belongs.

I want to add, however, that because we hold traditional values, we don't try to pretend we're perfect. As anyone who knows us will tell you, I have my weaknesses, and Sande has hers. A real advantage of using Reality Discipline in our marriage is being able to assign responsibilities to the most likely party—that is, to the one who will carry them through.

For example, at our house, we decided long ago that it would be better if Sande took care of the checkbook. A typical firstborn, she does a great job of keeping track of things, no thanks to me. Having grown up the lastborn baby of my family, I didn't develop that fine appreciation for order and sequence. I'm working at it because I know it's a weakness, but there is no question that I'm not equipped by natural ability and preference to handle the checkbook.

For instance, I'm always amazed when the bank sends us a detailed list of the checks we've written, once a month, and they even include the numbers of the checks. My response is, "What's all this for?" but Sande pounces on the bank statement in a flash. I guess she's afraid I'll mistake it for junk mail.

Turning the checkbook and bill-paying over to Sande was a partial answer to our problem. It was just too much trouble for me to carry my own separate checkbook around, so I made it a habit to tear a check or two out of her checkbook and put them in my wallet for "emergencies." Then, when I had the need to write a check, I would just go ahead and do so. But usually I would forget to record what I wrote. Later, when Sande tried to balance the checkbook with that once-a-month statement from the bank, she had to wrestle with check numbers that were out of sequence or checks that had not been returned because they were still in my wallet.

After some fairly serious "unbalanced checkbook sessions," I decided to use a little Reality Discipline on my lastborn ways. Since then, I've made a real effort to reform. Now I take blank checks only from Sande's checkbook, not from the supply in her drawer, and when I write a check, I really try to remember to give her a note with a check number and the amount. Yes, I know it would all be so simple if I just carried my own checkbook around and recorded all the checks I wrote in it. But old habits are hard to break, even for psychologists who tell other people how to use Reality Discipline in their lives.

I make this confession only to point out that I'm one of the lucky babies of the family who married a firstborn who knows how to take care of things—particularly financial matters. Woe unto the Leman family if Sande and I had *both* been lastborns!

I have talked with and counseled any number of couples who were both lastborn babies, and I have heard all kinds of horror stories about how they spent themselves into oblivion. One couple who had been married thirty-seven years told me they once had a lucrative little business going—a combination boutique and gift shop—but eventually it went belly-up straight into Chapter Eleven because neither one of them had bothered to keep consistent books.

"If we ever start another business," they told me, "we'll hire a firstborn to be our business manager and accountant."

Examples of how marriage partners value money differently are endless. Should a couple save for a new home, or should they keep renting the plush apartment and running up the credit-card total while they drive their matching BMWs? Different researchers and survey groups will tell you that one of the chief causes of divorce—if not the chief cause—is money, and it all goes back to how each marriage partner grew up. If she comes to the marriage from a well-to-do home where money was always plentiful (and therefore meaningless), it's going to be difficult if she marries a man whose family had very little.

If she has tastes running to Ethan Allen while he is more familiar with K Mart and Sears, reality says they are going to have to make some adjustments. If her family ate out a lot while his mother cooked seven days a week at home, they're going to have to make more adjustments. Making those kinds of adjustments starts with sitting down and talking about your individual backgrounds and your perceptions of life. Tell each other what is really important, what you really value. You will undoubtedly learn something—and strengthen your marriage while doing it.

VALUES DETERMINE YOUR PARENTING STYLE

Values come into play in a hurry when the children start to arrive. How were you and your spouse parented? How do each of you see the parenting task? If the husband was raised by authoritarian parents, for example, he may want to be authoritarian as well. On the other hand, he just could be so fed up with the "you'd better toe the mark" approach that he'll want to go completely permissive as his own personal vendetta against his authoritarian upbringing.

For the sake of illustration, suppose the husband wants to be authoritarian but his wife, who was raised by permissive parents, much prefers the laissez-faire approach to dealing with her kids. Every time he moves in to do some disciplining, she moves in to protect them. With piranhalike instincts, kids smell these inconsistencies in a flash, and they quickly learn how to pit one parent against the other while trying to avoid being disciplined.

A great proportion of the people I have counseled over the years have been children, and in more than 50 percent of the cases, one of the child's major problems was having parents who approached discipline from totally opposite directions. In part III of this book, I state my own values regarding childrearing, but the first rule any married couple should follow in using Reality Discipline with children is:

BE SURE YOU WORK TOGETHER
AS YOU PARENT YOUR KIDS.

My colleague Randy Carlson, who is also a counselor, and I host "Parent Talk," a daily call-in radio show that reaches across the country. One day our subject was "getting kids to cooperate at home," and our guests were Charlene and Dan, parents of a blended family who had grappled with this problem of learning how to work together in disciplining the children.

Dan was the quiet, passive type who hated hassles and preferred to avoid trouble whenever possible. Charlene had been reared in a military family, and after they had gotten married and had children, she had taken over the role of disciplinarian. Dan had allowed her to do so, but he would often "escape" by leaving the dinner table or a similar scene when things got hectic and Charlene started coming down with her "drill sergeant" approach.

Charlene finally realized she was very authoritarian because she had been parented that way herself and she was making all the rules. She and Dan talked—yes, and even prayed—about their problem and decided to move toward each other in the parenting task rather than further and further apart. Charlene learned to ease up and be more flexible, while Dan learned to take over more when the children caused tension—at the dinner table, for example.

WHY THE HOLIDAYS AREN'T ALWAYS HAPPY

Even something like establishing holiday traditions can become a bone of contention, because each partner has a different set of values. Back in chapter 3, I suggested that young parents try to establish their own holiday traditions as soon as possible. Instead of going to his parents' home or her parents' home for Christmas or Thanksgiving, have Christmas or Thanksgiving at your own place. Invite your parents over for a change, rather than always going to their home.

Holding out for practicing your own family traditions during holidays can be a challenging task. It can lead to friction, not only between the two of you, but also with other relatives. Just last Christmas, after nearly twenty-five years of marriage, I experienced my own holiday tradition "crisis."

Because I'm always eager to give my children a taste of their "Leman roots," I convinced the family that it would be great to spend a Christmas holiday back in New York State. By the middle of December, we had left sunny Tucson and were huddling around a roaring fireplace in the same cottage we live in during summer vacations, on the shores of Chautauqua Lake, not far from my sister's home in Jamestown.

A few days after we arrived, I took my mother and my firstborn sister, Sally, to breakfast at a local restaurant. Because it was still "very early" in the morning, around ten o'clock, Sande remained behind in her favorite place—bed. Mom and I got there first, and when Sally walked in, her first words were, "I've got a great idea. Why don't you come to our house for Christmas Eve?"

I gave this a couple of seconds' thought and replied, "I'm sorry, Sally, but I don't want to come to your house on Christmas Eve."

Looking back, I suppose I could have been a bit more diplomatic. Within seconds of my announcement of how I preferred to spend Christmas Eve, my mother was in tears and assuring her firstborn daughter, "I'll come, I'll come." Before the waitress even came for our order, my sister was also in tears, and my mother was saying through her sobs, "You're terrible—how could you be so terrible?"

"I don't think you understand," Sally sniffed. "It would be great to have Christmas Eve together. It hurts my feelings that you don't want to be together. We haven't been together on Christmas Eve for more than thirty years."

I pointed out that we were all going to have Christmas Day

together, with dinner at our cottage. All my children, two of her children, and even her grandchildren would be there. Gently, I tried to explain that as the lastborn baby in the family, I much preferred my hang-loose approach to Christmas Eve to the rather structured evening Sally and her husband, Wes, would have.

I tried to point out to Sally that her family would attend church services at eleven o'clock at night on Christmas Eve, but I didn't want to disturb or intrude on their traditions. With our three-year-old, we simply didn't want to go to church that late.

Our Christmas Eve plans would include going to church early, around five, then coming home and having a casual buffet featuring turkey sandwiches. Then we would put on Christmas records, and if any of us had any final gift-wrapping to do, we would slip away to take care of that.

"We always look forward," I concluded, "to having a very loose and spontaneous evening."

Sally didn't really hear me. "But we want you to be there," she urged. "Grandpa is going to read the Christmas story."

By Grandpa, Sally was referring to her father-in-law, who also lives in Jamestown and who always has Sally and her family come to his home on Christmas Eve. Again, I began feeling like an intruder on her family's traditions, which she was changing in order to invite us to her place.

"Sally, we also read the Christmas story on Christmas Eve," I said with what I hoped was a twinkle in my eye. "I believe it's found in the book of Matthew, and over in Luke as well. I think I'll read from Luke. I trust him more because he was a physician."

My little attempt at humor died in midair, frozen in an icy wall of gloom. The rest of breakfast was very quiet, but I stuck to my guns. I preferred risking disapproval, hurt feelings, and ruffled feathers to being forced to agree to something I knew I and the rest of my family would not enjoy. What we do on Christmas Eve may not seem like anything profound, but it's something we value highly, and I cared enough about that value to admit to my sister how I really felt.

I believe that every family is like a snowflake—different and unique. Every family needs its own way of doing things—its own traditions. When you are the head of a family, you have to protect those traditions and your integrity as a family.

As I said, sticking to your guns concerning your personal values takes fortitude and patience. After that breakfast meeting with Sally and my mother, I went home and told my family what had happened. Then I took a vote and wanted to know how many wanted to go to Sally's house for dinner on Christmas Eve and how many wanted to stay at the cottage. The Leman children voted unanimously for the cottage, but Sande, firstborn pleaser that she is, felt we should go to Sally's.

Sande is so kind and gracious that she would not dream of offending anyone. I told her she was outvoted five to one and that I had probably offended Sally already anyway, but that it would all work out. Sande went along, reluctantly. I knew she really preferred for our family to have Christmas Eve alone, just as I did, but her pleaser personality was giving her a few guilties.

The Saturday before Christmas, I was doing the "Parent Talk" radio show over the long-distance phone with my partner, Randy, back in Tucson. Just before we went on the air, I asked him what our subject was for the day, and he said, "'Your in-laws and the holidays.'" Immediately I told Randy about my breakfast conversation with Sally and my mother. He commented, "You know, this happens in a lot of families. Let's talk about it today on the air."

So with a national audience listening, we got into it during the program, and Randy asked people to call in and vote on: "How should Kevin spend Christmas Eve?"

Some people called to say I was being childish and should just go over to my sister's and have a good time. But other people said, "No, I think you're doing the right thing. I admire your stance." As

I recall, those who agreed with my decision outnumbered those who didn't by at least two to one.

Interestingly enough, it all did work out. Our family had its usual Christmas Eve, as did Sally's. Then on Christmas Day, Sally and her family came over for dinner, and everything went beautifully. The children played together, the adults relaxed, and the proverbial good time was had by all, including Sande. We survived our Christmas crisis. Mom, whom I love dearly, no longer thinks her cub is terrible. Sally is still my special sister. I'm her favorite cub-brother, and we love each other as much as ever.

A CRUCIAL BUT OFTEN-NEGLECTED AREA

Whenever I talk about values, I can't help but think of the need for using Reality Discipline on your marriage in the area of the spiritual. I believe a husband and wife make a big mistake if they allow a spiritual void to occur in their marriage and in their family.

Early in our marriage, Sande and I made worshipping together one of our most important values. We realize that reality has a way of confronting us daily with tough questions about truth, morals, and right and wrong. Without a biblical base, how do we give our children answers that make any sense?

I often hear parents say, "We don't want to cram anything down our children's throats. When they're old enough, they'll figure it out for themselves."

That sounds open-minded, but as someone said, "You can be so open-minded, your brains fall out." Real life demands that we establish a relationship with almighty God through His Son, Jesus Christ. And if that base is to mean anything, we will take time to train our children in the faith. We will practice it before them daily.

Despite the many benefits of cultivating the spiritual in life, I find many people who get away from doing this. Because we live in an age of "rootlessness," I often run into couples who were reared in a church somewhere back home, and now they've moved across the country and "dropped out" as far as church attendance is concerned. It can be sensitive to bring this subject up with clients, but I do it anyway because I believe that there are three sides to life. Not only are there the physical and the mental/emotional, but there is also the spiritual.

Often I deal with clients who obviously want peace that goes beyond physical or emotional concerns. I ask them where they are spiritually, and they may come back with, "I really don't want to talk about religion." Then they usually tell me they grew up in a very strict religious home where God was depicted as the big policeman in the sky, always looking down on them with a baleful eye, ready to pounce at the slightest infraction of the rules.

"I'm not talking about 'religion,'" I reply. "I am talking about what I believe is a basic need deep within all of us—the need for a relationship with the Creator."

In more than twenty years of counseling, I have met people with all kinds of faiths or what they believe is no faith at all. But I've never met anyone without spiritual needs. It is my firm conviction that every marriage needs a spiritual base, with both partners tuned in on the same wavelength, if at all possible.

It's encouraging to see that during the late 1980s and early 1990s, there has been a "spiritual revival" of sorts, particularly among the baby boomers, that huge chunk of the U.S. population—some 76 million—who were born between 1946 and 1964. According to a cover article in *Newsweek,* roughly two-thirds of the boomers had dropped out of organized religion. But in recent years, more than one-third have returned. Around 57 percent—about 43 million people—are attending a church or synagogue, and about 60 percent of them are married with children.[1]

When interviewed by *Newsweek,* one man said that during the past year, he had felt a need to stop and reassess his life. "I had reached a certain level of success," he said, "and what does it all mean?"[2]

That's exactly my point. It's hard to get a handle on what life means without developing your spiritual values. Some people wonder how they can begin. I simply encourage them to start talking to their Creator—a process that often goes by the name of *prayer*—and reading the Bible. It's also important to find Christian fellowship in a church where the Word of God is preached.

What happens when two people of radically different religious backgrounds marry? For example, a conservative marries a liberal. They know they have different backgrounds, but love blinds them to any problems this might cause later. They will work it out—love will find a way.

Once they're married, however, love doesn't find a way as much as Reality Discipline does. The couple with very different backgrounds needs to sit down and discuss this thoroughly and make some decisions. Suppose she is the conservative and really wants to practice her faith. He is the liberal and has slipped in church attendance since leaving home. If they have children, how will they be trained—in the conservative tradition or in the liberal? These are hard questions that must be dealt with, and if they're not dealt with before a couple is married, they should be dealt with as soon as possible, preferably before the children arrive.

An important consideration is the religious motivation and involvement in each spouse's family. Suppose, for example, her family are all fervent conservatives, and they put pressure on the couple to have the children trained in that kind of church. They may even pressure their daughter's husband to convert to conservatism. Meanwhile, his family are fervent liberals, and they are putting on pressure from their side of the family.

How will the couple handle all these questions and pressures? Whatever they do, they must come together and make a stand. Otherwise, they may find one set of parents or the other running their lives. The key Reality Discipline principle to use in this case is, "The whole—your marriage and your family—is more important than what your in-laws think."

How Do You Deal with Differences?

Differences in background, differences in perceptions, differences in values—all these can add up to a lot of pressure and stress unless you know how to cope. I have two basic suggestions for using Reality Discipline to deal with your differences.

1. Care enough to confront each other (lovingly, of course).
2. Care enough to work at changing yourself for the good of your partner and your marriage.

I have already touched on caring enough to confront in the story of why I turned down my sister's invitation to bring my family to her house on Christmas Eve. I could have accepted Sally's invitation and spent the evening masking my resentment and other uncomfortable feelings. Instead, I chose to communicate how I really felt.

There's a lot of discussion today about "the need to communicate"—especially in marriages and in families. I believe *communication* is an overused word and an underdeveloped skill. The reason it is so underdeveloped is that many people are too lazy or too fearful to try.

Communication starts with being honest—what David Augsburger (in *Caring Enough to Confront*) calls "truthing it in love." Augsburger points out that conflict in marriage is natural: "Conflict is viewed as neutral (neither good nor bad) and natural (neither to be avoided or short-circuited). Working through differences by giving clear messages of 'I care' and 'I want' . . . is most helpful."[3]

There are two basic approaches to dealing with differences in a marriage: You can let those differences drive you apart by attacking and criticizing each other, or you can learn to appreciate your differences and even celebrate them. But always remember:

Go after the problem without going after each other.

A key word is *adjustment.* Adjusting means changing and adopting different behavior, not because you're trying to ignore problems, but because you're trying to face reality and work them through.

THE CONTROLLER, THE PLEASER, AND VALUES

In chapter 4, I mentioned that people with a controller life style often marry pleasers, who believe they count only when they are making the oceans of life smooth for everyone around them. In the typical controller-pleaser marriage, the partners usually have radically different values.

Controllers value winning at any price; pleasers value peace, also at any price. Controllers value being right, and they aren't that concerned about being liked; pleasers value being liked, and they will let people walk all over them, even when they know they are right or not to blame.

The most common pairing finds the husband as the controller and his wife as the pleaser. This was the case with Frank and Judy, two firstborns who had five children. Judy was a beautiful brunette, color coordinated from head to toe, with dark eyes, a flashing smile, and a perfect figure, even after five children, most of whom were now in their teens.

Frank was equally well dressed, a tall, imposing man who exuded confidence. They appeared to neighbors and friends to "have it all," but it turned out they had very little going in their marriage. They came to me after Judy finally had enough of trying to please a man who "couldn't be pleased." Frank's attitude seemed to be, "Let's get this over with—I have to get back to the store." It was quickly apparent that Frank's values centered on a strong work ethic and his business, which he had inherited from his parents.

Actually, the "store" was a chain of retail stereo outlets that sold at wholesale prices. Sales had gone flat, and Frank was in danger of losing everything. Two of the stores were up for sale, and the remaining three were limping along. On paper, Frank's accountant was trying to make everything look good, but the empire was crumbling.

Frank's answer to the crisis was to increase his normal twelve-hour day to eighteen. He had also resumed drinking, which he had stopped completely a year before meeting and marrying Judy. The fact that Frank was supposedly a nondrinker had attracted Judy, because she had an alcoholic father, which had caused extreme pain and suffering in her own family as she was growing up.

Now that Frank had started drinking again and the marriage was coming apart, everything that Judy valued seemed to be coming apart as well. She felt betrayed and was at the end of her patience.

"We never see him—he might as well not even be alive," she complained with bitterness in her voice. "Sometimes I even wish that he would just die."

Judy admitted to feeling "nothing inside." They slept in twin beds, and there had been no sex between them for almost two years. "I'm just his maid and housekeeper," Judy continued, "someone to keep up the perfect front he thinks is so important."

The tension between Frank and Judy was bad enough, but as often happens in a dysfunctional family, the children had picked up on their parents' problems and were causing some of their own. The oldest son, nineteen, had gotten his girlfriend pregnant and was pushing her to get an abortion. Their sixteen-year-old daughter had gone from straight A's to F's and had recently run away for three days with her boyfriend, who had introduced her to the "wonderful world" of drugs.

THEIR PRIORITIES REVEALED THEIR VALUES

Obviously, much more was crumbling than Frank's business. His marriage and his family were in deep, deep trouble. When I asked each spouse what the other's priorities were, the values popped up thick and fast. Judy said: "Number one is his job, by far. Number two is his family—not *our* family, but his—especially his mother. Number three would be certain other people, all business related. Number four would be the children, and I might come in as number five."

When asked the same question, Frank replied: "Judy's number-one priority is the kids. Number two is God—her faith. Number three is animals—we have three dogs, a couple of cats, two riding horses, and a parakeet. Number four? Me, I guess."

When Frank mentioned animals as one of his wife's main priorities, I made a mental note to explore how she had been hurt in life and by whom. People who have been hurt, particularly women, often have a great fondness for animals. Judy desperately needed a husband who was attentive, caring, and loving, but obviously that wasn't happening, and she was filling the void by pouring her life into her children and pets.

Next, I asked each spouse to describe the other. Judy said of Frank: "Very reliable, responsible, impatient. He has little paper piles all over his desk. He's a lonely guy, and he rarely makes any of the kids' games or activities."

Frank described Judy this way: "A wonderful mom, very loving and affectionate. She's emotional, disorganized, and unprepared. She also has very high expectations, particularly of me."

Things were getting a little clearer. Even though she was a pleaser, Judy showed tendencies toward being a flaw-picker. As I learned later, besides being an alcoholic, her father had been critical and authoritarian. She had spent her growing-up years trying to please her father, but she had never measured up. Ironically, she did adopt his flaw-picking tendencies, and that's what had brought her into her marriage with Frank with a lot of high expectations.

Judy's pleaser personality, mixed with her high expectations of Frank, had proved to be a double whammy. The more she had tried to please him, the more disappointed she had become as he had buried himself in his business and failed to meet her needs for attention and caring.

Frank, on the other hand, was so focused on his business that all he could see was that "Judy doesn't care about what I've worked for all my life, what my father and mother worked night and day to create."

"Have you ever talked with Judy about what she values, what she thinks is important?" I asked.

"*Talked* with her?" Frank asked with a sardonic smile. "Well, I've had to do a lot of listening to her complaints. Frankly, doc, I can't figure her out. I give her everything she wants. I tell her I work the long hours because I'm doing it for her and the kids, but she doesn't hear me. Doc, I've tried, but I learned a long time ago that I'll never measure up to what she wants—whatever that is."

"Let me ask you this, Frank," I continued. "Would you rather lose your business or your family?"

That stopped Frank cold. He sat for almost a minute before answering as he tried to sort out what he valued most.

"That is a very difficult question," he finally responded. "Maybe it's even a moot point. It looks as if I'm going to be losing both."

"I can't speak for your business—that's your area of expertise. But I can speak for your marriage and family. You can salvage this if you want to change your priorities. If you value your family at all, it can be done."

Frank left that day, not at all sure he wanted to try. In fact, after that first session, I almost had to admit the marriage was brain dead.

FRANK'S CONTROLLER NATURE WAS CHALLENGED

I was surprised when Frank and Judy came back for their next appointment. Frank was not overly enthused, but something I had said challenged his controller's entrepreneurial nature. The idea that his life was totally out of control was more than he cared to admit. He was willing to try to change things, but he had to admit he wasn't too hopeful.

I began by suggesting to Frank that he start by doing two things: First, stop the drinking that he had recently started. Judy's background in a co-dependent home, where alcohol had reigned supreme in her father's life, was a critical issue, and Frank had to realize it.

"You can't really appreciate how much Judy values a home where alcohol is not even present," I told Frank. "If you're interested at all in trying to salvage your marriage, you've got to lay off the booze."

Second, I suggested to Frank that he take control of his own schedule and simply refuse to pour eighteen hours a day into his business, six and seven days a week. Frank wasn't enthused about either suggestion. He loved working, and he didn't see anything wrong with a glass of wine now and then "to calm his nerves." Grudgingly he laid off alcohol completely, and he also agreed to try coming home at least three nights a week by six o'clock.

It wasn't much of a start, but at least Frank was trying to take some baby steps back toward his family. Later, he told me that leaving by 5:30 to get home by 6:00 was so out of character for him that on at least two occasions, some of his employees followed him out to the parking lot to ask him what was wrong.

"Nothing's wrong," Frank would snap. "I'm just going home for dinner. I don't live here, you know."

On Judy's side, she was impressed by Frank's efforts, but not very. I had to stress to her that she must bite her tongue because of all the garbage that had accumulated in the past.

"Even when a husband starts trying to change, a wife will often refuse to believe he means it, and she can actually torpedo the marriage with more complaints and accusations," I explained to Judy. "A wife who has been hurt as you have is so used to it that she is looking for more of the same in almost everything that happens."

Judy said that all she could do was try. She still felt nothing for Frank, and she was sure he felt nothing for her.

It's almost a year later at the time of this writing, and their marriage is still on the bubble. Frank has made some progress with trying to rearrange his priorities, but rearranging his values will take longer. Values are so deeply ingrained, you don't change them in a few months because some counselor tells you to do so.

Since her initial outburst of bitterness and threats of divorce, Judy has softened slightly and is trying to confront Frank gently rather than holding it all in in typical pleaser fashion and then dumping the whole load when her frustration becomes unbearable.

Both of them are taking small steps toward changing. They have a chance, but they must fight slipping back into earlier learned behavior—the old values. In fact, what they will need to do is hammer out new values together.

If they make it, it will be one day at a time. It won't be because of some "Eureka!" decision on his part or hers. Much will depend on whether they can start thinking about each other's needs instead of their own.

Ten times out of ten, husbands and wives end up in my office because of unmet needs in one or both partners. In the next chapter, we take a closer look at the needs of husbands and wives and how Reality Discipline can insure that everyone's needs are met every day.

Don't Forget . . .

- Differences in personal and spiritual values are one of the most powerful and pervasive forces working on any marriage.
- One of the major battlegrounds in many marriages is money, and values are often at the bottom of the problem.
- Values in parenting style become crucially important when the children start to arrive. Spouses should strive to work together as they parent their children.

- It's important to work out your own family traditions and to value them enough to fight for them, if necessary.
- Spiritual values could possibly be the most important of all for any family. Without a spiritual anchor, the family is morally and ethically adrift.
- When dealing with differences in values, as well as backgrounds and perceptions, care enough to confront each other lovingly, and work hard at changing yourself, not your partner.
- No matter what your background, your life style, or your values might be, always try to go after the problem instead of each other.

And Why Not Try . . .

- Sit down and talk together about values. Ask each other, "What are your most important personal values—what do you think is really most important about how to live and function in a family?"
- When parceling out different household roles and duties, keep well in mind the personal values of each spouse. For example, don't turn a lackadaisical lastborn loose with a checkbook if there is a firstborn partner who is more orderly, organized, and financially minded.
- Talk together about how you are parenting the children. Take inventory on how you are handling any disagreements you might have. Do you always make sure you disagree in private and never in front of the children? Plan how you can give more encouragement and support to each other in situations requiring discipline.
- Analyze where you are spending holidays as a family. Are you creating your own family traditions, or are you always going to the home of one set of parents or the other? Discuss whether this is satisfactory and if you might not want to start creating traditions of your own.

- Encourage each other to keep the spiritual life central and make worship a regular part of family life. If spiritual values have not been that important in your family, make plans to try churches in your neighborhood. Find some setting in which you can worship together as a family.
- Discuss the way the two of you typically resolve conflicts. How can you do that in a more loving manner?

Chapter 6

Her Needs and His

The Most Important Differences of All

RECENTLY I WAS TALKING WITH A YOUNG WIFE AND MOTHER OF TWO children under the age of ten. She was ready to end her marriage because she was sick and tired of carrying the entire load. Her husband was totally inattentive and disinterested in his family. Whenever she wanted to talk, he wanted to watch TV.

"Not now, another time," he would say. This went on for years, and finally she said, "I can't live like this anymore. He doesn't help. It's all on me. I do it all."

High mortgage payments and debts up to their eyeballs didn't help. When her husband suggested that she get a full-time job to help with the finances, she flatly refused. As she related the story to me, she said, "Do you know something? I don't even care anymore. It's easier when you don't care."

For more than ten years she had complained, but she had not really confronted in love, and neither had he. When she nagged, he simply went deeper into his shell, and the gulf between them had widened.

How different it could have been if they had used Reality Discipline early on and decided to "truth it in love"! He needed to know that when he walked in from work after his wife had been grappling all day with two young children, she didn't see only a husband come through the door. She saw *relief.* To put it in baseball terms, she was ready to call in the bullpen so she could rest for a couple of innings. But when she tried to get him to help, he wasn't interested. He didn't hear her because it was his habit to tune her out.

We are all creatures of habit, and we do what we do because we have done it that same way over and over. For example, we drive to work, and we don't even have to think about it. It's six blocks down and then five blocks to the right, and we pull into the parking lot.

Without thinking about it, this husband let his wife continue to do all the work while he simply plopped on the couch to watch TV. After all, he had been out there "busting his tail" all day for her and the kids, and what else did she expect him to do?

I met this woman during one of my travels, and as she talked, it became apparent that she was long past the point where counseling might have done any good. Her story was saddening because it really didn't have to be that way. If they could have learned how to care enough to really confront each other, both of them could have made changes. He might have started realizing that he had certain bad habits and that he needed to replace those habits with good ones. He could have started thinking differently. Maybe it would be more accurate to say that he could have started thinking, period.

Then, when he caught himself reverting to the old habits, he could have stopped and come to his wife to say, "I'm sorry. Please forgive me. What can I do?"

As for the wife, her husband's constant neglect had caused her to develop a bad habit as well—nagging. By learning to think differently, every time he irritated her she could have communicated her needs rather than her anger.

THE TEN BASIC NEEDS IN A MARRIAGE

When married couples finally decide to get some counseling, she usually comes willingly, but *he* is there only after leaving heel marks on the rug from the front door of the office all the way back to my desk. By then, their problems seem overwhelming, or so they both tell me. But I don't let that discourage me. I'm committed to saving every marriage I can, and I use every weapon in my arsenal to do so.

One of those weapons centers on that short but very big word: *needs.*

In his best-selling book *His Needs, Her Needs,* Willard F. Harley, Jr., lists five basic needs men expect their wives to fulfill and five needs women want their husbands to meet. He has seen these needs surface over and over in more than twenty years of counseling literally thousands of couples with troubled marriages, particularly those that are torn by extramarital affairs. What are men's five basic needs, according to Harley? In marriage, men want:

1. sexual fulfillment,
2. recreational companionship,
3. an attractive spouse,
4. domestic support (a well-maintained, peaceful home), and
5. admiration (as in "respect").

And women's five basic needs? From their husbands, women want:

1. affection,
2. conversation,
3. honesty and openness,
4. financial support, and
5. family commitment.

For the most part, Harley's lists, compiled basically from his experience in Minnesota, coincide with what I've seen in more than twenty years of counseling in Arizona. I might have described some things in slightly different terms, but overall he touches on the nerve center that can cause the most trouble in marriage. I highly recommend *His Needs, Her Needs* everywhere I go. It is one of the most practical and helpful books on marriage in print today.

While Harley gives equal weight to all ten of the needs in his list, I believe husbands and wives can do a lot to strengthen their marriages if they honestly confront both the man's need for sexual fulfillment and the woman's need for affection. What we must understand, however, is that even though a man's basic need is for sexual fulfillment, that doesn't mean he doesn't like affection—to be held, talked to lovingly, and even comforted. And because a woman's basic need is for affection, that doesn't mean she doesn't enjoy sex.

After I discussed the man's need for sex and the woman's need for affection at a seminar, a woman came up afterward to challenge me: "Were you trying to say that men like sex and women don't? Were you trying to say that women only want affection?"

"Not at all," I responded. "I believe that when a man shows a woman the right kind of affection, it prepares her to enjoy tremendous sex. Many women can enjoy sex to a higher degree than men."

WITH MALES, "SEXISM" COMES NATURALLY

Having said that, I must admit men are still men, particularly when it comes to how they see women, what they think of them, and how they relate to them.

The basic male attitude starts very young and really kicks into gear when a boy hits puberty. Eavesdrop on any group of junior high boys, and you'll understand what I mean. It's my guess that the conversation hasn't changed much in several thousand years. When puberty starts, a boy becomes very interested in a woman's body—her looks in general. The male is sexually stimulated by sight, and the conversations of young boys, soon to be men, are peppered with comments about how women look, how they are "built," and other enthusiastic observations.

Earlier I discussed how boys can become sexist when they have a sexist father for a role model, but there are other ways for sexism to rear its ugly head. On our "Parent Talk" radio show, a mother called in and told me about the trouble she was having with her twelve-year-old son. When she would ask him to take out the garbage or dry some dishes, he would retort, "That's not a man's job—that's your job because you're a woman."

"Where does he get that from?" I wanted to know, suspecting her husband.

"I really don't know," she answered. "My husband treats me with respect, helps with the housework—we have a very healthy operation. But my son has other ideas."

It's my best guess that her boy is getting these "other ideas" from his peer group. Perhaps some of his friends have fathers who are sexist, and they are simply passing the word along to him.

MEN BRING A PHYSICAL APPROACH TO MARRIAGE

Another interesting male behavioral phenomenon that starts in junior high school can be seen when a boy chooses a girl he likes and proceeds to tease, push, and even sock her hard on the arm. If you tell that junior high girl that the boy is getting physical with her because he likes her, she can't believe it.

"He *does?*" the girl might say. "Then why does he keep shoving and hitting me?"

It's hard for a young girl to understand that a boy can't always express his liking for her without getting physical. He will outgrow this (at least, boys who become men outgrow this) and learn more acceptable ways to show her he is interested. But until then, the young teenage girl will just have to tough it out as she learns that boys are truly a different breed.

When boys grow up to become men who get married, they bring this basically physical approach to the marriage. And when they aren't well-informed about a woman's needs and how a woman functions, they often appear to have only one idée fixe— sex, sex, and more sex. I hear this complaint over and over in my own office, as Dr. Harley has heard it in his. The answer is to blend the man's need for sexual fulfillment with the woman's need for affection. As Harley puts it:

> When it comes to sex and affection,
> you can't have one without the other![1]

When a man gives his wife the right amount of affection, she is usually more than happy to meet his sexual needs. And with a "slow hand and gentle touch," he can find himself with a tiger in his bed.

WHEN "I DON'T CARE" MEANS SOMETHING ELSE

A husband can show affection to his wife in many ways if he really knows the person to whom he's married. To a woman, affection is having her husband know what she likes and be willing to go out of his way to say in different ways, "I love you, I care about you."

Some husbands don't have a clue about how to do this, and they often excuse themselves by saying, "She knows I'm not the affectionate type." Others at least try to do the affectionate thing, but they blow it because they don't work hard enough at knowing their wives and what they really want.

I often tell a story at seminars that gets a tremendous response—at least from the women in the audience. I ask them to picture the following scene:

It is Friday night, and the wife has arrived home first from work. She is just starting to think about preparing dinner when her husband drags in after his week of fighting deadlines and freeways.

This is the man who used to leave her love notes under the windshield wipers of her car when they were in college. And who slipped love notes under the door of her apartment when they were dating. This is the same handsome lover who walked her down the aisle and before God and man said, "I do." Now, after several years of marriage, he comes home on Friday night and mutters such romantic nothings such as "Is there any mail?" and "What's for dinner?"

Questions like these make the typical wife just want to soar—as in "go straight up." Just then, however, the perceptive hubby notes that something is missing: "By the way, where are the kids?"

"The kids? They're all at Grandma's to stay overnight—it's just the two of us for dinner."

"Just the *two* of us?" The weary knight of the freeways is starting to come to.

"Yes," replies his wife.

"Put that stuff away—forget about making dinner. I'll take you out to dinner."

His wife needs to hear those magic words *out to dinner* only once. She's in the car in a flash. Her husband joins her a few seconds later because he *walked* to the car!

(Sometimes I think that the three little words every woman loves to hear are not *I love you* but *out to dinner*. I've had many women tell me I'm absolutely right.)

But let's continue our story. The husband and wife are driving into town, and he turns and says, "Honey, where would you like to go to dinner?"

Now, to give him credit, he's trying to be a good guy. He's trying to find out where his wife wants to go for dinner. What does she say? As only wives can do, she responds, "Oh, I don't care."

Using his naturally keen insight, our perceptive hero concludes: *Well, she doesn't seem to care where we go.* His male mind continues to function with computerlike speed as he reasons, *I'm dead tired anyway, and the kids aren't home, so maybe we'll just get a quick bite to eat, and then . . .*

"Honey," he says as he turns back to her with what he thinks is an adoring look, "what do you say that we go down and see the Colonel?"

Her mouth agape, his wife stares back at him and says, "The Colonel? As in Kentucky Fried Chicken? *You want to take me to see the Colonel?*"

At that moment, a deep freeze instantaneously fills the car. This husband had better like his chicken cold, because that's the way things will be the rest of the evening.

You see, this husband missed the point. When his wife said "I don't care" where they went for dinner, she didn't exactly mean "I don't care." Of course she cared. Furthermore, she thought: *If he really loves me, he will* instinctively *know where I want to go for dinner.*

Some husbands throw up their hands in exasperation and exclaim, "She wants me to read her mind!" But that's not quite it. What women want their husbands to do is *anticipate their needs well in advance,* not after the fact.

THIS HUSBAND REALLY KNEW HIS WIFE

I know of an insurance agent who won a trip to a resort hotel in San Diego. His wife loves San Diego, and he wanted to surprise her with the news. Instead of offhandedly mentioning his special prize to her between helpings of broccoli and baked potatoes, he decided to make all kinds of secret preparations. He waited until the day they were to leave, and then he came home unexpectedly at 10:30 in the morning and said, "Honey, we're going to San Diego."

"What do you mean, we're going to San Diego?" she said incredulously. "I don't know what you're talking about."

Whipping out the plane tickets, hubby said, "Here—see for yourself."

"That's *today!*" she practically shrieked. "What about the children ... ?"

"My mom is due here in about two minutes. She's going to take care of the children."

"But we can't leave right now. Look at my hair!"

Long years of experience had taught this husband not to be dismayed by one of the most common female ploys known to mankind—"But what about my hair?"

"Honey," he said soothingly, "an hour and a half after we land at Lindbergh Field in San Diego, you've got an appointment to get your hair done at the Hotel Coronado."

At this point, all the wife's objections and defensiveness melted like a snowman in the San Diego sun. Her scowls of consternation were replaced by smiles of anticipated pleasure. She put her arms around her husband and simply said, "Honey, I love you," and off to San Diego they went for an affectionate—and passionate—weekend.

The difference between this husband and the one who wanted to visit the Colonel is huge—maybe light-years apart. One man at least thought of taking his wife out to dinner, but he didn't know her well enough to follow through and make "out to dinner" something special. The insurance agent, however, had his surprise planned down to the final details. He knew his wife would be worried about her hair, and he covered that. He knew she would be worried about the kids, and he covered that, too. In fact, he covered a multitude of details to make the trip special. And in doing so, he communicated to his wife, "I know you, I know you intimately, and I want to meet your needs. I want to make you happy."

In a way, he "reached into her soul" to tell her he wanted to do something special just for her. I believe every husband can do the same with his wife—in his own way, with his own timing. It's simply a matter of wanting to bother, wanting to take the time, wanting to learn who your mate really is—what she likes and why.

A HUG HAS AWESOME POWER

Perhaps an even more basic way a man can show affection to his wife is through the simple power of touch. No, I don't mean sexual touching. I'm talking about simple little things like hugs and back rubs.

A hug says, "I'll take care of you and protect you. You are important to me." A hug says, "I'm concerned about your problems, and I want to be there for you." A hug can say, "You've done a great job—I'm really proud of you!" As Willard Harley puts it, "Men need to understand how strongly women need these affirmations. *For the typical wife, there can hardly be enough of them.*"[2]

Something I admit having had to learn in my own marriage is the importance that women give to being physically held without necessarily having sex. I tell husbands that they must learn to give foot rubs, back rubs, and the like to their wives—without sex. Let me emphasize that—*without* sex. When a husband performs simple acts of affection like hugs and back rubs, his wife concludes, *He really does care. He cares for* me. *He doesn't just love my body.* As I said above, it's all-important to "know your mate." It's vital to know *when* she likes a back rub or a foot rub the best.

My wife, Sande, is a sleeper, as in "sleep in until eleven in the morning." She doesn't sleep in on weekdays, of course, but on Saturdays, that's where you'll find her. Personally, I think sleeping in is a waste of time, but if I go in there, bang around, and say in a painfully loud voice, "*Seems to me you ought to be up!*" it could be a very long day. In fact, it could be a very long winter.

Suppose we arrive at Saturday morning after a long week during which I took a quick trip out of town to do a seminar, a talk show, and a banquet talk. I'm lonesome for Sande's company, but there she is, fast asleep with the day already half gone.

To get her going, I use my best strategy. First, I make her a good cup of coffee and bring it to her bedside. Then I begin to scratch her back. She wakes up on the first scratch—don't ask me why—she just loves to have her back scratched. Then I rub her arms, her feet, and her legs, and by now she's purring like a kitten. That way, the day starts off on a very good note.

Of course, I could plunk the coffee down, spill most of it on the nightstand, and say something brilliant like, "Time to get up—the early bird gets the worm!"

But then all I'd get for my trouble would be, "I don't like worms," and she wouldn't be up for another two hours.

Through the well-known school of experience, I've learned not to do that. I've learned that when Sande is in the rack on a Saturday morning, it's because she doesn't have to run Lauren to preschool or do the dozens of other chores that make up her typical day. She may hear the doorbell, she may hear the phone, she may even hear our dog, Cuddles Marie, barking at who knows what. She isn't going to stir. Why? Because she knows I'm home. I'm not in Los Angeles or New York or some other town. This is the one day when she can just "veg out."

If I want to be a good lover to her, I have to understand this, and it's not always easy to do. I'm as normal as any other husband. Through the week, she's poured all her energy into our kids. Here we are on a Saturday, and why can't she pour a little energy into me?

But I know that isn't how it works. As I've said in other books like *Sex Begins in the Kitchen*, what goes around comes around. Sex isn't something that has to be a ritual or a duty, squeezed in just after the late news and just before Jay Leno. Sex should be "the result of a whole day of affection, consideration, love and one-ness."[3]

USE REALITY DISCIPLINE TO MEET EACH OTHER'S NEEDS

Do you recall the seven Reality Discipline principles discussed in chapter 2? Here they are again in brief form:

1. The whole is always more important than the parts.
2. Have values, and live by them.
3. Always put your spouse (not the kids) first.
4. Balance responsibility with forgiveness and love.
5. Stick to your guns.
6. Keep responsibility where it belongs.
7. Treat people like persons, not things.

All these principles can be applied to marriage, but I'd like to focus on how three or four of them particularly relate to recognizing your spouse's needs and trying to meet them.

If I really believe that *the whole is greater than the parts*, I will be aware that my wife's needs are different from mine but that they are equally important. My job is to try to meet her needs, not judge her or criticize her for having them.

And it goes without saying that if I believe in *always putting my spouse first*, it follows that I will be interested in meeting her needs. And if she believes equally in Reality Discipline, she'll want to put me and my needs first as well. As we look at Willard Harley's list of the five basic needs of men and the five basic needs of women, it's interesting to see how this can all work in real life.

For example, according to Harley, one of the five basic needs in a man is "recreational companionship." In other words, husbands need wives to be with them in their recreation—what they do for relaxation and fun. I have always been impressed by Sande's willingness to sacrifice in this area.

We love living in Tucson, a cow town that made good and happily became the home of the University of Arizona. But Tucson is not exactly the center of the universe when it comes to professional sports, stage shows, or other forms of "big city entertainment," so it's easy to understand why the University of Arizona Wildcats are the only game in town. As an alumnus of the U of A, as well as an avid sports fan, I am a season ticket holder for all football and basketball games. Rain or shine, win or lose, you will find Leman and his family out there, singing the Arizona fight song and urging our Cats to "bear down!"

Sande has been faithfully attending these games with me for many years, even though she is hardly what you could call a "sports fan." I am fairly sure that if Sande had her druthers, she would not attend another football or basketball game for her entire life. Nonetheless, she's there with me because she knows I like her to be there. Over the years, she's become a knowledge-able fan, but that doesn't mean she doesn't bring along a few of her own interests as well.

Whenever I think of "recreational companionship," it brings to mind doing different things together or, for even more fun, "doing things together differently." There are a lot of football games where Sande and I go together, but we certainly wind up doing things a bit differently. I sit there screaming for the Cats as they make a goal-line stand, and I look over at Sande to see her flipping through, of all things, a recipe book. The pure and simple truth is that she loves to look at recipes, and when she tires of the game, she whips out her latest collection to see what she can find. So there we are. I'm wondering why the Cats don't try an end run, and she's contemplating zucchini au gratin.

Please understand, however, that not all the "sacrificing" is just on Sande's part. We have learned to compromise. While she goes to my games, I go with her to antique shops. As you might guess, I'm not really into antiques, but it's one of Sande's favorite sports. While spending our summers back in western New York State, she loves to prowl old and dusty antique shops on the back roads around Williamsville, and that's where we can be found on many a hot summer day.

I admit that I don't necessarily repeat phrases like "The whole is always more important than the parts" and "Always put your spouse first" as we head down the road to look for antiques, but those are the principles I'm living out. And Sande does the same for me when she goes to watch the Cats do or die on the gridiron or the hardwood.

YOUR SPOUSE IS NOT A THING

Whenever husbands and wives start thinking about meeting each other's needs, they are using Reality Discipline Principle No. 7:

TREAT PEOPLE LIKE PERSONS, NOT THINGS.

Every week, I hear amazing stories in which husbands and wives treat each other like things instead of persons. If you and your spouse are serious about treating each other like persons, you will put each other's needs first. If you fail to meet your spouse's needs, reality has a way of coming home to roost. When a husband or wife's personal needs are not met at home, that spouse will look elsewhere to meet those needs.

Not meeting your partner's needs doesn't always drive him or her into an affair, but it happens all too often. The good news, however, is that meeting your partner's needs is a sure-fire guarantee that your marriage will be *affair-proof.* In chapter 7, I'll explain why.

Don't Forget . . .
- All marriages revolve around a short but very big word—*needs.*
- Husbands and wives have basic but not similar needs that must be fulfilled by the mate.
- Men and women both want great sex and affection. Generally speaking, men want more sex and women desire more affection, but the reverse can also be true.
- Women want their husbands to anticipate their needs in advance, not after the fact.
- The typical wife seldom gets enough hugs. She can always use another hug—and another and another.

- Always treat your spouse like a person, not a thing.

And Why Not Try . . .

- Talk together about the basic needs for men and women listed in this chapter. Which of these is most important to each of you, and why?
- Think through how you can do a better job of anticipating your spouse's needs consistently. Concentrate on the need that he or she said was most important.
- For husbands: Try giving your wife some extra hugs and see what happens. Remember, your goal isn't more sex but to make her feel more cherished.
- For wives: Try joining your husband in some of his favorite recreations, like spectator sports or even hunting or fishing. Later, you can suggest he join you when you shop or make new decorating plans for your home.
- Over the next month, make a conscious effort to treat your spouse like a person, not a thing. Keep track of examples of how and when you did this.

Chapter 7

The Union Fidelity Love Bank Is Always Open

How to Affair-Proof Your Marriage

T HE EXTRAMARITAL AFFAIR IS THE MOST TRAGIC RESULT OF UNMET needs in a marriage. Whenever I deal with a couple who have been torn apart by his infidelity or hers, I can always count on one thing: Details of the affair will tell me exactly what is wrong within that marriage. I call it the Marital Litmus Test because it clearly reveals what is lacking in the relationship.

A straying wife will tell me: "John was so attentive before we got married, but in a few months everything changed. At least Bruce would *talk* to me. I was starved for that. The afternoon we wound up in bed was after we had a long talk about what it takes to be fulfilled."

Or a husband with a mistress will say: "My wife hasn't been interested in sex in years. I didn't mean to fall in love with Shirley, but working together day after day . . ."

Affairs are often depicted in films or television shows as therapeutic "one-night stands" or brief flings to let off steam.

"Yes, I had an affair," the heroine tells her friend at lunch, "but now it's over, and I'm able to cope at home a little better."

I suppose this kind of thing happens in real life as well as in soap operas, but the affairs that come to my attention arise out of deep unmet needs at home. Two key words describe every hardcore affair: *disillusionment* and *license.*

Typically, disillusionment sets in because he is starved for sex, or she is starved for affection and conversation. I say "typically" because sometimes it is precisely the reverse: the wife complains about not having any sex, or he complains about a lack of communication.

Whatever the complaints of either partner, their disillusionment is plain. Before marriage, they think they will have the perfect life: openness, sharing, doing everything together—and, of course, terrific lovemaking. And it seems to work out that way for a few months, maybe even a few years. But then the children arrive, schedules change, and life gets busier. Soon they are going their own separate ways, passing each other like two radarless ships in the night, and intimacy becomes a vague memory.

In most cases, one spouse tires of the disillusionment first and decides she or he deserves better. "I have a right to meet my needs," says the disappointed spouse, and consciously or unconsciously, this husband or wife starts navigating toward ports of call where other arms are open. Disillusionment leads to license, a feeling you can get when life doesn't work out and you begin to think, *I have the right to do things* my *way.* And when a spouse gets that disillusioned, it often leads to deep involvement with someone else.

INTIMACY DIES OF SHEER NEGLECT

For any affair to start, there must first be the erosion and rusting of something very important at home—what I call the "intimate connection." The most graphic description of many marriages that find their way into my office is found in the following poem, appropriately entitled:

The Wall

Their wedding picture mocked them from the table, these
two whose minds no longer touched each other.

They lived with such a heavy barricade between them
that neither battering ram of words
nor artilleries of touch could break it down.

Somewhere, between the oldest child's first tooth
and the youngest daughter's graduation,
they lost each other.

Throughout the years each slowly unraveled
that tangled ball of string called self,
and as they tugged at stubborn knots,
each hid his searching from the other.

Sometimes she cried at night
and begged the whispering darkness to tell her who she was.

He lay beside her, snoring like a hibernating bear,
unaware of her winter.
Once, after they had made love,
he wanted to tell her how afraid he was of dying,
but, fearing to show his naked soul,
he spoke instead about the beauty of her breasts.

She took a course in modern art,
trying to find herself in colors splashed upon a canvas,

complaining to other women about men who are insensitive.

He climbed into a tomb called "The Office,"
wrapped his mind in a shroud of paper figures,
and buried himself in customers.

Slowly, the wall between them rose,
cemented by the mortar of indifference.

One day, reaching out to touch each other
they found a barrier they could not penetrate,
and recoiling from the coldness of the stone,
each retreated from the stranger on the other side.

For when love dies, it is not in a moment of angry battle,
nor when fiery bodies lose their heat.
It lies panting, exhausted,
expiring at the bottom of a wall it could not scale.[1]

As this poem so starkly puts it, intimacy erodes as he lies beside her in bed, snoring like a hibernating bear, unaware of her winter. Intimacy rusts as she takes a course in modern art to fill the void, but all she does is complain about her husband's insensitivity to the other wives taking the same course for the same reason.

Intimacy starves as he climbs into a tomb called The Office and buries himself in business, and she climbs into a hearse called a minivan to spend her days playing cab driver as she "pours herself into the children."

And one day intimacy dies, not in angry battle, but of malnutrition, expiring from sheer neglect.

In many marriages, when the intimacy connection goes, an affair takes its place. It seems someone is always waiting in the wings or at the office water cooler who is more than willing to fill the void. And this someone seems to meet the needs that are not being met in a marriage that started full of promise and is now as empty as a house the day after the movers have come and gone. Or perhaps a better analogy is that the Love Bank is now empty, with both partners' accounts at zero.

THE LOVE BANK IS ALWAYS OPEN

In *His Needs, Her Needs*, Willard Harley uses a Love Bank analogy to describe what happens as a man and woman meet for the first time, start to date, fall in love, get married, and then move in one of two directions: toward more and more intimacy or toward the destruction of intimacy and very possibly the tragedy of divorce, triggered by one partner's affair (and sometimes both).[2]

Harley believes that every person has an emotional recorder deep inside, which he calls the Love Bank. This recorder registers the effects of positive and negative experiences, which cause deposits and withdrawals of "love units." Every person you know has an account in your Love Bank, and your spouse should be the major account holder.

When a husband does something to make his wife comfortable, he gets a deposit worth one unit in her Love Bank. If he makes her feel good, he gets two; making her feel very good gets him three; and superterrific rates him a plus four. But if he makes her uncomfortable, it's a minus one; if he makes her feel bad, it's a minus two; very bad, minus three; and terrible and depressed would result in a withdrawal of four units from her Love Bank.

Meanwhile, his wife is doing banking of her own. What she does to make him feel comfortable or uncomfortable, good or not so good, very good or very bad, and terrific or horrible all register as deposits in, and withdrawals from, his Love Bank, where she has her account.

Harley admits the Love Bank is an artificial device, but it describes perfectly what goes on during every waking moment of a marriage.

The Love Bank concept gets particularly interesting when you realize that different husbands and wives register deposits and withdrawals differently. What may be an "uncomfortable" encounter for one partner may be a "feel very bad" encounter for the other. What may be a "feel good" encounter for one can be a "terrific" experience for the other. That's why it's so important to know your partner, be aware of the different ways you react to each other and the rest of the world, and then say and do the positive things that keep both Love Banks filled to overflowing. There is no better way to affair-proof your marriage.

In the rest of this chapter, I focus on using three simple strategies to affair-proof your marriage:

1. avoiding temptation,
2. rekindling romance, and
3. developing couple power.

All three of these strategies are based on Reality Discipline. That's why they're simple, but that doesn't necessarily mean they're easy. Using Reality Discipline is often difficult but always worthwhile. And the more you use it, the easier it gets.

WANDER NOT INTO TEMPTATION

When Steve Kerr tried out for the University of Arizona basketball team, it was obvious he was a great shot, particularly from twenty feet and beyond. But he also had some liabilities. As Coach Lute Olson put it tongue-in-cheek, "He's short, but he's slow."

Kerr got his chance, however, and went on to become one of the best three-point shooters in college history. After helping lead the Wildcats to the final four NCAA tournament in 1988, Kerr signed with the Phoenix Suns of the NBA. Later, he was traded to the Cleveland Cavaliers, who wanted to use him as a three-point specialist. In 1990, he posted one of the best three-point shooting marks in the league.

How could someone who isn't all that tall and not gifted with natural speed be so effective in the toughest competition on earth? Coach Olson summed it up best when he said, "The key to using Steve is to keep him out of situations where he is overmatched."

Olson's remark contains a nugget of wisdom for all of us, whether we play basketball, backgammon, or the game of life. If you want to affair-proof your marriage:

> STAY OUT OF SITUATIONS WHERE YOU
> ARE OVERMATCHED.

In other words, there are definitely times to say no—to working late in certain situations, to casual invitations to coffee, lunch, or dinner with certain people, to accepting certain little gifts or favors. As the apostle Paul wrote regarding temptation in 1 Corinthians 10:12, "So, if you think you are standing firm, be careful that you don't fall!" To put it all another way, in Reality Discipline terms: "Know your limits. If you're a tricycle person, stay out of the fast lane."

ADMIT YOU CAN'T ALWAYS "HANDLE IT"

One of the best ways to stay aware of temptation and avoid the danger of being overmatched is to be sure you keep a strong spiritual influence working on your marriage. As I deal with people who have become entrapped in extramarital affairs, I often hear them admit, "I thought I could handle it" or "I didn't think it would go that far" or "I was trying to be a good friend. I didn't really know how lonely I was myself."

One of the greatest strengths and advantages to developing the spiritual values you practice together in church weekly is that you learn that you *can't* always "handle it." You learn to know yourself and your weaknesses. Most important, you learn you can call on God's resources for strength. Turning once again to the apostle

Paul, he said in Philippians 4:13, "I can do everything through him [God] who gives me strength." That same assurance is ours as well.

Because some people immediately link the word *spiritual* with religion, they complain that they may wind up on a guilt trip. My answer, which may sound a bit odd coming from a psychologist, is, "What's wrong with a little healthy guilt?"

If your Christian values are really important to you, it's entirely possible that God's still, small voice might speak to you when you don't realize you are about to drift into a situation where you are definitely out of your depth. If you feel a bit of guilt at that point, I say that's all to the good. Better to feel a twinge of guilt and stay out of trouble than to wander into an affair that will cause a flood of guilt later.

Fatigue Can Make a Fool of Anyone

But as you develop your spiritual resources, don't be a spendthrift with your physical and emotional resources. In other words, don't get so busy, so weary and run-down, that you aren't thinking straight.

Keep in mind what Vince Lombardi, legendary coach of the Green Bay Packers, once said: "Fatigue makes cowards of us all." Fatigue can also make a fool out of anyone. When you tear through life overscheduled, overcommitted, and overworked, your resistance has to drop. And when resistance is low, you can catch just about anything. Ironically, it is often when a person's resistance is low that the person takes temptation too lightly and wanders into questionable or even dangerous territory.

Even ministers can fall into the fatigue trap. In fact, they are often more vulnerable because they're notorious for working long hours, trying to handle too many things, and trying to please too many people. As I was talking to a pastor in a church where I was conducting a weekend seminar, he took me aside to say confidentially, "Kevin, these people are killing me."

"What people? Are you talking about people in your church?"

"Yes—that's exactly who I'm talking about. I—"

Just then, a woman hurried up and interrupted our conversation: "Pastor, can I see you right now?"

The pastor looked at me as if to say, "See what I mean?"

Making a spur-of-the-moment decision, I turned to the lady and said, "I'm sorry, the pastor can't talk to you right now. I'm sure if you call the church on Monday, he'll be able to set a time for you."

The woman blinked and looked at me as if to say, "And *who* are you?"

Actually, she knew very well who I was—the speaker for the weekend. After staring a hole through me, she turned back to her pastor to repeat her request: "But Pastor, it won't take but a minute. I just want to see you about—"

"No, seriously," I interrupted her again. "He really can't talk to you right now."

With that, the lady let out a loud, "Hmmmph!" and stalked away in what I assumed was a huff.

"I can't believe you said that!" my pastor friend said incredulously.

"I probably lost a participant in my seminar, but I did it for one reason," I explained. "That's exactly what you're going to have to do—get better at saying no to people, or all your good intentions and work will go against you, and you won't have anything left for your own family."

As far as I know, this pastor wasn't in danger of wandering into an affair, but who knows what pressures were really working on him? When you are tired, hassled, and feeling as if your own church flock is "killing you," anything can happen and often does. I've had more than one pastor come to me for counseling after becoming enmeshed in an affair to say, "I don't know what happened. She had just gone through a divorce, and I was just trying to help her . . ."

SATISFIED PARTNERS DON'T WANDER

As you work on staying out of questionable situations yourself, do everything you can to help your partner do the same. Although there is no 100 percent guarantee, as a general rule, satisfied partners do not wander.

One of the best "satisfied partner" illustrations I ever saw was on a Donahue show that focused on fidelity versus infidelity in marriage. Well into the program, a cute little lady who must have been close to eighty got up to tell the audience that her husband had died recently, but she looked back at fifty-five years of marital happiness. How had they done it? I can't recall her exact words, but she said something to this effect: "I got all the juices out of him and didn't leave any for anyone else."

There was a roar of laughter, but people weren't laughing *at* her—they were laughing *with* her, because they knew her words were full of wisdom. If marriage partners are getting enough attention, affection, and sexual fulfillment at home, they're not likely to stray into an affair.

WHAT IF YOU'RE THINKING OF CHUCKING IT ALL?

As I offer these different ideas of how to stay away from temptation, I'm well aware that some readers are so discouraged, they're not even sure they *want* to stay away from temptation. They don't feel there is much of their marriage to save, and they've lost their will to work at it. I feel deep sympathy for this problem, but as I counsel people who have reached the point where they're ready to chuck it all and have a fling, I don't use sympathy—I switch to some hard-nosed Reality Discipline.

"I know how empty you must feel," I respond. "I know you believe you have a right to happiness and fulfillment. But think of the children—your four-year-old or your five-year-old. Imagine yourself holding the child on your knee and explaining that you're not all going to be living together anymore. That Mommy and Daddy haven't been getting along too well and you have found somebody else."

Some clients think this kind of speech is "hitting below the belt." Maybe it is, but then, so is having an affair. Think it through carefully before you take the plunge, and remember that the whole is always more important than the parts—even your own part.

In recent years, it has been encouraging to see that divorce is "going out of style" to some degree. Increasing numbers of people are realizing the high cost of "disposable marriages," particularly where children are involved. According to Bickley Townsend, a vice president in the organization that conducts the Roper poll, "There is definitely a turning-away from the acceptability of divorce and from minimizing the impact of divorce."

In 1990, the Roper poll asked two thousand people to define the most important aspect of success, and the top choice was "Being a good wife and mother or husband and father." In 1986, the most popular answer to the same question had been, "Being true to yourself."[3]

Michele Weiner-Davis is one therapist who used to be overwhelmed by problems that husbands and wives expressed in marital counseling, and she would suggest to them how they could "dissolve things peacefully." In recent years, however, she has switched to believing that it's better for people to do all they can to save their marriage.

Weiner-Davis, who now calls herself a "divorce buster," tries to help counselees be aware of the serious postdivorce problems they will face, such as disastrous financial situations for the woman and the pain and hurt for the children who may be involved. Years later, children may still have wounds that haven't healed. She also points out: "Half of first marriages and 60 percent of second marriages end in divorce. If people got rid of problems by getting rid of their spouses, we wouldn't be seeing those statistics. Many people say, 'If I knew then what I know now, I'm not sure I would have gotten my divorce.'"[4]

ROMANCE KEEPS YOU OUT OF THE RUT

I'm glad the idea of working at marriages is back in vogue because, for me, "working at it" has been the cornerstone of Reality Discipline. While some situations are truly incredible, I begin every case assuming there is hope if I can get both partners to agree to at least try to work at their relationship. The typical couple that comes for counseling is convinced that romance has long since faded from their marriage and cannot be revived. But I believe any couple can do many things to make plenty of deposits in each other's Love Banks.

For example, I sometimes suggest to my clients, "Have you ever thought of keeping your mate off balance?" I realize this sounds a little odd. Why would marriage partners want to keep each other off balance? It all depends on how they do it and why.

If there's anything that kills romance, it's sameness. Every married couple experiences the "letdown" that follows the first glow and breathlessness of falling in love, tying the knot, and then discovering that reality seems to leave out romance. But it doesn't have to be that way if you're both committed to keeping each other off balance with little surprises that say, in different ways, "I love you," "I'm proud of you," "I really like being married to you!" And sometimes the surprises can be big ones—wild and crazy stuff, perhaps, or just taking time to make a date or a weekend a lot more special and intimate.

THE NAKED LADY WHO NEEDED A LIFT

One of the more outstanding examples of the wild and crazy category that I've seen involved a couple whose marriage had fallen into the sexual doldrums. During a counseling session I had with the wife, I mentioned that sometimes it really helps when the woman is more aggressive and takes a more active role in initiating sex. I never cease to marvel at what people can do with a rather simple suggestion.

Not many days later, this couple went to a party. Due to their busy schedules, they had to drive there separately. As the party ended, the wife managed to leave before the husband. She arrived several minutes ahead of him at the long, common driveway they shared with the family next door. After going down this driveway almost a quarter of a mile, she pulled off to the side and removed every stitch of clothing she had on.

In a few minutes, she saw headlights turn into the driveway off the main highway, and she got out of the car and stood there, stark naked, with her thumb out as if she were hitchhiking. As the headlights approached, it occurred to her that she hadn't reached the Y where the driveway split, with one part leading to her house and the other to the neighbors'. *What if this isn't my husband?* she thought. *What if it's the neighbor instead?*

But by then it was too late to change her plan. The headlights caught her in their glare, the car stopped, and the door opened. Fortunately, it was her husband, who went along with the gag and asked, "Hey, lady, do you need a lift?"

Needless to say, this woman's willingness to do something wild and crazy gave their love life a lift—and then some! I've seen it happen so many times. When a woman becomes assertive and aggressive with her husband sexually, it does wonders for his self-esteem, and it puts her more in the mood for lovemaking as well.

On the other side of the coin, when a man tones down his natural male aggressiveness and gently centers his thoughts on pleasing his wife, she becomes more interested in sex and possibly becomes more aggressive herself. My first law for a strong family advises, "Always put your marriage first." A good corollary to that law says:

> For more romance in most marriages, the wife should
> become more sexually aggressive, and the man should
> become more patient and gentle.

Hitchhiking naked and hoping your husband comes along first may not be your style, but there are other ways to do something a little crazy if you're so inclined. One man, a friend of mine, came home from work and found his wife on the dresser, ready to leap into his arms. That might not sound very unusual in itself, but you must realize that she had dressed for the occasion in nothing but Saran Wrap! When my friend told me what had happened, my only explanation was that his wife might have been reading "one of those books" again (maybe it was one of mine!).

No matter—he admitted he had had a lot of fun seeing how long it would take to peel off the Saran Wrap. "Kevin," he said, "if you think getting Saran Wrap off a sweaty body is easy, just try it sometime!"

THE MORE CONVENTIONAL APPROACH WORKS, TOO

I doubted Sande would be interested in Saran Wrap—that would be a little too rich for her own conservative firstborn tastes. She does, however, have more conventional ways of being creative.

Recently, she and I wound up in Toronto, Canada, to celebrate our anniversary, and as we were about to head out for dinner, she said, "Let's just eat in the room. I've already ordered room service."

Because I was tired, I thought that sounded like a good idea, but things got even better. Sande excused herself and disappeared into the bathroom. About then the dinner arrived, and after the bellhop left, Sande came out of the bathroom dressed in a sexy, new, red negligee. Then she reached into her purse and brought out a big, beautiful, red candle. In minutes, its delightful fragrance filled the room as it illuminated our dinner together.

It was a wonderful evening—one I'll never forget. The four children were safe at home with relatives, and I was trapped in a hotel room with a beautiful woman in a red negligee. What made it especially memorable was Sande's extra planning and creativity, not to mention her aggressiveness, which tickles me as much as it does the next husband.

The moral of all these stories is that husbands and wives should become very adept at surprising one another. All it takes is a little planning and then taking the trouble to pull it off. With these two simple principles in mind, anyone can cook up something that will be a surprise, something you can both talk about, laugh about, and enjoy long after it's over, because the memories of the good times you had together will be there. In other words, the Union Fidelity Love Bank will be operating on a deposit basis for both of you. Keep in mind that when you both have a superterrific time, deposits are made in both Love Banks, not just one. This is what the intimacy connection is all about.

Also remember that while you may want to do a special production now and then, it's the little things that really matter. Little things like coming home early and taking her out to dinner at a place she really likes (not the Colonel's). Like sending her a note home from the office, handwritten, that says, "I want you to know how much I care. I want you to know how much I appreciate all you do for our family. You do so much for me and for the children. I'm so proud of you."

And, of course, the notes can also flow in the other direction—from wife to husband. Don't forget that one of a husband's five basic needs is admiration and respect. You'll never know how many points you can put in his Love Bank by slipping a note into his lunch or jacket pocket that says, "You're such a wonderful husband and such a great dad. The kids and I are so lucky that you belong to us."

There are endless ways to keep the spark of romance burning brightly in your marriage. For some additional ideas, see the box on pages 162-63. But do more than read those ideas. Use some of them regularly, and your account in your spouse's Love Bank will grow into a nice IRA!

COMMUNICATION BUILDS COUPLE POWER

In chapter 5, I mentioned that *communication* is an overused word and an underdeveloped skill. I find this to be especially true on the part of husbands. There is no question that one of a woman's five basic needs is for communication—and that means communicating about more than "What's for dinner?" or "Want to watch CNN or a rerun of 'Cheers'?" When a husband doesn't try to communicate with his wife, he's setting her up to be drawn into an affair with a man who is *willing to talk—and listen.*

Frequently, when women tell me about marital problems, I can sense that there has been infidelity on somebody's part. Finally, I may ask, "Have you engaged in any affairs?"

At that point, I get "the look" that tells me more than any of her words could say. But when she goes on to describe her affair, it's often a story not of passionate, nonstop sex, but of caring, conversation, and communicating. In many cases, her eyes will drop slightly, and then she'll look up and say, "I suppose you won't believe me, but we've been together now for six months, and there hasn't been any sex."

She's quite sure I won't understand, but I do understand because I know there is a one-to-one correlation between an extramarital affair and a void in a marriage. She has found someone who will listen to her, talk to her, share feelings with her, and be excited over the little things in life with her.

Obviously, that wasn't happening at all at home. As I've already said, the only good thing you can say about an affair is that it tells you exactly what's wrong in a marriage.

That's why I'm convinced there are many kinds of affairs. Yes, there are the torrid sexual marathons, where the straying mate and the lover can't get enough of each other physically. At the other end of the spectrum, there are liaisons where an unhappy mate finds someone who will just listen to her for hours, sometimes long distance on the phone. She will say, "What feels so right about it is that I can just tell him anything. I don't feel as if I have to measure up, jump higher, or do anything but be myself."

In other cases, it's a combination of sex and communicating. She will say, "Yes, we've had sex, but that isn't really it. There are so many other things, like the time we went for a walk by this lovely stream to a waterfall, and we stood together underneath the falls, getting soaked and just laughing and enjoying each other. And there was the time we just lay on the leaves together and looked up through the trees at the sky. I never felt like doing any of that with my husband. Why do I feel like doing it with him?"

The answer is simple. He listens, he takes time, he's gentle, he's interested in *her*. For the woman who craves intimacy, I advise marrying a man who enjoys lying on the leaves on a warm autumn day and gazing up at the blue sky. When a man has that kind of sensitivity, warmth, and spontaneity, the intimacy connection is much easier to maintain.

HOW TO FAN THE COMMUNICATION FLAME

For husbands and wives who want to work on communication, I suggest two approaches that are exactly 180 degrees apart in strategy. The first is designed particularly for wives who have the notorious "Harry the Turtle" for a husband. No matter how much they nag, no matter how much they beg him to talk, he just seems to go deeper into his shell.

In severe cases of this kind, I sometimes advise the wife, "Don't say anything." In other words, quit nagging, quit pounding on the shell, quit demanding he come out to play or at least to talk. In other words, wait him out by backing off and not asking so many questions.

When you ask question after question, you only succeed in putting Harry on the defensive. Even the most innocuous question, such as, "How was your day today, honey?" can irritate him. Instead, work at making statements instead of phrasing questions, because questions always encourage the same deadly routine:

"How was your day?" she asks.

"Fine," he grunts, and the conversation dies a quiet death.

When Harry the Turtle thinks he sees his wife coming with her long list of questions and pry bar in hand, he simply retreats into his shell until she goes away.

But suppose a couple is eating dinner, and the wife is dying to know how a big meeting went at work. Instead of asking, "Harry, I'm dying to know, how did it go with your boss today?" she should try a simple command: "Tell me about the meeting." Believe it or not, with Harry the Turtle, gentle commands go down much easier than questions. "Tell me about . . ." is open-ended and not as threatening as a direct question.

SHOULDS AND OUGHTS ARE DEADLY

At the other end of the spectrum is the approach of fanning any flicker of conversation into something resembling communication. One of the big mistakes many couples make is that when a tiny flame of communication does spring up, they manage to douse it immediately with a big bucket of *shoulds* and *oughts*. It's not an original observation, but it's still all too true: people don't like to be told what to do. And that goes double for your spouse.

Along with the *shoulds* and *oughts*, husbands and wives are very good at saying *always* and *never*. If there's anything we can say about the use of such absolutes, it's this: *Absolutely never* use them!

Here are some other tips about how to communicate. They apply equally to husbands and wives, but admittedly, husbands may profit more from using even one of these ideas to rebuild the intimacy connection.

Deliberately plan for some time together. Examine your typical schedules, and pick times when you can focus on each other's feelings, concerns, and interests. This could be at dinner, but it may work better just before going to sleep. Try lying in each other's arms and talking about how you feel—what's causing joy, what's causing anxiety and concern. Make it a time to be open and honest, but avoid attacking and complaining.

As one mate talks, the other should listen. Books have been written about the need for couples to listen to each other, and everything those books say is true. The trouble is, few people know how to listen, and perhaps even fewer *want* to listen. It's a human weakness to want to think about what you're going to say next in a conversation rather than listen to a person who is trying to say something to you.

Try sitting comfortably facing each other. Choose a subject—something a little more intimate than the weather—and let one spouse—the wife, for example—begin telling her husband how she feels about it. The husband is not to interrupt, but only to listen. When his wife stops talking, he must say back what he believes she said. Then his wife can either affirm, deny, or modify what she meant and what he heard.

Then the partners should switch roles and let the wife listen and feed back what she thinks she heard her husband say.

Admittedly, this little exercise is artificial and "unnatural," but if you're having trouble communicating, it's a great first step toward better conversations in the future. What you're learning is the art of listening—really hearing what your mate is trying to say.

Don't talk to your mate to try to change him or her. Communicate with one purpose in mind: to learn how to be a better marriage partner. Stay away from should-ing, ought-ing, always-ing, and never-ing each other. I like the way Willard Harley puts it: "An intimate conversation cannot include an argument."[5]

Kidnap Him and Communicate

The above ideas are nothing new. You can find them along with many others in any marriage manual or book on communication. The important thing is to determine together that you *want* to try to communicate. I realize many wives reading this will say, "But that's just the point—he doesn't want to communicate. How do I get his attention? How do I let him know my ideas have merit?"

One approach I've suggested that has worked for many wives revolves around "kidnapping" the husband—either for a weekend or even for a night out to dinner. I don't care how you arrange it, but get him into a situation where you can say, "You may not think what I'm going to say is important, but I want you to know that I'd really like to do more of this with you. Something keeps stopping me, however, and I want to explain what that is."

Then the wife can explain her feelings—quietly, lovingly, without using *should, ought, never,* or *always.* Yes, I realize some husbands will not listen and that some will possibly even become angry. But if your Love Bank is growing empty and the intimacy connection is frayed, if not broken, what do you have to lose? On the other hand, it's just possible he may listen. I know of many husbands who have listened and who are now taking tiny steps toward reconnecting with their wives on an intimate basis.

What Does Your Mate Really Want You to Do?

One of the best conversations Sande and I ever had happened a few years ago, when I decided to solicit her ideas on how I could be a better husband. I asked her to name at least ten things that she really appreciates and wants me to do regularly. Here is what she told me:

1. Whenever I'm sick, take the kids to church anyway.
2. I like it when you scratch and rub my back to wake me up in the mornings—and bring me coffee.

3. I like it when you help with the dishes and picking up around the house, when you see what needs to be taken care of and you take care of it and I don't have to point it out.
4. I also like it when you don't call attention to what you're doing to help. Rattling the empty coffee cups to let me know you're taking them to the sink doesn't impress me.
5. I love it when you say, "You need a weekend away. I've made arrangements for you to spend some time alone." Along with that, I want *you* to take care of the kids, not just dump them off at my mother's.
6. Oh, yes, I also really appreciate what you do for my mother, like providing her with transportation and helping her get things fixed around the house.
7. I like it when you take my car out to be washed and serviced—and then I'm sure it's safe to drive.
8. You don't know how much I appreciate it on those days I'm at the end of my rope with the children and you take over when they really get wild and start arguing with each other.
9. I like it when you make the plans for us to go out. You get the baby-sitter, you call up our friends and set a time to meet them—everything isn't left for me.
10. And finally, I love it when you're patient and understanding—especially if I've had a bad day. Like the time you came home after I drove the car through the garage door. You had to have seen the door when you drove up, but you walked in and said, "Honey, how was your day?" I said, "Oh, fine!" and I was almost ready to cry when you said, "Let's go out to dinner."

Obviously, any wife or husband would have a different list of ten things they appreciate having their spouse do or say. Try exchanging your own lists soon. You will probably learn a great deal—about needs you're meeting and some you aren't. You will also get ideas about how to do better Love Banking and build stronger intimacy connections. And while you're at it, you will be affair-proofing your marriage, because you'll be putting your marriage first—where it always belongs.

A Baker's Dozen Ways to Fill Her Love Bank

1. Treat her as important. Let her know you want to understand how she feels.
2. Ask her opinions. Don't surprise her with arbitrary, unilateral decisions.
3. Give her frequent hugs, especially if she is feeling down or depressed. Just hold her, no lectures or advice.
4. Talk to her about how she spends her day—at work or at home. Be *interested.*
5. Always handle her with care in every way.
6. Accept her as she is; change yourself, not her.
7. Get rid of habits that annoy her.
8. When you help around the house, don't expect a twenty-one-gun salute.
9. Let her know how proud you are that she is your wife.
10. Call if you're going to be late.
11. Besides remembering birthdays, anniversaries, and holidays, surprise her with a card or some flowers for no special reason except that you love her.
12. When she shares a problem with you, don't immediately jump in to be The Great Fixer. Chances are she knows how to solve the problem already and just wants you to listen and empathize.

13. *Never* give her a toaster on *any* special occasion, not even a four-slicer. And that goes double for frying pans, waffle irons, and can openers.

A Baker's Dozen Ways to Fill His Love Bank

1. Admire his achievements; let him know you're aware of the stress he's under at work.
2. Keep your "honey-do" list down to a reasonable number of items. Show him special thanks when he takes care of something on the list.
3. Don't second-guess him in front of the kids. Disagree in private.
4. Ask him how you could be more sexually aggressive.
5. Handle his "male ego" with care. Always try to preserve his self-esteem.
6. Accept him as he is; change yourself, not him.
7. Get rid of habits that annoy him.
8. Make it a point to pay special attention to him rather than always centering on the children.
9. Thank him for his contributions to the family without adding, "Only I wish . . ."
10. Call if you're going to be late.
11. If you give him something to read, don't bug him about it.
12. Instead of always waiting for him to remember your anniversary, kidnap him and take him on a special anniversary dinner or weekend yourself.
13. If your husband is the "Harry the Turtle" type, try not asking him any questions for a week.

Don't Forget . . .

- Extramarital affairs are almost always the tragic result of unmet needs in a marriage.
- Marital intimacy often dies of sheer neglect.
- Everybody—especially your spouse—has a Love Bank, and it is always open for business.
- To affair-proof your marriage, avoid temptation, rekindle romance, and develop couple power.
- Always stay out of situations where you may be over-matched or tempted beyond your limits.
- Admit that you can't always handle certain situations or temptations.
- Satisfied partners don't wander.
- Romance improves in most marriages when the wife becomes more sexually aggressive and the man becomes more patient and gentle.
- *Shoulds, oughts,* and banal questions often kill communication.

And Why Not Try . . .

- Use some of the communication tips in this chapter—everything from listening more closely to sitting facing each other, to practicing talking and listening (see pages 158-59).
- Try at least one of the baker's dozen ideas for filling his or her Love Bank this week. See how many of these ideas you can use within the next month. Then take inventory on what kind of difference they have made.
- Sit down together and exchange lists of five or more things each of you could do regularly to make the other happy.
- Discuss those times and settings when each of you is most vulnerable to being tempted by another person. How can you help each other avoid or otherwise deal with those situations?

Part III

Leman's Second Law:

To Keep Your Balance as Parents, Always Be Ready to Pull the Rug Out From Under Them

Chapter 8

Are You Preparing Your Kids for the Real World?

Reality Discipline Can Be Their Secret Weapon

I HAD JUST FINISHED A SEMINAR SESSION ON "WHY CHILDREN SHOULD Be Treated Differently, According to Their Age, Ability, and Personality" when an anxious-looking mother came up to me and said, "Dr. Leman, I've been listening to what you're saying, and it seems to me that my youngest child is going to feel very slighted if I do what you suggest."

"You mean, you're concerned about giving children different bedtimes and different allowances, for example?" I asked.

"Yes, I am. I think the younger boy is going to feel like it's just not fair. Why should his older brother get more allowance than he does, and how come his older brother can stay up later? They're only two years apart."

I understood this mother's concern, because I hear a lot of this as I travel the country. Many parents just don't want the hassle of sorting out who should go to bed earlier, who gets how much allowance, who can see what movie, and the like. They'd rather treat everyone the same and save themselves all kinds of time and trouble. What they don't realize is that by doing that, they are creating all kinds of problems for themselves—and their children—in the future.

"Tell you what—I have an idea you might want to consider," I told the mother. "Why don't you wait until your boys are fourteen and sixteen. The sixteen-year-old will have his driver's license. Then you can suggest to your fourteen-year-old that he beat his fist on the counter at the DMV and demand that *he* have a driver's license, too."

"That's silly," the mother scoffed. "They wouldn't give him one."

"You're absolutely correct," I answered. "That's the way life is. We can't all be treated the same all the time, because that's not how the real world operates. Out there in the real world, your sons are going to find all kinds of inequities. They're going to find laws and rules. And they're going to run into all kinds of things that 'just aren't fair.' I believe parents have to start somewhere, very early in their children's lives, preparing them for reality, and that's why I suggest that they always establish different treatment for different children, even if at times the younger ones, especially, wail that it isn't fair."

The mother went away still unconvinced, but all I could do was smile and hope she would think about it. The real world is not only unfair, it's also dangerous. Anything parents can do to prepare their kids will pay off in the future, and often in the present as well.

THE REAL WORLD IS A RISKY PLACE

Even a casual look at the newspapers and magazines, along with the eleven o'clock news, proves it's no secret we have become a more violent society and that many of the violence makers are youngsters. All parents need to consider: "What am I doing to prepare my kids for a real world full of inequities, temptations, and dangers?"

They can start by being aware of what's really going on out there. I sometimes suggest to parents that they visit their local junior high school and walk down the halls, just observing and listening. What will they hear? The chances are good to excellent that their ears will be burned by language that would make the proverbial sailor blush.

But the foul language is a relatively mild pollutant compared to many others out there. The U.S. Senate Judiciary Committee reports that adult bookstores outnumber McDonald's restaurants in the United States at a rate of at least three to one.[1]

According to a report out of the University of Utah's department of psychology, a study of six hundred junior high boys and girls showed that 91 percent of the boys and 82 percent of the girls had been exposed to X-rated, hard-core pornography. Two-thirds of the boys and 40 percent of the girls reported wanting to try some of the sexual behaviors they had witnessed, and 25 percent of the boys and 15 percent of the girls admitted to actually doing some of the sexual things they had seen in pornography within a few days after exposure to it.

The point is, the modeling effect of pornography on youth is very powerful. The same Utah study showed that lengthy exposure to pornography (over six weeks) changed the attitudes and feelings of people using it so that they were far more likely to condone sexual improprieties and think that sexual transgressions were really not so bad, and that victims of such transgressions didn't really suffer all that much.[2]

Reports like the University of Utah study are powerful evidence that pornography encourages sexual assault and rape. There is a "hidden epidemic" of rape throughout the United States. The number of rapes in this country increased 526 percent between

1960 and 1986,[3] and rapes by boys eighteen or younger rose by 14.6 percent between 1983 and 1987, according to the FBI.[4]

In a recent survey of six thousand students on thirty-two college campuses, one in six female students reported being the victim of rape or attempted rape in the preceding year. At the University of Arizona, located in our fair city of Tucson, one of every fifteen men said he had committed or attempted rape in that same period. Another survey found that 90 percent of rape victims had not reported their assaults to the police.[5] Some experts say that only about one out of ten rapes is reported to college officials at all.[6]

A growing phenomenon is what is known as "date rape"— attacks on girls or women who have been taken out on a date. Various surveys of thousands of women show that in some cases, 90 percent of the women who were raped knew their assailants and that anywhere from 47 to 57 percent of the rapes happened on dates, depending on which study results you read.[7]

Rape isn't the only crime of violence in the real world. Across the land, kids can get killed for the clothes they wear on their backs. In Chicago, Starter jackets representing pro sports teams have been a hot item in recent years. Teenagers are stealing more than fifty a month from each other. Four Chicago youths have been killed for their seventy-five- or hundred-dollar jackets.[8]

Kids have even been murdered for their shoes. A fifteen-year-old boy left home for school but never made it there. A day or so later, his shoeless body was found in a vacant lot. He had been murdered for his hundred-dollar pair of Air Jordans. Later, a seventeen-year-old was picked up wearing the Air Jordans and was arrested for murder.[9]

In some metropolitan areas, particularly New York City, expensive sunglasses are another motive for teenage crime. "Cool dude thugs" there regularly mug youngsters for their sunglasses.

It isn't even safe to go out for the cheerleading squad anymore. As I was driving home one day a few years ago, I heard on a newscast that a mother in Texas had been charged with attempting to have her daughter's rival's mother murdered to give her own child a better chance of becoming a cheerleader!

THE REALITIES OF "STRANGER DANGER"

In recent years, many parents have taken advantage of a children's fingerprinting service that has been offered in malls throughout the country. The reasoning: In case the child is kidnapped or murdered, the prints would be on file, and the child could be identified.

Across the country, kids are waking up, trudging down to breakfast for their bowl of Crispy Critters, and finding faces of kids their own age staring back at them from the missing-children posters on milk cartons.

Many children go to bed at night afraid that someone will break in and steal them. I advise parents to give their children "stranger danger" instruction. While we want our kids to trust people and be friendly and cooperative with adults, the fact is that not all adults are friendly or even safe. Children need to know there are people who will hurt them if they give them a chance.

Children should be instructed that if someone drives up to the curb when they are walking home from school, they should never get closer than ten or fifteen feet from the car. Actually show your child how far ten to fifteen feet is. The idea is for the child to stay far enough away that someone can't just reach out, grab the child, and pull him or her into the car.

If someone drives up and asks a child for directions, the child can give them if he knows, or he can simply say, "I don't know" and keep walking. If someone gets out of the car and comes toward the child, he should run to a house or an adult working in a yard. Some volunteer parents keep special signs in their windows to signal children that this is a place where they can find help.

I advise parents to tell their children: "Remember that we would never send a stranger to pick you up for any reason—at school, at church, or even at somebody's house. Never go with a stranger, for example, if he comes to your school and tells you, 'Your parents were in an accident, and I'm here to take you to the hospital.'"

Another safeguard I suggest is having a family code word. If anyone tries to say he represents Mom or Dad, the child is to ask, "What's our family code word? If my parents had sent you, they would have told you."

The intent of many strangers who kidnap children is sexual abuse, which often leads to murder. But many young girls are also abused within their own families in every kind of incestuous situation imaginable. Statistics vary on how many women were sexually abused at some time while they were growing up. Some say one out of four, but I believe the figure is much higher in some groups. Some studies show that up to 40 percent of women polled had been sexually abused when they were very young.

If you think I've been quoting all these grim statistics and probabilities to get your attention, you're absolutely right. The real world is a very dangerous place. Kids need all the help they can get in order to cope. And I know—I don't just think—that rearing them with Reality Discipline will give them an edge that could save their lives someday.

DOES EDUCATION PREPARE KIDS FOR THE REAL WORLD?

Even if our children successfully avoid sexually transmitted diseases, AIDS, porno peddlers, rapists, and other sources of violence, the real world is still loaded with pitfalls, from elementary school all the way up through junior high and high school and on into college. The media constantly carry stories of highly qualified teachers—the cream of the crop—who leave their profession to find work that will pay them a living wage. In many high schools, particularly in the inner cities, teachers face physical danger, along with being overworked and underpaid and often having to take on responsibilities that really should be assumed by the students' parents.

On the other side of the coin, we have teachers who stay on but who lack the motivation or ability to do a good job. In their perceptive and savvy book *Real World 101,* co-authors James Calano and Jeff Salzman look back at their own college careers and claim that, in general, the teaching was lousy. They don't want to indict the entire profession, and they are well aware there are many college profs and instructors who are "talented, committed and competent professionals."[10] Nonetheless, many more of them were just plain mediocre-to-terrible.

I know some colleges can rightly claim they offer top-notch teaching to their students, but across the board, I agree with what Calano and Salzman are saying, because I've seen it myself. The average pay for professors is quite low, and in addition, there is little incentive for them to excel in classroom teaching. The usual scenario is for a professor to get tenure, bury himself in research, then plug along with mediocre classroom work without fear of being tested, evaluated, or criticized.

Occasionally, however, a professor is willing to confirm that the problem really does exist. This surprisingly candid statement was made by a professor during a speech at recent commencement exercises for Brown University:

> We the faculty take no pride in our educational achievements with you. . . . With us you could argue about why your errors were not our errors, why mediocre work really was excellent, why you could take pride in routine and slip-shod presentation. For four years we created an altogether forgiving world, in which whatever slight effort you gave was all that was demanded. When you did not keep appointments, we made new ones. When your work came in beyond deadline, we pretended not to care.
>
> Why? Despite your fantasies, it was not even that we

wanted to be liked by you. It was that we did not want to be bothered, and the easy way out was pretense: smiles and easy B's.

Few professors actually care whether or not they are liked by peer-paralyzed adolescents, fools so shallow as to imagine professors care not about education but about popularity. It was, again, to be rid of you. So go, unlearn the lies we taught you.[11]

The professor's words are hard ones—even harsh—but he was being honest with these Brown students, maybe for the first time since they had come to the university. He was telling them they had better unlearn the lie that you can get by with slipshod work, the lie that you can be late for appointments or cancel appointments and new ones will be made with no problem. The truth is, this kind of behavior in the real world can lead straight to disaster.

In general, the typical college or university protects incompetency at all levels, from the faculty and staff down through the students. In a lot of ways, college is a great place to hide out, where you can believe the lie that says you can get by with little or no effort because it's a forgiving world out there. The truth is, the real world demands excellence, punctuality, dependability, responsibility, and accountability. The sooner your kids learn this, the better they can cope.

I can't give you a lot of direct help with how to pick a college for your children. But I can give you the key to starting them off right, literally from the day they're born, by rearing them with Reality Discipline. It's designed to build into them the psychological, emotional, and spiritual muscles they need to cope in a dangerous and unforgiving world.

In parts I and II, we looked at seven principles of Reality Discipline that apply to all facets of family life. Now I want to add three more principles that apply especially to parenting:

REALITY DISCIPLINE PRINCIPLE NO. 8:
USE GUIDANCE, NOT FORCE; ACTION, NOT JUST WORDS.

REALITY DISCIPLINE PRINCIPLE NO. 9:
BE CONSISTENT, DECISIVE, AND RESPECTFUL OF
YOUR CHILDREN AS PERSONS.

REALITY DISCIPLINE PRINCIPLE NO. 10:
HOLD YOUR CHILDREN ACCOUNTABLE FOR THEIR
ACTIONS, AND HELP THEM LEARN FROM EXPERIENCE.

WHAT IT MEANS TO "PULL THE RUG OUT"

To implement Principle No. 8, "Use guidance, not force; action, not just words," I use a strategy that some parents don't quite understand at first. With tongue in cheek, I tell seminar audiences: "Sometimes you have to pull the rug out and let the little buzzards tumble."

Mothers cringe and think I'm suggesting some kind of cruelty that could actually harm their little darlings. Furthermore, they aren't at all thrilled to have their children called buzzards. I explain that down Tucson way, we affectionately refer to children as little buzzards and no offense is intended—it's a loving term.

As for "pulling the rug out," I am not talking about doing something that would actually cause a child physical harm. I explain that the parent who is willing to pull the rug out is ready to follow through with Reality Discipline and back up words with action. The biggest mistake many parents make is to just talk and use the same old lines kids have heard for centuries:

"You'd better shape up or . . ."
"I don't know what I'm going to do with you—what do you want me to do?"

"If you do that again, you're going to get smacked."

"I've had it with you."

"You've got to quit hanging on to me. I'm getting tired."

"What's wrong with you? I swear, you're going to end up just like your uncle Milton."

With Reality Discipline, you never use empty threats or words. You quietly explain what the consequences will be if certain behavior is continued or if certain responsibilities aren't met. When the child fails to listen, the rug is pulled, life closes in, and the price must be paid. None of this is designed to be painful punishment, only effective training the child will not forget.

TONY HELD HIS MOM'S CAR POOL HOSTAGE

I once talked with a frustrated mom who came to see me because she couldn't get her nine-year-old son up in the morning for school. Not only was the daily battle to get Tony out of bed driving her bonkers, but she also had an additional problem. Because she was part of a mothers' car pool, little Tony's dawdling was making not only him late, but the other children in the car pool as well. This mother was getting it from the other parents, especially from her friend Margaret.

"It's getting embarrassing just running into Margaret at the store," Mom told me. "She keeps letting me know how many times per week Tony makes her son late for school. I feel terrible, and I dread talking to her."

"Why don't you use Reality Discipline?" I asked.

"Oh, yes—I read about that in your book on making children mind, but I don't see how it can help me in this situation."

"Why not?"

"Because we're in this car pool—it just wouldn't work."

"Excuse me," I replied, "but I really don't see the problem. Just use Reality Discipline."

"Dr. Leman," Mom told me firmly, "I'm sorry, but that just won't work in this situation."

"It will if you're really willing to pull the rug out," I told her.

"Pull the rug out? He doesn't sleep on a rug. He sleeps in a bed. What do you mean, pull the rug out?"

"It's just a little expression I use. I suggest that you try giving your child an alarm clock. Tell him it's his responsibility to get himself up and that you are sick and tired of coming in every few minutes to remind him, then always having to leave late to boot. Tell him he has to get up, get dressed, eat breakfast, and be ready to leave by a certain time—say, 8:20—and if he's not, there will be consequences."

"Consequences? You mean give him a whipping?" she said with a twinge of horror.

"No, not at all. If he's not up and ready, just be brave enough to leave on time and take the other kids to school."

"Do you mean leave him behind? Do you mean leave him at home?"

"Exactly."

"Oh, I couldn't do that!"

I looked at Mom for a few seconds, then asked her mildly, "Do you want to solve your problem?"

"Oh, yes," she answered.

"Are you really willing to listen to what I have to say?"

"Well, yes, I am."

"Then try Reality Discipline with your son. I assure you that you won't have to do it every day for six months or even every day for a week. Once or twice ought to do the job, but you have to be brave enough to pull the rug out."

"I'm not sure I know how to go about doing this," she said with a worried look. "All I see is that I'll be leaving my son home alone unsupervised while I take the other kids to school."

"Okay, let's talk about that. How long is it going to take you to pick up the other kids, get over to school, and then get back home?"

"Oh, no more than thirty-five to forty minutes, at the most," she said.

"Fine. Then do it. I'm sure your son has been home alone for thirty-five to forty minutes on occasion. Go ahead and leave, pick up the other kids, drop them off at school, and then stop in at the assistant principal's office to tell him you have a little problem with your son Tony, and you're wondering if he can help. He'll probably be more than happy to help. You'll explain that he will probably want to call Tony in later this morning because he is going to be at least an hour and a half late for school. Then explain to him what you've done and why. I'm sure he'll be more than happy to cooperate—he may even want to give you a medal."

Mom took my advice—a little reluctantly, to be sure, but nonetheless, she followed through. She gave Tony an alarm clock and told him the rules and what the consequences would be if he didn't get up on time. Being nine years old and used to getting his own way, Tony didn't take Mom seriously. The very next morning, she left him snoozing away while she took the other kids in the car pool to school. When she got back, guess who was standing in the carport, hands on hips? Yes, it was Tony, not only ready for school, but also ready for battle. Suddenly he was very concerned about what time it was. He had never been concerned about the time before—but he was *now*.

"Where have you been?" Tony practically shouted. "Do you know what time it is? I've got to get to school!"

"Well, honey," Mom replied rather glibly, "why don't I run you down to school right now?"

Note that she resisted the temptation to remind Tony that he was undoubtedly going to grow up like Uncle Harry and be irresponsible. She didn't give him the "I told you so—that you were going to have to get up and get yourself to school and if you didn't there would be consequences." She didn't spit in Tony's soup. Everything she did was loving, kind, and full of positive regard and happy smiles.

On the way to school, Tony still wanted to fight. He was bristling, but Mom wouldn't go for it. She just kept her eyes on the road, wheeled up to school, and dropped Tony off, saying, "Honey, have a good day."

Off Tony stamped to school, and his first hurdle was trying to slip into class late. Somehow his teacher didn't seem to notice, and he slid into his seat in the back of the room, heaving a deep sigh of relief. Five minutes later, however, the school intercom loud-speaker boomed, "Will Tony Jones please report to the assistant principal's office."

Tony walked down the hall with fear and trembling. He knocked tentatively on the assistant principal's door, and a voice boomed out, "Come in!"

Tony timidly took a seat, and the assistant principal said, "Tony, what time does school start?"

"Eight-thirty," Tony replied carefully.

"What time did you get to school this morning?"

"Uh . . . about 9:40, I think,"

"It was actually five minutes to ten," the principal corrected him. "What time are you going to be here tomorrow?"

"Eight-thirty, sir," said a chagrined Tony, who was already planning to put that alarm clock his mother had given him to better use, starting tomorrow morning.

The next time Mom came in to see me, she told me there was no longer a problem with getting Tony up for school.

"Do you know why?"

"Well, I guess I used Reality Discipline."

"To be specific, you were willing to pull the rug out and let your little buzzard tumble. That's the whole idea behind Reality Discipline. If you're not willing to pull the rug out, Reality Discipline is just another paper tiger. But when you put some gentle teeth into what you say, Reality Discipline *always works."*

PERMISSIVENESS IS MISGUIDED LOVE

Tony's mother was amazed at how well pulling the rug out on her son actually worked. "But what about next time?" she wanted to know. "Tony isn't going to become a model kid just because I made him get up and go to school on time."

"Correction," I reminded Mom. "You didn't *make* Tony do anything. Reality taught him he can't sleep in. You just stuck to your guns and didn't bail him out, as you had been doing in the past."

Once parents commit themselves to Reality Discipline Principle No. 8, "Use guidance, not force; action, not just words," they must go on to use Reality Discipline Principle No. 9: "Be consistent, decisive, and respectful of your children as persons."

This is where parenting style is important. In my seminars, I talk about three typical parenting styles you can find in most families. Depending on the day of the week or the hour of the day, you can find any or all of these styles in the same family, and that's just the problem: Parents aren't *consistent.* They don't stick with the best style that will get the job done and treat their kids like persons, not things.

The two styles that inconsistent parents use the most are *permissiveness* and *authoritarianism.* Before Tony's mom learned to pull the rug out, she was a good example of a permissive parent. By permitting Tony to sleep in every morning and then rushing around to accommodate him, she was saying to Tony, "It's okay—do whatever you want. It doesn't make any difference—I'll back you up."

In another case, two parents came to me for help with their eleven-year-old son who had been stealing them blind. It had gotten so bad, they had been forced to put all their valuables (even their wallets) in a safety box that they kept locked in their bedroom closet.

As we talked, the mother let slip a telltale remark that told me

I was working with two classic permissive parents. Proudly she said, "You know, Doctor, since he was born, we've never left little Johnny at home alone."

I looked back at the mother, searching for words that wouldn't condemn her, but I did want to let her know her strategy had not been the best.

"That's unfortunate," I finally said. "By never giving Johnny a chance to stand on his own two feet or operate independently, even for a brief time, you've robbed him of something very precious—becoming accountable and responsible for his own life. Now he's paying you back by acting in a very irresponsible way."

Johnny's parents were shocked. In classic permissive style, they had literally given Johnny "everything he had ever asked for." How, they wondered, could he possibly repay them in this way?

"Very easily," I told them. "When you parent a child permissively, you teach him to be a taker who isn't interested in giving much of anything, whether it's cooperation, obedience, or acting responsibly."

It was difficult for Johnny's mother and father to change their style, because they were truly loving parents. Parents like Johnny's and Tony's often let their love for their children mislead them, because they bend over backward not to be authoritarian. That's why they often slip totally into permissiveness. On the other hand, authoritarian parents never worry about bending over backward. They make their children bend over backward to obey their strict rules, standards, and demands.

AUTHORITARIANISM SEEMS TO WORK, BUT . . .

Authoritarianism is the autocratic, iron-fisted approach that tells the child, "You will do it our way or else," "As long as you live under our roof, you will toe the mark," or "We are the bosses—what we say goes."

I've dealt with any number of kids who have rebelled under the yoke of authoritarianism. Oh, they didn't necessarily rebel at first. That's one of the tricky things about authoritarianism. For a while it seems to work—in fact, it can seem to work all the way up to when a child becomes an adult. But why do you think so many college kids seem to go slightly berserk once they get away from home? In many, many cases, they are finally out from under the thumb of their parents, and not knowing how to handle freedom, they waste their opportunity by flunking out or getting into all kinds of drinking, drugs, and sexual promiscuity (what a lot of so-called experts like to refer to as "being sexually active").

And a lot of children don't wait until they're in college. Teenagers who have lived under the iron fist all their lives finally learn how they can retaliate by punishing Mom and Dad for a change. I think of one fifteen-year-old girl who turned up in my office pregnant. Throughout her childhood, her parents had never trusted her. She had never been allowed to go on anything that resembled a date, or even an outing with a group of other youngsters. Finally, she climbed out the window one night to meet her nineteen-year-old boyfriend, and that's when it happened.

When I talked with this young girl, she told me her parents were so overly strict that they "didn't care about her feelings." As far as she was concerned, she had been punished all her life, and now she had decided she had a right to punish them. In effect, she had gotten pregnant on purpose to get back at her mother and father.

When the parents learned what had happened and why, they were deeply grieved. They had meant well. They had only been trying to keep their daughter "safe" from temptation and harm. But because they had used an authoritarian style that communicated no love or concern, it had all blown up in their faces. Now the girl's life was in ruins, and they blamed themselves for what had happened.

Although these parents had made a mistake, I counseled them not to blame themselves for their daughter's decision. Parents should always remember that no matter what kinds of mistakes they make, their children make their own choices in life. The best we can do as parents is to guide children in the best way possible and then pray that they will make the right choices.

REALITY DISCIPLINE IS FIRM BUT FAIR

If permissiveness and authoritarianism are not the best ways to parent kids, what's the alternative? I call it the "firm but fair" approach. The parent maintains a certain amount of authority in order to guide and train the child, but that authority is countered and softened by an attitude of "Look, I want to hear your side. Let's talk this over. What do you think we can do as an alternative?"

A big difference between the firm but fair approach and authoritarianism and permissiveness is that the parent gives the child an opportunity to make rule-decisions about life and then to accept the consequences of those decisions, all within an atmosphere of love and forgiveness, not one of judgment or disinterest. In the firm but fair approach, you give your child guidelines that are worked out ahead of time, often by asking the child what would be fair to him or her. Then the child can make choices based on those guidelines as decision-making opportunities arise.

The key to the firm but fair approach is that when a child does make a wrong choice, you must stick to your guns and hold the child accountable. In other words, you let reality be the teacher. Here's where Reality Discipline Principle No. 10 comes in. By holding a child accountable for his or her actions, you help the child learn from experience. You show the child respect, and you're consistent and loving, even when Reality Discipline moves in to cause the child a certain amount of pain.

That's what happened to Tony. It was painful for him to get down to school late and be called into the principal's office. Tony was embarrassed and also afraid. Actually, he got off easy compared with what has happened in a lot of other situations. But

Tony learned that the alarm clock was for real, that the getting-up time was for real, and that being ready to go with the car pool on time was for real. Above all, he learned that Mom was for real and that she wasn't going to be his slave any longer. Actually, Tony's mom had been robbing him of self-respect and self-esteem with her permissive approach because she had been doing everything for him, including getting him to school even after he had slept past a reasonable time.

In a way, Tony's mom had been providing him with what I call the "Disneyland experience"—making things as easy as possible for him, but giving him no chance to learn what life is all about. I've counseled many a Tony who has grown up without having to worry about getting up in time for school. Now these people can't get to work on time. They can't get their reports in on time. When it comes to the clock or the calendar, they seem to be helpless.

On the other side of the coin, the authoritarian parent offers the child no opportunity to make choices. In effect, authoritarians make all their children's decisions for them. Authoritarians see themselves as better than their children, superior beings who must be obeyed because they have a God-given mandate that says they must be obeyed. And it's true: The Bible does say children should obey their parents. But it also says parents should not provoke their children to wrath and rebellion by lack of love and fairness.[12]

It's not easy to be a consistent parent. And as every parent knows, it's impossible to always call the shots perfectly. As parents, we aren't God. We can't be everywhere at once, watching two siblings as they get into a scrap and knowing who really caused what. But I still believe that the best way to approach parenting is with the firm but fair style. That approach is the balancing factor that makes Reality Discipline really work. Firm but fair parents are the ones who are willing to use action, not just words, and to be consistent and decisive as they hold their kids accountable.

REALITY DISCIPLINE DOES PAY OFF

Above all, I've seen it work in my own family. Today we have five children who range in age from their late teens down to infancy. We began using Reality Discipline with our oldest child, Holly, and we continue to use it with her sister Krissy, her brother, Kevin, Jr., and with our little "surprise packages," Hannah and Lauren.

How do we know it pays off? Sande and I can't say our children never want to do anything wrong, that they never misbehave, act up, get moody, or do any number of things that kids do all the time. But we do get some awfully good indications that something right has been happening over the years. One example we treasure is how Holly, then Krissy, responded to getting their driver's licenses.

I suppose that one of the most traumatic events parents can think of is the day their teenager gets licensed to drive. That license means the teenager has wheels and is free to roam in a high-speed machine, fully capable of killing himself and many other people as well. Teenage auto tragedies happen daily, and I have had to deal with more than one family who has been shattered by a teenager's irresponsible use of a car.

Being the oldest, Holly got her license first and immediately went about obeying the Rules for Using Our Family's Car. The only catch was, I didn't write the rules—she did. In a letter addressed to Sande and me, Holly set the following rules for herself:

- I will at all times be a cautious and responsible driver. (Driving as if there's a cop behind you at all times.)
- I'm responsible for my life, the people in the car, and many other lives. I'll be responsible with your car since it is a privilege.
- I'll never drive with another questionable driver. I'll be alert when I drive, and I'll *never* be under the influence of anything.

- There will never be more passengers than seat belts, and everyone must wear one.
- No one will ever drive your car except me. (It won't be lent out.)
- I won't get a ticket.
- Loud music won't be played.
- I won't be on Speedway on Friday and Saturday nights (the place where the kids cruise).
- I'll be considerate of your needs with the car.
- I'll use good judgment. I won't leave the tank on empty.
- I'll be responsible and make you proud.

Holly Kristine Leman
November 12, 1988

P.S. I won't pick up hitchhikers.

Not to be outdone by her big sister, when Krissy got her license almost two years later, the following appeared under our bedroom door:

Krissy's Rules

1. I will *ALWAYS* wear my seat belt. (This is easy, seeing as they are automatic.)
2. I promise to be a defensive and good driver.
3. I'll do my very best in letting you and Mom know where I'm going and who I'm with.
4. I'll be home when you request that I am. (If something happens that makes me ten minutes or more late, I'll call.)
5. No hitchhikers will be allowed in my beautiful Honda.
6. There will be no crazy driving, racing, etc., of any kind.
7. I'll be responsible for keeping my car full of gas and clean (donations are accepted!).

8. Mom, I won't go driving around at night after a movie or cruise Speedway.
9. Under *no* circumstance will I drink and drive.

Kristin Sarah Leman
May 15, 1990

Obviously, these two sets of driving rules are not proof positive that Reality Discipline always works, and I'm well aware that all the returns aren't in yet. Holly and Krissy are as capable of making mistakes as anyone else. So far, they haven't made many, although Holly did get a ticket for supposedly going through a stop sign in our neighborhood. Oddly enough, the traffic officer followed her for a mile and a half before pulling her over.

"Dad," Holly told me, "I stopped the way I always do."

"Well, I guess he thought you rolled on through," I said. "I don't know what you want to do, but I think you ought to go down to court and tell your side of the story."

Holly went to court, and I accompanied her, never saying a thing but longing to give the judge a "character reference" on my daughter.

Holly told her side of the story, and then the policeman told his. To be kind but candid, the officer stretched the truth into a pretzel, saying that Holly had come up to the stop sign, "slowed down just a little," and gone right on through it.

After hearing both sides, the judge ruled against Holly, and she had to pay the fine. We talked about it afterward, and Holly said, "Dad, I can't believe it. The policeman lied about what really happened."

"Holly, it's a perfect example of how life isn't always fair. You know the truth, you told the judge the truth, and I'm proud of you."

As far as I'm concerned, Holly didn't violate any of her personal driving rules that she had written on her sixteenth birthday. She may have made a "rolling stop" at that stop sign. I make one now and then myself, as everybody else does. But she certainly hadn't driven recklessly or irresponsibly. It was a good lesson for her as she makes her transition into adulthood and takes on other adult responsibilities.

What I like is that Holly and Krissy have written their own rules, and now they are trying to obey those rules—not because their parents want them to be "good little girls," but because *they have made the decision for themselves to drive responsibly.* For my money, that's becoming ready for the real world, something we have been trying to help them do since they were born.

Believe me, they didn't start out that way. When they came into this world, they needed lots of training and nurture, just as every child does. In the next chapter, I want to show how Reality Discipline can be used with young children to give them the head start they need in life.

Don't Forget . . .

- Parents need to do all they can to prepare their children for how to cope in the real world, which can be an unfair, even dangerous place.
- Reality Discipline can build a child's psychological, emotional, and spiritual muscles and prepare him or her to cope in a dangerous and unforgiving world.
- A key strategy in using Reality Discipline with children is to always be ready to "pull the rug out"—in other words, follow through to be sure that children are accountable for their actions and that they understand that any act always has its consequences, positive or negative.
- Reality Discipline never uses empty threats. When the child acts irresponsibly, the rug is pulled out.
- If you are not willing to pull the rug out, Reality Discipline is just another paper tiger.
- When you are *consistent* in your use of Reality Discipline, it always works.
- Authoritarianism and permissiveness may seem to work

for a while, but in the long run they produce rebellion and misbehavior.

- The best parenting style is "firm but fair." The parent is in charge but is loving, reasonable, and always willing to listen.
- Your goal in rearing your children with Reality Discipline is to bring them to the point where they *decide for themselves* to act responsibly in certain situations.

And Why Not Try . . .

- Commit Reality Discipline Principles No. 8, 9, and 10 to memory:
  8. Use guidance, not force; action, not just words.
  9. Be consistent, decisive, and respectful of your children as people.
  10. Hold your children accountable for their actions, and help them learn from experience.
- If your child is constantly misbehaving by refusing to get up on time for school, refusing to eat when food is served at mealtime, or anything else, try using Reality Discipline and "pulling the rug." Use the example of how one mother dealt with her son when he wouldn't get out of bed in time for school—see pages 176-80.
- Talk with your spouse about your parenting styles. Is one of you authoritarian while the other is more permissive? Or are you both one extreme or the other? Discuss how you can move toward the middle ground of firm but fair.
- Think back over the past couple of weeks, and analyze how consistent you've been in your parenting. How can you become more consistent?
- Read "Parents Need Common Sense" (pp.190-91), and discuss it together. I totally agree with family psychologist, syndicated columnist, and author John Rosemond regarding his six-point plan as a prime example of what Reality Discipline is all about.

PARENTS NEED COMMON SENSE*

Once upon a time, people got married, had children and reared them.

It wasn't something our forebears spent a lot of time fussing and fretting over—it was just something they did, along with most everyone else.

When a young couple had children, grandparents and other extended family provided whatever support they needed to get their feet on the ground. "Parenting" hadn't been invented yet.

Along came a war, and then a baby boom. Young parents took their children and went looking for the promised land. From the ashes of the extended family rose a host of childrearing experts.

It wasn't long before rhetoric replaced reality as the primary shaper of our childrearing practices. Nonsense replaced common sense. American families became child-centered, American parents became permissive and democratic, and American children became spoiled and sassy and out of control.

It's high time we returned to a more traditional, common-sense vision of childrearing. Specifically, we need to start rearing children consistent with what I call The Rules of the Game.

These are the realities by which they are going to have to live their adult lives, and the sooner they get used to them, the better. Here they are:

Rule One: *You're never going to be the center of everyone's attention. Not for long, at least.*

This simply means that children should not be the center of attention in their families. Parents should be the center of attention. If they aren't, children won't pay attention to them.

Rule Two: *Everyone must obey a higher authority.*

Therefore, parents should expect children to obey. They

should not *wish* that children would obey, they should not *plead* with children to obey, they should not *rant and rave* at children to obey. They should simply, without apology, expect them to toe the mark.

Rule Three: *Everyone is expected to be a contributing member of society.*
Too many children are "on the dole." They take from their families, but are rarely, if ever, expected to put anything of consequence back into them.

Ask yourself this question: Do I expect my children to perform a regular routine of chores in and around the home, for which they are not paid? The only acceptable answer is yes.

Rule Four: *Everyone is responsible for his or her own behavior.*
Quite simply, a child who does something bad ought to feel bad about it. All too often, however, a child does something wrong, and the parent feels bad. Why should a child accept responsibility for his own behavior if someone else is doing a fine job of accepting it for him?

Rule Five: *You can't always get what you want, and what you do get, you get by working and waiting.*
Therefore, children should receive all of those things they need, and a conservative amount of those things they want. Today's child desperately needs more "vitamin N"—the most character-building two-letter word in the English language.

Rule Six: *You experience happiness, which is the elixir of success, in direct proportion to how sensitive to and considerate you are of others. Self-centeredness and unhappiness go hand in hand.*
Parents who raise their children according to Rules One through Five don't have to worry about Rule Six.

*From John Rosemond, *Six-Point Plan for Raising Happy, Healthy Children* (Kansas City, Mo.: Andrews and McMeel, 1989). Used by permission.

Chapter 9

We Have Met the Enemy, and They Are Small

---●---

Using Reality Discipline with Younger Children

A QUESTION I OFTEN HEAR AT SEMINARS AND DURING CALL-INS TO OUR "Parent Talk" program is: "When can I start using Reality Discipline with my children?"

My answer is: "As soon as they are born." I advise all new parents to follow the advice we took from a wise obstetrician who told us when our first child arrived, "Get a baby-sitter at least one night a week, and go out. Get the child used to knowing that you aren't always there."

We did this with our first child, Holly—with some trepidation, of course—but it did work. It gave both of us, and especially Sande, a much-needed break from the routine of caring for a newborn. At least once a week, we were able to concentrate on each other and our marriage, rather than on this new little intruder who happily had taken over our lives. It also sent a message to Holly even in her first weeks and months of life that there is a discipline and order to life, that the universe does not revolve around her.

When children come into the world, they are soft, cute, cuddly, and the object of our total adoration and unconditional love. One thing we tend to forget is that they are also totally self-centered, insatiable in their demands, and *very* conditional in their love for us. Children need our love, and studies have shown that if they don't get this love, they can literally die. Because they are so help-less and needy, infants are, in essence, little tyrants whose every whim is to be obeyed—at least in their own minds.

As children move through infancy, into the crawling and then the walking stages, this self-centered attitude continues, and it is the parents' task to help them learn how to share, how to wait, how to obey, and numerous other basic lessons. Children aren't neces-sarily going to cooperate with all this. In fact, I often tell parents, tongue in cheek:

"Children are the enemy."

In other words, they will do all they can to get their own way. They will do all they can to divide Mom and Dad and get them dis-agreeing over bedtime, who should do what chore, and so on. Make no mistake about it—children are very shrewd and very per-ceptive. They can smell inconsistency and indecision in Mom or Dad in a flash, and they are quick to try to take advantage of the slightest opening.

Another thing the parents of a very young child can do any-time between the ages of a few months and two years, for example, is to bring in a powerful ally: the playpen. I sometimes tell brand-new parents that this is a "new invention" that can be very useful. Young parents of the 1990s seldom seem to know what a playpen is, and if they do, they dismiss the idea as unfair and unloving.

Nothing could be further from the truth. A playpen is an excel-lent and safe place to put a child who is just going too far, becoming what I call "a little ankle-biter" by being too clingy, overly fussy, and demanding. The playpen is a "time out" place, not only for the child, but also for Mom (at least, it's usually Mom), who desperately needs a bit of respite.

Some mothers say a playpen would never work because the child would scream bloody murder at being put in one. That's why I encourage moms to start putting the youngster in the playpen as early as possible, so that he or she gets used to it. If you haven't started your child out early with the playpen but want to start at thirteen months, for example, it is quite true that he may protest loudly at being confined (sometimes a different toy to distract the child may help). At this point, you must be strong—and also just a bit deaf. I guarantee that the child will stop screaming. Of course, it may take a while. At last count, I believe the record for screaming—as reported by parents from southern Arizona, at least—is something like two hours and fifty-three minutes.

Seriously, the child will usually stop in a few minutes. Simply go about your business making dinner or doing whatever needs to be done, realizing that the screaming has not come to stay, but has come to pass; and pass it will when the child either runs out of energy or finally gets the message that "Mom or Dad is not going to pick me up."

Also, keep in mind that if you start putting a child in a playpen at an early age, the child will get used to it and may even like it. Granted, some children will like it less than others, but parents must be resolute. Some children aren't going to give in easily. They want their parents to give in, and if the parents do give in, they simply teach the child, *If I cry long enough and hard enough, I will get my way.*

I always tell new parents, "You want bonding, but not binding." In other words, parents certainly want to care for, love, and nurture their child (bonding), but at the same time they are not to be the child's servant or slave (binding). Children need love balanced with training, teaching, and discipline. Again, I use the word *disci-*

pline with some reservations, because I know so many people think it means punishment. If I want to get across one point in this chapter, it is this: *Reality Discipline is not punishment.* It is teaching and training to help a child grow up to be capable, responsible, and accountable. As you work with your child to teach and train, you need to keep three major points in mind:

> Every child seeks attention.
> Every child is unique.
> Every child learns through watching—you.

CHILDREN GET ATTENTION ONE WAY OR ANOTHER

As children grow from infancy into the preschool and grade school years, they continue developing the basic skill that they had the moment they were born—getting their parents' attention. Three levels of behavior in children can lead to problems for the parents. The first and mildest is what I call the *attention-getting child* who says, "I only count when others pay attention to me," then proceeds to try to fulfill that need. All children want attention, and all children try to get it in positive or negative ways. When the negative outweighs the positive, problems usually start.

Moving up the scale a notch, we come to the *powerful child* who is definitely using power-trip tactics. The powerful child says, "I only count when I control, dominate, or win." In other words, the powerful child wants to control his parents and others around him and, if possible, even dominate them. He wants to win in every encounter. He says in so many words, "I'll *make* you pay attention to me!"

The most serious kind of behavior is seen in the *revengeful child* who tells himself, "I only count in life when I get even—when I hurt you back." Most revengeful children grow up to do time in prison.

For our purposes in this book, I want to focus on attention-getting and powerful children. All children learn through experimenting with what psychiatrist Alfred Adler called "purposive behavior." All social behavior is purposeful—that is, it serves a purpose in the child's life.

For the powerful child, purposeful behavior is really a power trip. The child is trying to keep Mom and/or Dad under his thumb or needlessly involved in his life. Early on, the child starts probing the kind of resistance he's up against. He learns what works with his parents and what doesn't. He experiments to see what gets him what he wants and what fails.

Occasionally, even a shy child is very powerful. Early in my counseling career, I recall working with a five-year-old who spoke softly—very softly. I soon found myself leaning forward to catch her words, and soon I practically fell over on top of her because I had leaned so far, I was losing my balance! Suddenly it occurred to me: *This child is controlling me with her shyness—and her soft voice.*

I decided to sit back and speak to the child in a normal tone. When I couldn't hear her, I gently asked her to speak a little louder. At first she didn't like it, but eventually we got on a much better conversational basis. I had taught her she could not control me with her shyness. At the same time, I was careful to not badger her or demand that she speak up and quit acting "so shy." I've always found that when you treat children in the way you expect them to act, chances are they will act that way.

THE PICKY-EATER SYNDROME

While all children choose their own ways to take power trips, there are certain "universal" areas of life that become battlegrounds. One of these is the kitchen table, where every mother has heard: "Yuck! I hate peas . . . I hate soup . . . I hate fish . . . I hate salad." Sometimes, to the complete dismay of parents, children who loved spaghetti, fried chicken, or hamburgers yesterday or last week will say, "I hate spaghetti . . . I hate fried chicken."

President George Bush made the news with his admission that he never liked broccoli as a child and still doesn't. While that doesn't make the president a picky eater, it illustrates the kinds of battles that are familiar to all parents.

What can a parent do with a child who is taking a power trip by being a picky eater? Reality Discipline comes to the rescue. One mom told me, "This kid is driving me nuts. He doesn't eat a thing. He eats like a bird. What do I do?"

"Why don't you try not setting a place for him at the table?" I responded. I guarantee mothers that not setting the child's place at the table will gain his immediate attention. All of us—even young children—view the dinner table much as people view their favorite pew at church. We all have our favorite seat. When the child walks in and sees that his place is not set, he's going to protest, "Hey, Mom, what's going on?"

At this point, Mom must do her Reality Discipline thing. She must be strong but not judgmental, severe, or uptight.

"Why, honey," she should say glibly, "nothing special is going on. We're just about to have dinner, and we're having spaghetti, and I know how you hate spaghetti."

The child may say, "Yuck, I hate spaghetti. What else can I have for dinner?"

Now Mom must reply, "Nothing. That's why I didn't set a place for you at the table."

The child will probably react in one of two ways. One is to stomp out of the room, accusing his mother of child abuse and maybe even murder. Mom must not panic. The child will simply miss dinner, and she will undoubtedly see him at breakfast—much hungrier and less picky about what he's going to eat.

Or it just may be that, with his bluff called, he will go over and look in the pots on the stove containing the tomato sauce, the meatballs, and the spaghetti. He will take a big whiff of all this, think about how empty his stomach is, and very possibly say, "Mom, I think I could eat that spaghetti after all."

To which Mom can reply, "All right, I'll set a place for you, honey."

And the child will sit down and eat his spaghetti, even though every time it has been served before, there has been a discussion that would make the United Nations Security Council look like a quilting bee.

I believe that even with very young children—three, four, and five years old—there is no need to turn the dinner table into a debating society or battleground. Suppose you have just sat down to dinner with your three-year-old and five-year-old. Suddenly, without warning, the five-year-old decides everything is "yucky!" and little "Me, too" chimes in. Kindly but firmly, excuse both children from the table and tell them there will be no bedtime snacks and that the next time they can eat is at breakfast.

Parents sometimes accuse me of being "cruel and hardhearted," and I agree that at the moment Reality Discipline is being used, it can cause some tension. But that's just the point. It's tempting to succumb to the expediency of the moment rather than see the long-range benefits. By being firm with the children, you help them develop habits that will pay off in the future.

Speaking of habits, you want to start the child early with good eating habits. Don't bring junk food into your house. If all the food in the house is basically good, healthy food, you will be on a much better basis for getting children to eat when it is served at mealtimes.

It all goes back to early training. We have interviewed many parents who called in to our "Parent Talk" radio show to tell us that their children have not developed a taste for candy because from earliest ages on, candy was never served to them in any way, shape, or form. For these children, about as close to candy as they ever come is yogurt-covered raisins.

The consensus among all parents who operate this way is that you must start when the child is very young. And, of course, you must not be a candy or other kind of junk-food eater yourself.

If junk food has been part of the menu at your house—as in the form of snacks, for example—and you want to change things, the only way you can hope for any success is to go cold turkey on the junk food yourself. It will do little good to try to tell your children they can't eat candy or other junk food when they see you gobbling down your share.

Another tip is to not put a portion of food on the child's plate and then present the plate to him. This says, in effect, "I have decided what and how much you are to eat." Parents do this for speed and expediency as dinner is getting started, but if you want to use Reality Discipline, it is far better to offer a three-year-old, for example, a bowl of food and ask, "Honey, would you like some?"

If the child says yes, you put a small portion on his plate. If the child says no, you pass the food on to the next person. What you want to avoid is saying to the child in any way at all, "Here, kid—the stuff I put on your plate is good for you—eat it!" Let the child decide what he or she wants to eat.

Does this put the child in control of the situation? I don't believe it does, although it does make the child responsible for his own choices. Suppose a child refuses to eat all but one thing being served. So be it. As a pediatrician in whom I have great confidence once said, "Don't worry about it. The more you worry about what the child eats, the more it becomes a power struggle. The child will work it out, and if you don't make a big deal out of what he eats, he may try a lot more things of his own volition."

Remember, if you have a well-balanced meal on the table, the child will survive by eating only one thing. I sometimes talk to mothers who insist that their child "must have some fruit."

Again, I suggest that instead of demanding that the child eat fruit, they try to capitalize on what I call "oppositional behavior." In other words, for children who say they don't like fruit, practically make fruit forbidden.

Suppose you have three or four children, and one of them will eat fruit, but the rest won't. Serve the child who likes fruit, complimenting him on his choice and saying how good that fruit will taste. Serve yourself next, and then remove the fruit from the table. It is my experience that in many cases, one or more of the other children will suddenly decide he wants to try a piece of fruit after all.

Even if the other children don't want to try fruit, do not press it. Simply wait them out. One meal doesn't make a childhood. Perhaps by next week they will be willing to try fruit. In the meantime, ten out of ten pediatricians will tell you, "They will *not* die!"

Another question that often comes up is time limits. Suppose a child picks at his food, barely eating anything. In this case, simply set a time limit, and have the child understand that the dinner will be over by, say, 6:30 or 6:45. When the time limit is up, remove the child's plate. Do not make a special exception and wait around for another thirty or forty minutes for the child to finish. Oh, yes, two other points that the child must understand are: He gets nothing more to eat that evening, no snacks; and because he has only picked at his main course, he is obviously not hungry for dessert!

SOLVING SIBLING RIVALRY

Another familiar battleground to many parents is sibling rivalry, which is a dignified way to describe bickering, fighting, and all-out juvenile warfare.

I was once talking with a mom and dad who were having real problems because of all the tension at the dinner table. They were trying to settle it "diplomatically," and when that didn't work, the father would yell at the two boys to make them "shape up." One of their approaches was to get both boys to leave the table and come up with their own solution to their problem. Then they were to come back to the dinner table and present their solution to their parents. At that time, the parents would offer their point of view and maybe, just maybe, dinner could continue.

I suggested to the parents that that was not at all how I would handle it in my own home. By the time all that would go on, my dinner would be cold, and I would be quite unhappy, because I like my food warm for dinner. Especially with young children (in this case, the boys were six and seven), parents have to be action-oriented. They have to be right on top of what's going on, and if there's going to be discussion, that comes later.

In this case, *action-oriented* means that when children act up at the dinner table, they are immediately removed from the table and forfeit the prospect of having anything the rest of that evening. Give them no warnings, no second chances. *Use action, not words.*

Again, that sounds heartless to some parents, but it isn't really heartless at all. It is allowing reality to teach children the consequences of bad behavior. It is using reality to teach them that the dinner table is where we come together as a family for a good, positive time. All this can be clearly spelled out to children who have a history of arguing and fighting.

When they come to the dinner table, they know full well that if they start fighting, they forfeit their dinner. In addition, they are separated and placed in different rooms or at different ends of the house, which prevents them from doing what they are really after—getting their parents' attention through powerful behavior. There's no argument. This is the reality of the situation, and when Mom and Dad use action, not just words, children learn quickly that this kind of power trip simply will not work.

I talked to one father recently who used this approach with boys twelve and thirteen. They'd always engaged in plenty of sibling rivalry, and they still do to some extent, but never at dinner. They've now learned that this is one place where a power trip ends in disaster.

In dealing with any kind of powerful behavior, parental attitude is crucial. The parent should never show extreme displeasure, but should be calm and matter-of-fact. If the child senses the parent is upset, he has still won the day in some respects and may continue the behavior even though he has to pay the price of not eating.

WHAT TO DO WHEN KIDS ARE "MESSIES"

A third battlefield that causes a great deal of friction between parents and children falls under the general description of "keeping the house clean, especially your room."

Lori, a mother of two sons, nine and six, and a daughter, five, was really struggling with how to get her children to do an acceptable job of cleaning their rooms. They were to do it on Saturday mornings, but their concept of what was clean and Mom's were at least 180 degrees apart. Lori would start out by saying, "Okay, kids, I want your rooms cleaned this morning."

Then she would leave it totally up to them. Back they would come in no time at all to report that the job was all done, then off they would go to play. When Lori checked their rooms, she learned the truth. What her kids thought was "clean" was still very messy.

"I'd really like to know how to handle it when I think they haven't done it well enough," she asked me. "I don't want to hurt their feelings, especially when they really think they've done a wonderful job."

"Lori, I think it's great that you want to respect the children's efforts, because that's very important. But when the job isn't done to your satisfaction, you don't have to let that go. What you should do is not let the children leave until you have inspected their rooms. While they're saying, 'Can we go out and play now?' you're going to have to be saying, 'Well, I'm sorry, but your rooms just aren't ready yet. You're not ready to go out.'"

"But they'll howl like crazy and tell me I'm mean," Lori protested.

"You'll just have to be ready for that," I answered. "Telling Mom she's mean is the oldest line in the book. All you have to say is, 'I'm sorry, the rooms just aren't ready.' Then you can do one of two things: just walk out and leave the kids to finish them up because you're sure they know what you mean, or stay and give them direction and encouragement as they finish the rooms."

A solution that can be used in a case where one child does a nice job of cleaning the room and another child does a poor job is for the parents to hire the child who does a good job to clean the room of the brother or sister who is sloppy. This will achieve two things: It will give the neat brother or sister an excuse to "trespass" in the sloppy child's room—something the sloppy child will equate with Saddam Hussein's invasion of Kuwait. Second, and more important, the sloppy child will have to pay his brother or sister out of his allowance to get his room cleaned.

Again, all this is to be spelled out ahead of time. Always pave the way for Reality Discipline by helping your children clearly understand that, no matter what, they will be held accountable for what they do and don't do. Then, when children misbehave and you pull the rug out, you aren't punishing them—you're only using Reality Discipline to train them.

What Lori must remember particularly is that her nine-year-old and six-year-old sons are not going to be that concerned about "clean corners." The last thing she should do is demand perfection of them. If she feels the corners aren't really clean enough, she might go back in their rooms periodically when they're at school and shape things up to her liking. Chances are her sons won't even notice.

The important thing is to establish a routine in which the boys are made responsible for cleaning their rooms. My personal preference is twice a week. If you want to inject a little humor into the conversation, tell the child, "You are responsible for at least shoveling out your room on Tuesday and Saturday."

The key to Reality Discipline is that *parents must not be afraid to pull the rug out.* If the child's chores aren't done, there is no need to remind or to coax. Simply let it ride, but at six o'clock or at whatever time they're supposed to go to Little League practice or some other activity, the parent can say, "The car isn't going anywhere."

"What do you mean, Mom? We've got to be there!"

"I'm sorry, but the job I asked you to do today isn't done, and we simply aren't moving."

Many children will immediately say, "I'll go do it right now."

And they probably will want to "do it right now"—usually in a big hurry and even more slipshod than usual.

But the point is, they don't get to do the job right now. They miss practice or club or whatever they're in, and they're still held accountable to do the job at another time.

Holding the child accountable is always the key, no matter what the situation. For example, pants-wetting is not always a simple problem, but one solution that often works with the younger child who keeps coming in from play with wet clothes, saying "I forgot," is to explain that he will get only one pair of pants for the day. If he wets those clothes, he has to come in for the rest of the day and will not go out again.

This kind of Reality Discipline usually communicates with the four-year-old who knows he can control his bladder but who tends to "forget" in order to get Mom's attention and involve her needlessly in his life.

Another good rule is to always give the child an opportunity to think a problem through for herself or himself. Don't simply intone the "rule" that was broken—explain exactly where the child failed to be responsible. For example, one day when Kevin was in junior high, he came to me at 9:50 P.M., saying, "Dad, can you drill me on my spelling words for tomorrow?"

"No, Kevin," I replied. "I can't because it's time to go to bed."

"But Dad, I've got a big test tomorrow."

"I know, but it's ten to ten. If you had come to me at ten to eight, I would have helped you."

"Some dad you are," he said accusingly.

"Think of me what you like, but I'm not helping you now.

You've been sitting around all night watching television. Now, all of a sudden, you want to be a Rhodes scholar. It's too late."

Kevin has learned that if he wants help with his schoolwork, he has to start before ten o'clock. He knows that it's his responsibility to get his studying done and that studying comes ahead of TV.

It's always important to make a child feel responsible and then hold him accountable for those responsibilities. In that way, you treat the child as an equal member of the family. Ironically, if you let the child get away with irresponsible behavior, it really degrades the child, and in the case of a junior high student, it keeps the young person at a more childish level when he should be developing more-mature habits.

EVERY CHILD IS UNIQUE

In chapter 8, I mentioned how important it is not to treat all children the same. Whenever you pull the rug out and invoke Reality Discipline, you should always do it by taking the child's individual characteristics and personality into account. Reality Discipline for one child can be a cakewalk for another, and vice versa.

There's a proverb in the Old Testament that you may remember hearing as you grew up: "Train up a child in the way he should go, and when he is old he will not depart from it."[1] The typical interpretation is that parents should rear their children correctly, take them to worship, teach them right and wrong, and so on, and when they grow up they won't forget what they were taught. There is, however, another way to interpret the proverb that is more accurate.

The consensus of Bible scholars who understand the original Hebrew is that a more correct translation is: "Train up a child *in his own way* . . ." That doesn't mean you let him do as he pleases. It means taking the child's personality, temperament, and life style into account.

As I pointed out when discussing the differences between men and women, all of us start working out our own personal "way" or "life style" from our day of birth. And one of the most powerful determinants of a child's life style is birth order. (See chapter 4 if you want to review the key characteristics of firstborns, middle children, and lastborn babies of the family.)

It's especially important to consider the child's birth order and his perception of his position in the family whenever you set up any kind of Reality Discipline situation. Over the years, I've become something of a champion of all firstborns, because I see parents putting too much pressure on their firstborn child. They fail to realize that with only adults for role models, the firstborn child is already putting tremendous pressure on himself to measure up. When parents add even more pressure, it can cause the child to feel bitter or actually make him buckle under the stress. Firstborns have enough problems with perfectionism without having parents discipline them in such a way as to increase them.

I was talking with one mother about how she was doling out the chores in her family, and she commented that Jonathan (her oldest child, at twelve) was usually the one who "takes the garbage out." She was quite happy with her system of delegating responsibilities and the consequences that were invoked if the jobs weren't done. For example, if the garbage didn't get out, the dishes didn't get washed, or the floor didn't get swept, the child who had failed to do his chores would be assigned three or four more different duties to perform in addition to the one he had failed to do.

I told this mother her system was good as far as it went, but I suggested that instead of making Jonathan the garbage person of the family, sweet little Abigail, their six-year-old, be assigned the job. Taking out garbage is a task well within the ability of a six-year-old, and Jonathan could be given other tasks. For example, how about helping pay the bills? Why couldn't a twelve-year-old learn to write checks and even balance the checking account? All the older Leman children—Holly, Krissy, and Kevin—have taken their turn at the checkbook without bankrupting us. In fact, their mother says they all do a better job than their father ever did!

The point is, there are all kinds of chores to be done around the house, but to leave Jonathan with the garbage is only to tell him, "Once you're a garbage person, you're always a garbage person. Until you leave home, that's your job."

I suggested to Mom that she ask Dad to assign Jonathan to check the oil in the cars every week and even wash them on Saturday mornings. Another job for Jonathan could be "family bulb snatcher"—being responsible to replace all burned-out light bulbs.

Actually, the possibilities are limitless. The parents could talk it over with Jonathan and undoubtedly find other assignments more challenging than taking out the garbage. Doing the more challenging tasks would give Jonathan important training and increase his self-esteem as well.

WHEN A FIRSTBORN DOES A LOT OF BABY-SITTING

In another case, Betsey was a mother with a nine-year-old, a three-year-old, a one-and-a-half-year-old, and an infant. She was wondering about how much responsibility to give the nine-year-old. My first observation was: "I suggest that you not lean on the nine-year-old too hard. It's my guess that he winds up having to baby-sit and watch his younger siblings on many occasions while you do something else, or even run to the neighbors for something for a few minutes."

I asked Betsey if she saw any signs of resentment in her nine-year-old for the chores he had to do.

"Yes," Betsey replied, "resentment in the cleaning department. The problem is, I'm messy, too, so how do I teach something I don't even practice?"

"To tell you the truth, I would be less concerned with your nine-year-old's cleanliness and more appreciative of the good help he's giving you with the three younger children. In other words, where I could, I would ease up on the nine-year-old's responsibilities—the things you want him to do specifically—because he's going to be doing so many generally helpful things. And then I'd always make it a point to tell the child, eyeball to eyeball, just how much you appreciate his efforts."

Sometimes, in our desire to cover all the bases as we try to maintain a household full of children, we get caught up in the means and forget the end. We aren't simply trying to get children to "do their chores." There's a lot more to what we're doing than getting them to take out the garbage, wash the dishes, and clean up their rooms. Yes, all those things need to be done, but what we're really trying to do is teach obedience, responsibility, and accountability. We are trying to put the child in a position where he can make choices and then learn that he has to live with the consequences of those choices.

TIDYING UP THE MESSY MIDDLE CHILD

Another example of dealing with children according to their birth order came up when a mother told me her second oldest child (she had three) had always been "the biggest mess-maker in the family and noncooperative about everything." Nancy had been trying to home-school her children and was having a real struggle with having him do his schoolwork and then his chores as well. Also, it was becoming very discouraging to the older brother and the little sister when the middle child wouldn't pitch in and do his share of the work. In this case, the oldest child was eleven, the middle child was nine, and the youngest was turning eight.

"Let's just call a spade a spade here," I told this mother. "Realize that your nine-year-old son is sandwiched between his 'perfect' big brother, two years older than he is, and his little sister, who is the baby princess. Here he is, smack in the middle between the two most special people in the family, the firstborn and the only girl, who is the baby to boot. It's my guess he feels life has been a bit unfair to him to begin with, and why should he worry about chores? It's also my guess that a lot of his negativity and lack of cooperation comes right out of his feelings that he is being squeezed in the middle and is not as special as he should be in your family."

"But what do I do?" asked Nancy. "Just last week he caused the whole family not to get to eat until 8:30 in the evening because his chores weren't done. Because he didn't do his chores, I couldn't get the meal on the table until then."

"Reality is reality," I told Nancy. "Even though your middle child is feeling squeezed and that life's unfair, he has to know that the rules are the rules and that when he doesn't do his job, he'll have to pay the price. In a case like that, I'd feed the rest of the flock and leave him with an empty bin."

One other thing I advised Nancy to do was to make a list of all the things her nine-year-old son really enjoyed doing. Once she had this list in mind, it could become her ally in using Reality Discipline with him.

"Suppose your son plays Little League baseball or soccer," I explained. "Or suppose he's in 4-H or the science club. Whatever the activity, you tie the Reality Discipline directly to that event. When he fails to cover his responsibilities, he can't enjoy the activity he really likes."

"I'm not sure how that helps him feel very special," Mom said dubiously.

"That's a good point," I responded. "I was trying to keep a balance here to help your boy understand that life is full of responsibilities and that when he doesn't meet them, the price has to be paid. At the same time, your middle child needs some extra one-on-one attention, where you show concern and interest in him as a person. Doing things one-on-one with all your children is a good idea, but it's extremely helpful to gain better cooperation from the middle child."

In addition, be aware that a middle child often feels, *Nobody cares what I think.* Look for ways your middle child can be allowed to lead or make a choice about where the family will stop for a treat, for example. Being recognized as someone who can make choices that affect the rest of the family will do a lot to gain better cooperation on things like cleaning his room.

LASTBORNS ARE NEVER LEAST

Lastborn children are a special challenge, particularly when it comes to Reality Discipline. The problem is, they are usually little charmers, so cute that it's often tempting to let them get away with things their older brothers and sisters could never get away with.

I have a lot of experience with lastborn children because I am one. I've told in other books how I came in third behind a big sister who was an A-plus student and a big brother who was a B-plus student and a big athletic hero as well. *I'll show them!* I said to myself, and I proceeded to carve my own niche in life by pulling D's and F's and being the family clown.

I clowned my way up all the way to high school, where I finally ran into a no-nonsense math teacher who understood how to handle the lastborn who is trying to get attention in negative ways. Miss Wilson pulled me aside one day during my last semester in high school. Looking me squarely in the eye, she asked, "Kevin, when are you going to stop playing your game?"

"What game is that, Teach?" I asked. Believe it or not, I actually did refer to her as "Teach." It was 1961, and I was trying to be "cool."

"The game you play the best," the math teacher said with a smile. "Being the worst!"

I laughed it off, but what she said that day turned me in another direction. She had seen through my facade and knew I was playing a self-destructive, attention-getting game.

The point of this personal illustration is that parents shouldn't wait until a lastborn is in high school to call his bluff. They shouldn't depend on a teacher to do it, either. At an early age, the little family clown can be appreciated, but he should never be allowed to take the behavior beyond what is acceptable. Lastborns, cute as they are, have to be as responsible and accountable as anyone else.

With Kevin, our third child, we thought we had seen the end of dealing with lastborn behavior, but not so. I've already described how Sande and I had to go back to "square one" in childrearing with the arrival of Hannah (and later Lauren, too), our little "afterthought" who was born when both of us were in our forties. Hannah sometimes reminded us of what it can be like when a lastborn uses a favorite weapon—the temper tantrum. Firstborns and middle children are quite capable of temper tantrums, of course, but lastborns often perfect them to a fine art.

We were walking through a mall one evening when Hannah spotted a Walgreen drugstore. No, we weren't pushing her to read yet, but she recognized the store front and immediately associated what she saw with *candy!*

"I want a candy treat!" she almost shouted.

"No," I said. "No candy treats this trip. You've had your quota for a while."

Now I suppose, gentle reader, you would assume that because Hannah is the daughter of an experienced child psychologist, she simply acquiesced demurely and contented herself with trying to find a toy store where she could do some window-shopping. No such luck. She promptly threw a temper tantrum right in the middle of Tucson's largest mall, complete with lying on the polished marble floor, kicking, and screaming. It was, by any measure, a masterful performance.

Following the same advice I've given mothers for years, we all stepped over Hannah and just walked away. We didn't get far when she was up and after us, only to throw herself down and try again to get her candy treat.

"No deal, Hannah," I said quietly. "*No* candy!"

We've tried to teach all our children that you don't always get treats when you're out with the family. Once in a while, okay, but a treat is not an everyday thing.

As we continued through the mall on the way back to our car, Hannah made two or three more attempts to get her way—all to no avail. By the time we got to the car, Hannah was kicking and screaming again. Her big sister Holly was trying to hold her in the front seat, and as I attempted to pull out of the parking lot, Hannah kicked the gearshift from drive into reverse! Needless to say, the car stopped rather suddenly. At that point, Hannah received one good swat to let her know her behavior had gone well past what would be tolerated. She let out a yelp of surprise, cried for a minute or two, and was fine the rest of the way home.

As we drove along, I talked to Hannah about why she had received a swat. She kept saying, "I'm sorry, Papa," and I assured her, "Honey, it's okay. Papa loves you very much, but you have to understand you just can't have your way every time you want it."

I also tried to explain that the people who had made our car hadn't designed it to go from forward to reverse while it was moving at twenty miles per hour. I'm afraid those technicalities were a bit above her head, but the hugs and kisses I gave her when I put her to bed that night weren't.

While I prefer reasoning with children and letting reality do the disciplining, there are moments "in the trenches" when a swat sends the only message they will hear. The important thing is to be under total control when you give that swat and then take time to reassure the child that you love him or her very much. Always take care to teach your children that the same loving hand that helps them up when they fall sometimes has to correct them in love when they're out of control.

Everything I've said in this chapter could be put under Reality Discipline Principle No. 5, "Stick to your guns," whether you're dealing with lastborns, middleborns, or firstborns. Teach your children early:

1. You don't always get your way.
2. Life isn't always going to be fair.
3. Once Mom and Dad say no, they mean it.

And to these three rules, add one more: Keep your cool, your sense of humor, and your perspective. Earlier in this chapter, I said tongue-in-cheek, "Children are the enemy." Of course, children aren't really the enemy. It just seems that way at times. During those trying times, Reality Discipline is indeed a parent's—and a child's—best friend.

We have looked at how children seek attention and how they work out their uniqueness as they develop their own personality and life style. In the next chapter, we'll consider how much your children learn as they watch and follow your personal example.

Don't Forget . . .
- You can start Reality Discipline with children practically from the day they are born.
- Children are born self-centered. They are lovable little ankle-biters who need nurture and training.
- The playpen can be a powerful ally for parents if they're brave enough to use it.
- All children seek attention, in positive or negative ways.
- Every child is unique and should be treated according to his or her personality, temperament, and life style.

And Why Not Try . . .
- Review the various suggestions for using Reality Discipline given in this chapter: with picky eaters, rival siblings, messies who won't keep their rooms clean, pants-wetting, postponing homework, getting children to help around the house, and temper tantrums. If any of these situations apply to your children at this time, adapt the examples and try Reality Discipline. If it doesn't seem to work at

first, be patient and stick to your guns. If you're consistent, it will eventually pay off in much better behavior.

• For additional ideas in using Reality Discipline to deal with specific behavioral problems in children, see *Making Children Mind Without Losing Yours* (New York: Dell Publishing, 1987).

• How do your children tend to seek attention? How can you train them to use positive ways rather than negative ones?

• Whenever disciplining your children, be firm but fair, and stick to your guns. Teach them they don't always get their way, life isn't always fair, and that once you say no, you mean it. For more ideas on how to respond to children in certain situations, see "Healthy and Unhealthy Responses to Children" on the following pages.

Healthy and Unhealthy Responses to Children

Behavior	Unhealthy Parental Response	Child's Perception of Self	Healthy Parental Response	Child's Perception of Self
Child forgets to feed the dog.	"You're grounded for life." (Later you may want to amend this to two weeks.) "The dog is going to die, and it's your fault."	"I'm a failure." "I can't be trusted."	"I have asked your brother to feed the dog for three days. He will get three dollars from your allowance."	"Mom is holding me accountable. I have a choice: Feed the dog or pay for the privilege of having my brother do it for me."
Child leaves kitchen a total mess while getting a snack.	"You are a total slob! Do you think that all I have time to do is clean up after you?"	"Mom thinks I'm a slob, so why try to be neat?"	"I'm very upset with the way you've left the kitchen. Will you please come with me immediately so we can get it cleaned up?" (Mom stays in the kitchen while child is working.)	"Mom doesn't want the kitchen messy, and I'm going to have to clean up after myself."
Your child gets all C's and D's on his report card.	"What's this? Are you really this stupid? You could do better if you'd just not play Nintendo and watch TV all the time."	"My dad thinks I'm stupid. I'd much rather play Nintendo or watch TV anyway, so who cares?"	"It's clear to see that you didn't get very good grades this time. We both know you can do better than this. From now on, homework has to come before Nintendo or TV."	"Dad knows I can do better than this, and he wants me to do better."

Behavior	Unhealthy Parental Response	Child's Perception of Self	Healthy Parental Response	Child's Perception of Self
Child wants to watch an undesirable TV program.	"You know that trash is off limits—besides, it's on too late. Only idiots or perverts watch garbage like that."	"I'm an idiot or a pervert—I wonder what this program would be like? I'll watch it sometime when I stay overnight with Billy."	"I believe this program isn't a good one for anyone in our family to watch. Why don't you (name alternative activities) instead?"	"Mom doesn't approve of the show I want to watch, so maybe I'll try one of the others—it's better than nothing."

Chapter 10

Guess Who's Teaching Your Kids Their Values?

They're Caught More Than Taught

I N A NEW JERSEY CLASSROOM, A TEACHER POSED THIS SITUATION TO HER
pupils: "A woman finds a thousand dollars lying in the street.
She decides to turn it in to the authorities. Did she do the right
thing?"

According to the story that originally ran in *The New York Times,*
all fifteen children thought the woman was stupid. "Why turn in
the money?" these kids wanted to know. The rule they preferred to
live by was the old, familiar line, "Finders, keepers."

But the story doesn't end there. The really chilling part is that
the *Times* reporter asked this teacher, "Why didn't you tell those
kids that turning in the money was the right thing to do?"

"That is not my job," the teacher said. "My job is simply to help
them find truth as they find it within themselves."[1]

This teacher was voicing a general tendency on the part of the educational community to refuse to teach children morals.

"That's not our job," teachers say. "That's up to the parents."

You can argue for or against the teacher's position, but the fact remains that parents who are interested in using Reality Discipline in their families can't count on a lot of support from the schools. There are exceptions, true, but the general attitude is, "This isn't our territory."

We could hope that the opinion of those New Jersey schoolchildren was a rare exception, but unfortunately there is too much evidence that their attitude is widespread. An obvious example is the rampant cheating that goes on at all levels and that really gets fine-tuned by the time students make it to high school. One study of high school students revealed that 75 percent of them cheated during exams for one reason: "To get good enough grades to get into a good college." The motto among many students is, "Why flunk when you can cheat?"[2]

IS LIFE ALL ABOUT BUCKS?

There seems to be a crisis in values across our nation. A lot of educators and other experts are asking, "Whatever happened to good, old-fashioned honesty, integrity, dependability, humility, teamwork, compassion—oh, yes, and that seemingly scarce commodity called love for one's fellow man?"

In a survey of fifteen hundred college students who were considered to be outstanding in scholarship and leadership, only one in five said they were interested in studying anything that would clarify ethical and moral issues. As one student put it, "Morality has nothing to do with the study of business."

Perhaps this student had seen the film *Wall Street*, in which Michael Douglas plays Gordon Gekko, a highly successful and experienced corporate pirate who takes Bud Fox (actor Charlie Sheen) under his wing to teach him the finer points of takeovers and insider trading. Toward the end of the film, there's a potent scene where Fox bursts into Gekko's office after he learns that Gekko plans to wreck Blue Star Airlines, where Fox's father works. Gekko has completely betrayed Fox, who wants to save the airline and make it a paying business. Instead, Gekko plans to sell off the corporation, take his profits, and run.

In a tense conversation, the two men argue, and Fox asks Gekko how he could do it: "My father has worked there for twenty-four years!"

Gekko replies with a sneer, "It's all about bucks, kid. The rest is conversation."

Or to put it in the college student's words, "Morality has nothing to do with business."

ARE WE TURNING OUT "SKILLED BARBARIANS"?

Steven Muller, president of Johns Hopkins University in Baltimore, was quoted in *U.S. News & World Report* as saying, "The biggest failing in higher education today is that we fall short in exposing students to values. We don't really provide a value framework to young people who more and more are searching for it."

Muller went on to say that many of the institutions in the United States "have lost a coherent sense of values. . . . The failure to rally around a set of values means that universities are turning out potentially high skilled barbarians." And he added that one of the main weaknesses of the kind of people coming out of the universities is that they lack the self-confidence to make choices and *take responsibility*.[3]

VALUES TOOK HIM FROM POVERTY TO UNIVERSITY PRESIDENT

With all this bad news coming out of colleges and universities, it was encouraging to get a little good news in a local Tucson paper that carried a lengthy story about Manuel Pacheco's appointment to the presidency of the University of Arizona. In July 1991, Dr. Pacheco became the first Hispanic president in the 106-year history of the university. His story reads like a Horatio Alger account of what values are all about.

One of twelve children, Pacheco was born in Colorado and later moved with his family to New Mexico, where he grew up in extreme poverty on a small farm that his father had managed to purchase. According to Pacheco, "We didn't even get electricity in the house until 1954." But while the family had little money, there was plenty of love, and the kind of values that would help little Manuel succeed were taught.

"There were values that were instilled in all twelve of us when we were growing up," Pacheco said. "We had a lot of things we had to do around the house. We all had our jobs. My mother and I ran a dairy by ourselves from the time I was seven years old.

"I'd get up at four o'clock in the morning, get the cows, milk them, and then get ready for school. During that whole growing-up period, the one thing that I very clearly remember is that there were no unreasonable expectations of the children. The expectation was that it didn't matter what we were going to do: if we were going to do it, we needed to do it well."

And did the values and work ethic of Manuel's parents pay off? Today, every one of the twelve children holds at least a bachelor's degree, and five of them hold advanced degrees. In Manuel's case, he scored high enough on a test during his junior year of high school to be admitted to New Mexico Highlands University without having to go through his senior year in high school.

At the age of sixteen, the future president of the University of Arizona financed his college education by working twenty hours a week in the library and pumping gas on weekends. During the time he was in college, his parents were able to send him a total of only twenty dollars or so, but that wasn't important. What counted for him was the "moral support they provided . . . that was critical."[4]

VALUES ARE CAUGHT MORE THAN TAUGHT

Manuel Pacheco's story is proof enough for me that you don't teach values to children after they reach the high school or college level. By then, their values are deeply ingrained from learning through their parents' example. In fact, it's accurate to say that values are "caught" more than they're "taught." Even if you attend church services every week, that's not what really does the job. Like the school, the church can only supplement what happens in the home.

Make no mistake: Your children are learning their values by watching Mom and Dad every day. It's in the everyday situations that you communicate values, whether you intend to or not. For example, suppose Mom and her three kids, all under the age of nine, are walking across a parking lot and they come upon a money clip loaded with greenbacks. If Mom wants to teach a simple value like honesty, she will put an ad in the lost and found section of the paper to see if anybody comes forward to claim the money.

Some of her children might protest and say, "Mom, you're nuts," echoing the value system shown by the kids in the New Jersey classroom described earlier. It's then that Mom has to hang tough and simply say, "Honey, that money doesn't belong to us. We have to try to find its owner." Or she might use Jesus' familiar words in Matthew 7:12 to make her point: "So in everything, do to others what you would have them do to you."

An even simpler and more familiar illustration, perhaps, is getting back too much change—at the supermarket counter, for example. Again, Mom or Dad has the children along, and the question is, do you try to give it back or do you just let it go?

Suppose you get change for a twenty when you really gave the clerk a ten? By now, the clerk is very busy with someone else, and as you come back to explain what happened, the clerk gets embarrassed and says, "I didn't make any error!" Now you can really teach values by sticking to your guns, making the clerk verify that an error has been made, and returning the money that does not belong to you.

VALUES CAN GET YOU AUDITED BY THE IRS

As the above examples demonstrate, money is a great tool for teaching values. As your children watch you handle it, they learn a great deal—not only from how you make it, spend it, and save it, but also from how you give it away. In recent years, I have been audited by the IRS several times because they have had questions about my tax return. The first time it happened, my children asked me, "Did you do something wrong, Daddy?"

"I'm not sure, kids," I replied. "I'll go find out."

When I got together with the IRS agent, I discovered that his main concern was the deductions I had taken for charitable contributions. I contribute substantially to my church, as well as to other organizations, and he felt that my giving far exceeded the amount the government normally allows for. Fortunately, I was able to produce canceled checks and other receipts that satisfied him. "Well," he finally said, "looks like everything is in order."

When I got back home, my children asked me again, "How did it go? Did you do something wrong?"

"No, kids," I told them. "As a matter of fact, we've done something right. We exceeded the government's guidelines for giving."

I hadn't bothered to tell the IRS agent that I also do a certain amount of what I call "natural tithing"—giving money to needy friends and other acquaintances with no possibility of a write-off. But my kids know, and that's what's important.

Other opportunities to teach values are everywhere. Obviously, as you drive along the city streets or the freeways, your children are watching the speedometer. Your children are listening as you talk about traffic cops and what you think of them, and of course, any parent who thinks his children don't know what a "fuzz buster" is for is naive, indeed.

Or suppose you discover that your child has stolen something. Instead of giving the child a spanking, a grounding, or some other kind of punishment, the best way to teach the child is to accompany him back to the store, march him up to the manager or the clerk, and have him make restitution right on the spot. This kind of experience will teach more than any spanking ever could.

Obviously, the values we most want to instill come straight from the Bible, beginning with the Ten Commandments. God is a holy sovereign; He has clearly told us, "This is right, and that is wrong." And parents are instructed to teach His ways to their children in Deuteronomy 6:6-7: "These commandments that I give you today are to be upon your hearts. Impress them on your children. Talk about them when you sit at home and when you walk [or drive, we might say today] along the road, when you lie down and when you get up."

By implanting biblical values in our children, we prepare them for lives of peace with God, with themselves, and with others. This is our greatest privilege and responsibility.

HOW TO TALK ABOUT VALUES

If a serious talk about certain values with your child is warranted, I suggest you go about it in the following way. First of all, arrange it so you can sit down quietly and be able to give your child your full attention. Try to insure that you will not be interrupted. (Take the phone off the hook, if necessary.) Also, try to pick a time when neither of you is in a hurry and has to be somewhere.

Next, set the stage by saying, "Honey, I need to talk to you about something that's very important. Can we talk now for a few minutes?"

After getting comfortably settled, say, "You know, honey, there are people who might think that what I'm going to say is pretty square or hopelessly old-fashioned. But this is how I see the situation that just came to my attention." Then go into the problem and the value involved.

It's important to stay low-key and calm. Do not come across as if you're saying, "Hey, I'm laying down the law, and you'd better listen." You will have much more authority—and effectiveness—if you speak quietly and with conviction.

Here's another opening you might want to use: "Your friends might think I'm out in left field, but here is what I believe is right." For a little humor, you might say, "You know, I was born in prehistoric times, BCTV—Before Color Television."

As you continue to discuss the problem, say something like, "I think what has happened is not right, and it needs to be corrected. This is what I believe should be done."

As you bring the conversation to a close, you might say something like, "Some people might think I'm an old fuddy-duddy, but I believe if you do the right thing, you'll feel better about yourself. You'll be able to look into a mirror, and no matter what anyone else says, you'll be able to tell yourself, 'I did what was fair. I was honest. *I did the right thing.*'"

TO TEACH ACCOUNTABILITY, BECOME ACCOUNTABLE

To have the kind of conversation outlined above, you need to be sure of your own values. Above all, you need to know that you back up what you say with what you do.

One of the best approaches to teaching responsibility and accountability to children through role modeling is the approach taken by Josh McDowell, a family speaker-lecturer who talks about spiritual and moral values to thousands of high school and college students each year. McDowell also talks to parents' groups, and when parents ask him how they can teach their children responsibility and accountability, his answer is always: "Try being accountable to your children."

By being accountable to one's children, McDowell is not suggesting that you put them in charge of the home and the family. What he means is that the parent is willing to go to the child and say something like this: "Honey, I need your help. I want you to hold me accountable as your mom (or dad). If you ever see me doing something you believe is wrong, unfair, or unloving, I want you to tell me."

Now obviously, this is risky. For one thing, children have a way of seeing things from their point of view that may not be accurate or fair to you, the parent. But I still believe McDowell has a great idea here, because children also have an incredible ability to "tell it like it is."

You can sort out the times when they have the wrong perspective or not enough information. And you can stay in healthy control of the situation by reminding them that they are free to tell you what you're doing wrong or when you're being unfair, but that they have to be respectful when they do it. It's my belief that most of the time, kids will be "right on the money" and you can have some tremendous times of learning—for both of you.

McDowell admits he has been embarrassed more than once when his own kids took him up on his offer to hold him accountable. On one occasion, he was on a street in the small town where he and his family live, and he was very short with someone who had just come up to speak with him. His ten-year-old son was with him, and as the man was walking away, the boy said, "Dad, you weren't very nice to that man." McDowell literally ran down the street after the man, and with his son standing there, he apologized for his rude behavior.

In another instance, McDowell and his entire family (four children in all) were planning to go out to dinner. The younger children voted for a well-known fast-food place in town, but the oldest daughter, a teenager, adamantly refused. She started calling the restaurant chosen by her brothers and sisters a "grease pit" and a "garbage dump."

McDowell corrected his daughter for her language and attitude, and then they compromised by agreeing to drop the younger children off at the fast-food place while he, his wife, and the older girl went on to eat somewhere else.

As they drove up to the fast-food restaurant, he let the three younger children off. Then, half in agreement with his teenage daughter, he said, "Everybody out for the gag bag."

The younger children scampered off, too excited about their burgers and fries even to register what their dad had said. But his older daughter had heard, and as they drove on down the street, she said to McDowell, "Dad, you just did what you told me was wrong. What's the difference between calling a place a garbage pit and a gag bag?"

This is what is known as "an embarrassing moment as a parent." McDowell had to swallow his pride, admit to his daughter he was wrong, and thank her for pointing out he hadn't been a very good role model. But in doing that, McDowell was actually being a tremendous role model, because he was humble enough to admit he was wrong. That went a lot further with his teenage daughter than any amount of lectures ever could.[5]

Don't be afraid to admit to your children that you are human. It's fine to place great value on being accountable and responsible, but let them know it's okay to make mistakes, and forgive them when they do have failures and own up to them. The benefit in being accountable to your children is that they can help keep you honest. They can help you break old habits and constantly remind you that your role in developing their young lives is crucial. Parents who are accountable to their children become better people, and they are also more sympathetic to their children when they goof up.

DADDIES, DAUGHTERS, AND VALUES

If you intend to try becoming accountable to your kids, be aware of questionable messages you can send them unintentionally. For example, while men have been making some progress toward becoming less chauvinistic, many of them still hold deeply ingrained values that negatively affect their children. Fathers often send their daughters wrong messages about what it means to be a woman, couched in words like:

- "So you flunked the test—that's okay, girls aren't supposed to be good in math."
- "That isn't something a girl should do—you should act more like a little lady."
- "Well, that's how women are—they're always more emotional."

In her hard-hitting (especially for many fathers) book, *How to Father a Successful Daughter,* Nicky Marone, a junior high school teacher of many years' experience, describes what often happens to the values of young girls between the seventh and ninth grades. In seventh grade the girl is bright, enthusiastic, unaffected, and eager to learn. She is anxious to continue achieving the typical female advantage that tests comparing the academic achievement of boys and girls in elementary school continually show she has. By ninth grade, however, this girl is someone else. She wears tight jeans, low-cut blouses, tight sweaters, and two shades of eye make-up. She has two basic looks: disdainfully petulant and that wide-eyed, vacant stare.

But even more unfortunate is her "drop" in academic ability. She answers fewer questions in class and seems to be holding back on purpose. Her tests and written papers drop from A's and B's to C's, and her grade-point average plummets. Writes Marone:

> The bright, assertive natural child is gone and is replaced by a shy, submissive, cutesy young woman who giggles too loudly at jokes made by boys, and pretends not to know the answers to questions that she does, in fact, know perfectly well.[6]

Marone believes this syndrome isn't rare—in fact, it's fairly typical among girls all over the country as they reach the age of puberty. The lesson they've been learning from society, the media, and their family, including Dad, has finally taken its toll. What is the lesson? To value femininity above everything else. As Marone puts it, "Boys still eat it up, and girls still play it to the hilt. The game is still on, as hot and as intense as ever."[7]

Marone fears that when any daughter believes her acceptance as a human being depends almost solely on her femininity, she may "never develop assertiveness, never cultivate any finer talents, never realize her dreams."[8]

From what I've seen, Nicky Marone's observations are right on the money. Despite whatever progress the women's movement has made, many, if not most, young girls are still tuned in to "learning how to catch a boy." When you add what's happening on television and in films, it's no wonder studies show that 10 percent of thirteen-and fourteen-year-old girls in the nation have had sexual intercourse. By the time they're seventeen, 53 percent of all teenage girls in America have had intercourse.[9]

Other researchers claim that the percentages are even higher. A *New York Times* report stated: "Some studies indicate that three-fourths of all girls have had sex during their teenage years and fifteen percent have had four or more partners."[10]

Fathers who are reading this may be wondering, *So what should I do? Teach my daughter how to be a linebacker, or maybe a lady Rambo? Should I send her messages that say "Don't be feminine at all"?*

The answer is that fathers should send their daughters *both* messages: Value being feminine, but value being assertive and achieving as well. Any father can help his daughter develop into an assertive, strong young woman if he is affirming and always there for her. That means spending uninterrupted, focused time alone with her—just the two of you. Maybe it means taking her fishing, hunting, or camping. Maybe it means teaching her how to swing a bat, shoot a gun, or dribble a basketball.

It could mean taking her down to where you work and showing her what you do all day long.

How about discussing finances and investments? Or maybe doing something as ordinary as taking her along when you run some of those "traditionally masculine" errands—to the dump, the auto parts store, or the lumberyard?

But along with all these "masculine" pastimes that will help teach her to stand up for herself instead of being an empty-headed bimbo, don't give up on the feminine messages completely. Tell her she's pretty, that her new dress is "terrific." And you may want to tease her a little about all the boys who are going to be lining up on the porch and how you're going to be giving every one of them the third degree before he can take her out.

Go easy on the teasing, though, when it comes to how her body is developing or whether she needs to lose or gain weight. With the onset of puberty, early teenage years are a precarious, sensitive time. A daughter doesn't need to hear her dad "put her down," even though he's just doing it in fun.

HELP YOUR CHILD BE GOOD AT SOMETHING

I do not want to leave the subject of values without touching on a subtle but extremely important area. I believe that all parents should start as early as possible to help their children be good at something by the time they reach adolescence. Literally make this a priority value in your home, and it will help your children value themselves all the more. Competency in some area, even an ordinary one, will help your children have an opinion of themselves that says, *Hey, I'm somebody. I'm different from everybody else. I've got my own gifts and skills—I can do this.*

I don't care if "this" is playing the tuba or playing defensive tackle. I don't care whether it's bringing home consistent A's with a few B's or earning all of his or her own spending money. The point is, there should be an affirmation in the child's life that says,

I am somebody. I may not be the prettiest, the smartest, or the strongest, but I am somebody.

When a child enters adolescence—ages eleven to nineteen—without a feeling of being somebody who can do something, the effect can be, at worst, devastating and, at best, a real burden for the child to carry through junior high and high school.

At the Leman house, our latest entrant into the adolescent hormone group is Kevin, who is fifteen at the time of this writing. Ever since he was nine years old, his thing has been magic. He's a creative young man, much different from me when I was his age. I'd always been the little clown and little ham who loved to entertain everyone, but if there was a ball to be hit, thrown, shot, or kicked, I was there. Kevin hasn't gone the athletic route at all. Instead, he has his mother's artistic ability to draw anything, which he combines with a droll sense of humor and clever skill with his hands when doing magic tricks.

He once got a threatening note from one of his junior high teachers that said, "If there are any more cartoons on the work you hand in, it will be minus five points."

I'm not quite sure how Kevin got started with magic. I think he saw David Copperfield on television and wanted to know more. The next day, I took him to a magic shop, which I found interesting for maybe five or ten minutes. Kevin, however, was enthralled and wouldn't leave. A wonderful magician was in the store for a demonstration, and he left Kevin with his mouth agape as he did trick after trick.

Since that day, Kevin has bought any number of magic tricks—with his own allowance, of course—and he's really become quite good. Recently at breakfast, he asked me to tear a small corner off a dollar bill and put my initials on what remained. After I did this, he asked me to get a banana. I covered the eight steps across the kitchen and brought Kevin a banana, at which point he said, "Would you just cut that banana in two for us?" I started to cut the banana in half, and about midway through I felt some resistance. I broke the banana open to see what the problem was, and there was a dollar bill. But not just any dollar bill. It was the one I had torn the edge off of and initialed!

"Uh—uh—uh, how did you do that?" I stuttered.

Kevin just laughed and said, "Dad, a magician never reveals his secrets."

On another occasion, Kevin came up to me and said with a serious look, "Dad, do you think . . . Dad—is there room for another David Copperfield in this world?"

I looked at Kevin just as seriously as he had looked at me and said, "No, I really don't think so."

Kevin's mouth fell, but then I continued, "I think there *is* room for a Kevin Leman."

My son just beamed. I'm not sure what Kevin is going to be doing in life, but whatever it is, I have a hunch it will be creative and very entertaining.

I believe every child can be encouraged to be outstanding at something, even if he or she shows no special interest or talent like getting straight A's or being a superathlete. To help your child find something he enjoys and can do well, try exposing him to as many different experiences and opportunities as possible. If you send him to summer camp, for example, ask the staff to keep a special eye on him and note what he likes to do best. Sometimes a child will do things away from home that he wouldn't dream of trying in front of his parents.

Keep your eye on your child. Watch his play patterns; even be aware of his favorite television shows. Any number of things can give you a clue to what he is really interested in.

ENCOURAGE THEM, BUT DON'T PUSH TOO HARD

While you want to encourage your children to be proficient in areas where they're naturally talented or where they at least feel comfortable, you don't want to push them too hard and produce what David Elkind calls "the hurried child," who has grown up too fast too soon. In the preface to the revised edition of his book *The Hurried Child*, Elkind asserts that "we are 'miseducating' young children by teaching them the wrong things at the wrong time for no purpose. . . . Children have had to pay the bill for many of the social revolutions that occurred in our society since the 1960's."[11]

For the past fifteen or twenty years, possibly longer, parents have been pushing and squeezing their children into a stereotype that Elkind calls the "Superkid." The best word to describe all this is that parents *overestimate* what kids can handle. Like their namesake, Superman, Superkids are presumed to possess incredible powers and abilities, even as infants. They are supposedly faster than speeding bullets at learning, more powerful than locomotives in stamina and staying power, and able to leap the tallest challenge with a single bound that will make their doting parents proud.

How do parents push their children to become Superkids? They tell their children more than they want to know, especially about adult relationships and adult problems. And they push their children into schedules, activities, and achievements that are really beyond what they are ready for. For example, Elkind lists starting children on reading too early, sending them to exclusive private kindergartens that are almost as difficult to get into as good colleges, and encouraging them to dress and act like adults while they are still young children.

Due to their own pride or a totally mistaken understanding of what a child is developmentally capable of at a certain age, parents have been led to believe their Superkids can handle certain tasks and challenges long before they are really ready. Far from developing a new superrace, all this pushing and hurrying of children has had negative instead of positive results. Just a few of the foreboding statistics that Elkind mentions include:

- The number of obese adolescents has increased by 50 percent over the last twenty years.

- Teenage pregnancy rates in the United States are the highest of any western society.
- Teenagers are committing suicide and homicide at triple the rates of twenty years ago.
- The SAT scores of high school seniors have gone down, while 15 to 20 percent of kindergartners are "flunking out."
- In the last few years, there has been a several-hundredfold increase in the millions of children in the United States who are being medicated to make them easier to handle at school and at home.[12]

EARLY READING IS FINE—FOR A FEW

To look more closely at one area where we are hurrying children, Elkind cites the push toward early reading that has been going on in kindergartens across our land, despite the consensus of many researchers that "reading is an extraordinarily complex process and that a certain level of brain development is required before the comprehension of symbols is possible."

Elkind admits that some children do gravitate toward reading early and almost seem to learn to read on their own with ease. But studies by Elkind and other colleagues show that "only one to three children in 100 read proficiently [at the second-grade level] on entrance to kindergarten. If learning to read were as easy as learning to talk, as some writers claim, many more children would learn to read on their own. The fact that they do not, despite their being surrounded by print, suggests that learning to read is not a spontaneous or simple skill."[13]

When schools press children to read, they are setting up a certain number of children in these classes for failure. Some of them just aren't prepared intellectually for the task. A little boy of seven who was struggling with reading told Elkind, "I can't read, I guess I'm a flop in life."[14]

HOME ALONE ISN'T FUNNY

Whenever you push young children to do more than they're ready for, you put them under tremendous stress. One of the most stressful experiences for many children across our country today is having to bear the label "latchkey kid." Because Mom and Dad are both working, the children have to come home to an empty house, where no child care is available—sometimes for several hours or more.

Some women's magazines claim that the latchkey experience is good for kids, but from what I've seen, the exact opposite is true. The movie *Home Alone* may have been uproariously funny; the little hero who had been forgotten at home by vacationing parents made fools out of the bumbling burglars. But in the real world, being home alone is stressful and scary for most children. Kids will turn on lights, television, or the radio. Many will call friends on the phone and talk for hours just to keep in contact with another human voice. Some younger children will do the reverse and hide in the closet until Mom and Dad come through the door.

It's true that in some cases, children have to be home alone at certain times. Parents shouldn't dissolve in guilt over this, but they should realize that being latchkey kids is not exactly fun, no matter what their children might say to the contrary because they want to please Mom and Dad.

Whenever possible, do everything you can to make latchkey time as brief as possible. There may be supervised activities in which your child can engage after school that will take up a certain number of minutes and hours. Perhaps there is someone across the street or across the hall who might be willing to keep an eye on your child or at least be available to be called if there were any problems. You might even consider taking off work early for a special "play date" with your child on certain days. Use your imagination, and work with your child to let him know you don't like the latchkey situation and you want to do everything you can to keep it at an absolute minimum.

When you have no choice and your child does have to be a latchkey kid, it's wise to give her instructions and strategies in dealing with potential problems or danger. She should know what to do when strangers come to the door, when a fire breaks out, or when any accident occurs. She should have the phone number of neighbors willing to help. You might even instruct her on how to use a small fire extinguisher and to do basic first aid from a simple first-aid kit in the medicine cabinet.

Even more basic, she should know how to reach Mom and Dad on the phone, and surely, she should be well versed in how to dial 911 or the local emergency number.

What does hurrying children have to do with values? Everything. One major reason we hurry our kids is that materialism has crept under the door and through the woodwork of our homes. As I mentioned in chapter 3, in many families, the pursuit of what is ironically called the "good life" makes it necessary for both parents to go to work, leaving children to learn how to fend for themselves.

In 90 percent of the cases I see, the woman has to go to work, particularly single moms (more on this in chapter 13). In many two-parent families, one check simply doesn't make ends meet, and that means both parents have to hold down a job. Before both parents go to work full-time, however, husbands and wives need to sit down and do some long, hard thinking about *why* ends don't meet. In these tough economic times, many families have no choice, but others do.

Parents can do many things to stave off the incredible bombardment of propaganda and brainwashing that goes on daily through the media, urging them to "have it all." For example, where can the "good life" be scaled back a bit to take off some of the financial pressure? And if both parents have to work, perhaps one of them can work part-time, freeing up valuable hours that can be spent giving children the basic care they must have. Other ideas, already mentioned in chapter 3, include sequencing, Mommy Tracks, and Daddy Tracks. The point is, there *are* options, and there *are* alternatives. Don't be stampeded.

> People, particularly your own children,
> are far more important than things.

"Having it all" is one of the most insidiously dangerous values threatening the American family today. When you push your child to develop at a rate much faster than he is comfortable with, you are teaching him to value "having it all." I am constantly dealing with adults in my counseling practice who never had a chance to be carefree children. They were always made to toe the line, to take responsibilities for which they weren't quite ready. They were pushed to have it all and to do it all from a very early age, and they never had a chance to be kids.

Many parents claim they are pushing their children to help them be successful, but a closer look reveals that they are pushing the kids for their own sake—the parents'—not the children's.

Parents need to realize that anyone under stress tends to center on himself or herself. Because parents are stressed, they tend to transmit their stress to their children, pushing them to do more and be more than they really can at their tender age.

Ironically, all this hurrying of children is not done because we have made the children our chief priority. We are asking children to perform in order to satisfy other priorities motivated by personal pride and ambition.

If values are caught more than taught—and I believe they are—then one way to help your children catch the right values is to simply slow down. Prioritize what's really important, and let the rest go for the sake of your family. To paraphrase Reality Discipline Principle No. 1: "The whole—your family—is far more important than the good life."

Don't Forget . . .

- If children are not exposed to good moral values in your home, don't depend on having it happen in school settings.
- The best way to teach values is to set a good example—be a good role model. Values are caught more than taught.
- Fathers can send their daughters wrong messages about what it means to be a woman, encouraging them to over-value femininity and "being able to catch a man."
- One of the best ways to teach accountability is for you to become accountable to your own children. Give them the freedom to tell you when they believe you are doing something wrong, unfair, or unloving.
- To ensure a smoother passage through adolescence, try to help your younger child find something he is really interested in or good at before reaching high school.
- The country is full of "hurried children" who have been pushed to grow up too fast too soon.
- At best, the latchkey experience is an unpleasant and even scary experience for a child.
- One of the best things you can do to teach your children the right values is to slow your own pace. Keep in mind that the whole—your family—is far more important than the good life.

And Why Not Try . . .

- Ask your kids what *they* think your values are. Don't react if you don't like what you hear (and you may not). Instead, with your spouse's help, analyze the example you've been setting, and begin modeling the values you want your children to have.
- Look for teachable moments to communicate values to your children—for example, when you see you have been undercharged at the supermarket counter.

- To make your children more accountable, make yourself accountable to them. Try the approach taken by lecturer-teacher Josh McDowell (see pages 226-28).
- Talk with your spouse about helping your children discover special interests and talents before they reach high school. Discuss what you have seen in your children and what you might encourage. Also, plan to take them to more plays, concerts, museums, and the like—anywhere that might trigger some latent interest or ability.
- Talk together about the danger of "hurrying" your children to grow up too fast. Are they in latchkey situations? Go over your family's priorities, and be sure you can say accurately, "Our family is more important to us than anything else."

Chapter 11

The Hormone Years Needn't Be Terminal

———————●———————

Using Reality Discipline with Teenagers

ACROSS THE PLANET, THE CHALLENGE, PLIGHT, AND CRISIS OF THE teenager is reported, broadcast, discussed, analyzed, and lamented in newspapers and magazines, on television and radio. Even U.S. Sprint, with its vast high-tech capabilities, admits in a TV commercial that it "has yet to solve the problem of the teenager."

Pick up your local paper, and you are apt to read that the high school valedictorian who was voted the most promising math student in the history of her school has just attempted suicide with an overdose of sleeping pills, and that only her mother's early return from work saved her life. Across the country on that same day, the wire services catalog the story of a sixteen-year-old boy, always known as a model child, who lurked in the shadows of his own front yard with a shotgun. As his parents drove up, he opened fire on them, then turned the gun on himself.

These kinds of tragedies have become so commonplace, we hardly bat an eye. We blame them on drugs or drinking, shrug, and go about our business—until they come too close to home. Admittedly, Tucson, Arizona, is a much slower track than New York City, Chicago, or Los Angeles, but we have all "the bad stuff," too. Rival gangs like the Crips and the Bloods are represented in more-than-significant numbers in our quiet, little cow town. Our police officials estimate that at least fifteen hundred gang members live here.

We also grieve over teenage suicides. A seventeen-year-old came to see me for a preliminary consultation before going into actual counseling. He was mixed up and confused about what life wanted from him, but on the surface he didn't seem to have any unique problems.

We talked a while, and he made a date for his first counseling appointment. Three days later, his parents found him sitting in his car, the garage door shut, the engine running, and a rock music recording by a well-known, drug-oriented band turned up full blast on the cassette player.

Why does a young man do something as mindless as that? There is never one simple reason why someone kills himself. His parents blamed the rock music, but while that could have been a contributing factor, it wasn't the root cause. For teenagers, life is full of pressures that add up to unbearable stress, so unbearable that between 500,000 and 600,000 of them attempt suicide every year, and some five thousand succeed.[1]

Even as I worked on this chapter, these impersonal statistics took on flesh and blood when a high school classmate of mine called to tell me that another classmate's fifteen-year-old son had just taken a gun, put it to his head, and killed himself.

When kids aren't killing themselves, they're putting themselves in situations where someone else might. It's estimated that every year, 1.5 million children and youths run away from home. This number includes children of wealthy socialites, as well as children of hand-to-mouth crack dealers. Yet there is one universal thread that binds them all together. Most of them, rightly or wrongly, say they believe their parents aren't interested in them. The director of a runaway shelter in New York City adds that three out of every four runaways he treats have some sexually transmitted disease.[2]

In chapter 1, I quoted a letter from a young woman to Ann Landers that eloquently recorded what kids face today: rampant divorce, a wide-open approach to sex that has many young people losing their virginity by thirteen or fourteen, and the threat of sexually transmitted diseases capped by AIDS, which is always fatal.

There is also the widespread use of drugs, alcohol, and TV. Yes, I equate TV with drugs because so many youths, not to mention adults, are hooked on this habit-forming electronic escape hatch, which brainwashes them daily with materialism, hedonism, narcissism, and violence. Between the ages of six and eighteen, the average American youth spends sixteen thousand hours in front of a TV set and witnesses some eighteen thousand dramatized murders.[3]

Representatives of the television and film industries scream indignantly whenever their ability to exercise their precious right of "freedom of expression" is even questioned. They constantly maintain that research shows that television and films have no proven influence on viewers who see programs and movies for what they are—fantasy designed to entertain. Yet practically every day, there are tragic reports of someone else who has failed to keep fantasy separated from reality.

The above statistics don't even scratch the surface. Look around you with an eye sharpened by Reality Discipline. How much more proof do you need that our culture is in big trouble? There's a lot of rough—and fatal—stuff happening among our youth. Kids are being shot down in school hallways and on playgrounds. Many high schools now have students pass through metal detectors before coming to class to be sure no one is entering the school with a concealed weapon.[4]

WHAT CAN PARENTS DO?

I talk constantly to parents who are worried, scared, and at the wits' end corner. They wonder what they can do to control and protect their teenagers. When I suggest Reality Discipline, they're dubious. How can that help? Maybe more to the point, how can they use Reality Discipline with *teenagers?* They aren't little kids anymore.

It depends on the situation. I'm not saying a sudden dose of Reality Discipline will keep a depressed teenager from killing himself while a rock band plays in the background, urging him to "do it!" One thing parents must realize is that extreme examples like suicides, murders, and other mayhem are exactly that—extremes. The entire teenage generation should not be written off as hopeless because of the kind of stuff that sells newspapers or makes the eleven o'clock news.

I believe the vast majority of young people are not hopelessly addicted to drugs, alcohol, or even bad behavior. Yes, rapid changes are happening in their bodies. That's why I call them the "hormone group." Sure, they are sensitive, often erratic, and even unstable as they search and sometimes grope for a handle on life. *But* they're also intelligent, willing to listen, and even sensible—if what they hear adults saying makes any sense. In short, I believe the hormone years don't have to be terminal. And Reality Discipline can certainly be used with teenagers with great results. The rules are the same as for children, with certain modifications:

- Use action, not just words—*but be sure to think before you act.*

- Be consistent, decisive, and respectful—*but remember that teenagers want to be treated like adults, not like little kids.*

- Hold your teenagers accountable for their actions—*but don't spit in their soup or rub their nose in it.*

"YES, YOU CAN KEEP YOUR BABY, IF . . ."

After talking with thousands of parents over the years at seminars, in my office, and on radio call-in shows, I can say unequivocally that one of their greatest fears is to have their teenage daughters turn up pregnant. And no wonder. The Centers for Disease Control report that one out of nine teenagers becomes pregnant in a year, one of two females has sex between the ages of fifteen and nineteen, and one out of twenty-three teenagers has an abortion each year.[5]

On our "Parent Talk" show recently, a woman called in to offer her story and a refreshing approach to getting "the news." Her teenage daughter, who was supposed to be at work, returned home, and when she walked in, the mother could tell by the look on her daughter's face that something was very wrong.

"Honey, what is it?"

"Mom . . . it's—it's the worst thing in the world, Mom."

"What's *wrong?*" Mom said, getting alarmed.

"I can't tell you—it's the worst thing in the world . . ." Finally, the daughter blurted out, "I'm pregnant, Mom!"

As she relayed the story to us over the phone, the mother said, "I grabbed my daughter and held her. I told her I loved her no matter what. And then I could see things flashing before my mind like Rolodex cards. Suddenly I said, 'It's going to be okay, honey, it's going to be okay.'"

"How did you know everything would be okay?" I asked the mother.

"I just realized this *wasn't* the worst thing that could happen. My daughter was alive, she was healthy, and maybe best of all, she had come to me to tell me what had happened rather than head for an abortion clinic."

This mother showed tremendous insight and understanding toward her daughter in what undoubtedly—up to that point, at least—was the worst moment of her entire life. The mother could

246 . KEEPING YOUR FAMILY TOGETHER

have misused Reality Discipline and simply said, "Well, that's too bad—it's your problem."

That kind of callous approach to someone in tremendous pain, awash with guilt and on the verge of panic, is not Reality Discipline. It's simple cruelty.

On the other hand, when teenagers get pregnant, there is a time for Reality Discipline to click into gear. I know of another mother whose sixteen-year-old daughter got pregnant, then announced she was going to keep the baby.

The mother didn't say much at first, but she began thinking. Suddenly it hit her: *I think I know who is going to raise that child.* She talked it over with her husband, and they called in their daughter to let her know how they felt. They told her they respected her decision to keep the baby—in fact, they really approved of her doing that rather than opting for an abortion. But at the same time, they made it clear the baby would not be reared in their home.

"We know what you're saying, honey. It's sounds wonderful, but we want you to understand that if you keep your baby, you will have to raise him somewhere else—not here."

The daughter took the news hard at first. She felt her parents were being unfair, but they stuck to their guns. The mother especially had finished rearing her own children and knew she couldn't start over again with that kind of stress and pressure.

Eventually, the sixteen-year-old made her decision. She went ahead with the pregnancy, then gave the child up for adoption. She realized that was the right thing for her to do because, at sixteen, she was not psychologically prepared or physically able to raise a child herself.

Her parents had struggled, too. It wasn't easy to let their sixteen-year-old daughter know she couldn't count on them for help. But they had the courage to tell her, and once that firm commitment was made, the daughter realized an awful lot of basic and vital options had suddenly vanished: the refrigerator, the furnace, the hot water, and maybe most of all, the built-in baby-sitter who could relieve the girl of the constant pressure of having to care for a tiny child when she was barely beyond being a child herself.

There is a virtual epidemic in America of children having children. Giving up the baby was traumatic for the sixteen-year-old, but it was by far the best choice for all concerned. Not only did the baby have a much better chance in life, but the daughter could also continue her life as an adolescent. A maxim I have always believed in is this:

IT'S IMPORTANT TO ALLOW ADOLESCENTS
TO HAVE THEIR ADOLESCENCE.

When teenagers are forced to grow up too fast, they often go through adolescence fifteen years later and wind up in my office.

WHAT A PARTY BLITZ COST THE FOOTBALL STAR

Another situation that recently came to my attention involved a teenager who was a football star in his local high school. His parents had left for the weekend with strict instructions to "not have any parties" while they were gone. Unfortunately, the popular athlete let some friends know he had an empty house for the weekend, and before he knew it, a lot of those friends had invited themselves over to "just hang out, not really have a party."

The football player's friends told other friends, and that night the police had to respond to calls by neighbors who were complaining about cars all over the block, rock music that sounded like a Gulf War bombardment, and at least two hundred teenagers running amok.

When the star halfback's parents got home late Sunday night, they found drapes ripped down, two windows broken, landscaping destroyed, and small bushes and trees broken down. As a "capper" to the whole affair, a couple of party guests had urinated in the parents' master bedroom walk-in closet.

"At least they didn't decide to rip out the plumbing" was the only thing the parents could come up with by way of being positive.

When they confronted their son about what had happened, he tried to explain that he really hadn't thrown a party. He had invited a few friends over to watch a video, but then a lot of other people had shown up, and things got out of control before he could stop it.

"Well, son," said his father, "I can understand how this might happen. Unfortunately, you were still responsible, and you will have to pay for all the damage."

"How much is it going to be?" the boy wondered.

"Well, I don't have all the quotes in yet," said his father, "but I would say in round numbers it ought to run close to two thousand dollars. The good news is, you don't have to borrow two thousand dollars and pay me all at once. I'll be glad to take it in regular monthly installments."

"But Dad, my allowance isn't that much. It will take an awfully long time."

"I believe you have some money in a savings account," Dad answered. "I know you'll want to handle this and be accountable for what happened. So I'm leaving it up to you."

With that, his dad went out to work and his mother went about trying to give first aid to a few surviving rose bushes. The boy thought it over, did some quick computations, and decided he would take twelve hundred dollars out of his college savings account and pay the rest off in regular monthly installments, using money he earned at a part-time job he had after school, which he increased from ten hours a week to sixteen. He finally did pay off the entire amount, although it took him more than six months.

"But What If I Start World War III?"

I tell these two stories from my files as examples of how parents must be willing to use little words like *no* and *pay the damages*. Too many parents are afraid that using this kind of discipline on their teenagers will set off World War III. In some cases, that may happen. Some teenagers project an image that they want no part of adults or of having to listen to adult authority. They are quite sure they can handle life and make all their own decisions with no help from adults—particularly their parents. When parents say no or invoke consequences, the rebellious teenager tries to bluff his way out of it with an emotional outburst.

At a time like that, the parents should not retaliate. Keep your cool and wait a while. Talk with the teenager later, after he has calmed down a bit. For example, suppose a teenager has used the car on a certain occasion when he was expressly forbidden to use it. The parent might say, "I know what I have said seems unfair to you, but we had an agreement that the car was not to be used. You used it anyway, and therefore, you will not be using it for a week. Also, if you continue to complain, I'll add another week."

The point is that you have to be strong and stick to your guns. The teenager won't like it, but he or she will eventually respect a consistent, firm, but fair approach.

I am well aware some teenagers have a short fuse. They fit the stereotype that is well described in the old joke that says, "Teenagers have only two emotional outbursts a year; the problem is, each one lasts six months."

I don't believe, however, that all teenagers are like this. It is my conviction, gained from more than twenty years of counseling, that many teenagers want guidelines and rules because they want their parents to be interested in them—to care. It's when they don't get consistent guidance and reasonable rules that trouble can start.

One of the most encouraging stories I've heard came from my son, Kevin, who was on the student council at his junior high school. Kevin told me that during that time, one of the junior high students had broken a window at the school and that the student council had offered to pay for it. The boy had not been malicious, just careless. While fooling around with another kid in the hallway, he had somehow turned quickly with his elbow sticking out, and it had gone right through a small window in a door.

It looked as if everything was settled. The student council was feeling noble for picking up the tab, and the boy who broke the window was feeling "off the hook"—a $43.65 hook, to be exact.

But before the check could be cut to pay the repairman, the boy's mother got wind of what was going on and called the school to say, "Wait a minute. My son broke the window. He is the one who is responsible to pay for it."

Bravo for that mom! She was determined to keep her junior high son on the right road and, hopefully, away from serious detours later in life.

BUYING HIM A MOTORCYCLE WAS A REAL MISTAKE

In another case I handled, some well-meaning parents who had been too permissive decided to mend their ways and their son's as well. Their eighteen-year-old had all kinds of potential, but he had never decided to use it. It was quite obvious his parents had done far too much for him as he was growing up, but when they bought him a motorcycle, that was a real mistake.

It was sort of like buying a young child a puppy when the child never really wanted a puppy. Oh yes, for one fleeting moment at the county fair, the child had admired a puppy and said, "I wish I could have one." And so Mom and Dad went out and bought him a puppy, brought it to him, and said, "Here's your puppy, take good care of him."

But pretty soon, guess who was feeding the puppy?

It was exactly the same story with Lance and the motorcycle. He admired somebody else's motorcycle in his parents' presence, and they immediately assumed their son "really needed a bike for transportation." So they went out and bought him one, and they were content with his promise that he would make the $159 monthly payments, plus pay for his own gas and other upkeep on the bike.

But just a month later, Lance got fired from his part-time job and was soon broke.

Naturally, his parents were understanding. Although they had only a modest income, they decided to bite the bullet. They would take care of the motorcycle payments and upkeep if Lance would be responsible for doing a few things around the house. Naturally, Lance didn't keep his end of the bargain.

As is typical with permissive parents who have been kicked in the teeth, these parents fought back. They took away Lance's motorcycle and told him he was grounded. He could no longer use his bike, because it now belonged to his parents.

The next day, when they both came home from work, Lance's room was cleaned out, and so was the garage. The bike was gone.

It didn't take too much tracing, however, through some of Lance's friends, to go get it and take it back. Lance remained out of the house, staying with a friend, and the parents proceeded to put an ad in the paper to sell the motorcycle.

So far, so good. But what about Lance and trying to get him to live responsibly and be accountable to people—especially the people who had given him so much? He was refusing to come home, and the parents wondered what would happen.

"Oh, he'll be home all right," I told them. "I believe you told me he has only temporary housing with his friend, who is going to be moving away in a month or two. When that happens, he'll be back, because he'll need a place to stay."

"But what do we do when he does come home?" they wondered. "We've never been able to get much cooperation out of him."

"Tell him the rules haven't changed. Give him responsibilities, and hold him accountable. You've made a great start by taking away the motorcycle, but you've got to be consistent."

Sure enough, Lance did come back, and he even started taking out the garbage and doing a few other chores as he had originally promised. This, in itself, was almost enough to cause the heavenly hosts to sing the "Hallelujah" chorus, but I especially liked the simple and loving observation made by his mother, who had faith enough in her son to say, "I know he's trying to grow up."

I told her she was right. Lance was trying to grow up, but it was slow going. He would continue to grow a little and then falter, grow a little and then falter. In fact, I counseled Mom and Dad to be prepared for the next time Lance might get fed up and leave again for a while.

"If he does," I told them, "so be it. He'll be back."

"If he leaves again, it will be the last time," Lance's dad growled. "He'll never get to live in my house again."

"Wait a minute," I said. "Think about it. You already have a tremendous investment in your son. If he does leave again but comes back hat in hand, wanting another chance, what do you really have to lose by giving it to him? If you don't give him another chance, I'd say you have everything to lose."

Lance's parents saw my point. They realized their son was not a piece of plastic that could be stamped out perfectly the first time through the mold. Human beings have a way of taking a long time to work off the rough edges. What Lance's parents needed was patience and, along with that, the courage to be consistent, decisive, and respectful. One of the best ways to respect their son was to treat him as an adult, even at times when he acted like a small child. Eventually, it would pay off.

LAURA SECRETLY WISHED HER PARENTS WOULD SAY NO

Laura's story is a good example of how parents can be so permissive that their child feels neglected and uncared for. I see this happen with a lot of parents who feel outgunned and overwhelmed by their teenager. Some even try to become the teenager's buddy. They pull themselves into Calvin Kleins three sizes too small and try to be hip, rad, and "with it." And all the time they seldom, if ever, say no.

At fourteen, Laura became convinced that her parents didn't love her or care much about her. When she approached them to tell them what she wanted to do, she secretly wished they would say no to some of her crazy ideas, which had been hatched, of course, in conversations with her friends. Instead, they tried to be her buddy.

"Well, honey," they said, "you do what you think is right."

What Laura thought was right was to take drugs along with her friends, because that was the way to fit in. From ages fourteen to twenty-two, Laura was on drugs, including marijuana and cocaine. She thought the drugs would make her happy, but of course, the exact reverse is what happened. She wanted her parents to be involved in her life, but they weren't. Behind the "Honey, you do as you think best" was an attitude that they just didn't care.

Not only did Laura turn to drugs, but she also moved in with her supplier.

All this went on until she was well into her twenties, and then she happened to meet a woman who accepted her as she was but would not accept her self-destructive behavior.

"That woman turned my life around," Laura told us in a telephone conversation over our "Parent Talk" lines. "The word *no* was definitely part of her vocabulary, and I made some radical changes."

Today, Laura is a thirty-one-year-old mother of three children, happily married and definitely willing to tell her kids no, and then some.

WALK WISELY AND PUT AWAY YOUR STICK

At the other end of the spectrum is the authoritarian parent who moves in on the teenager the way General Schwarzkopf rolled through Iraq's Republican Guard. I have seen it happen so often, especially with young girls. While the girl is growing up, the parents are lenient and understanding, especially if she shows some sense of responsibility, as many girls do. With her parents' approval and even urging, the girl starts wearing makeup and designer clothes at an early age.

But then the girl reaches puberty and adolescence. She begins to develop physically, and fearing she will fall victim to preying males, the parents suddenly pull back the freedoms they had so liberally provided earlier. They literally switch parenting styles and become authoritarian, leaving their daughter feeling confused and even betrayed.[6]

There is no quicker way to alienate a teenager than by being authoritarian. Authoritarianism may work with younger children, but teenagers are a different package. They're capable of fighting back, and they will do so with every weapon in their arsenal. As Dr. James Dobson, founder of Focus on the Family, has said:

> After we have appealed to reason and cooperation and family loyalty, all that remains are relatively weak methods of "punishment." We can only link behavior of our kids with desirable and undesirable consequences and hope the connection will be of sufficient influence to elicit their cooperation.
>
> If that sounds pretty wobbly-legged, let me admit that I am implying: a willful, angry 16-year-old boy or girl CAN win a confrontation with his parents today, if worst comes to worst. The law leans ever more in the direction of the emancipation of the teenager.[7]

COMMUNICATION IS BETTER THAN CONFRONTATION

If Dr. Dobson is right (and I think he is), it behooves wise parents to work on communicating with their teenagers and avoiding confrontations that can only lead to more problems and even disaster.

Parents often complain to me, "We'd like to communicate, but our teenagers just won't listen." My reply is that the parents are the ones who should do more listening and less talking. If you want to listen to your teenager better, try working on your listening from two different directions. First, be sure you tune in. In other words, don't make your teenager talk through your newspaper or get your attention while you're watching TV. Take time to look your teenager in the eye and actually hear what he or she is trying to tell you.

Second, listen actively—not just for the facts but for your teenager's feelings. What is your teenager trying to say? Often the words aren't what count—it's the way the words are being said, the look on the teenager's face. Active listening is a skill well worth cultivating.

And when you do talk, watch your words. Some of the least favorite lines parents use on teenagers include the following:

- "It's not that I don't trust you, it's just that . . ."
- "Just wait until you have kids of your own—I hope you have one just like you."
- "I thought you were going to school, not to a costume party."
- "Trust you? Why should I trust you—you've got to prove you're trustworthy."
- "You don't know how lucky you are. When I was a kid . . ."

Frankly, it's easier to use lines like those above than it is to think of tactful but honest ways to communicate with your teenager about something you don't like or you're not quite sure you agree with. For example, instead of ripping a teenager's outfit by suggesting it belongs at a costume party, you might say, "I'm sure you have your reasons for wearing that, but to be honest, it doesn't flatter you at all. You look so much nicer in the brown skirt and beige sweater."

Statements about hoping your teenagers will have "a kid just like you've been" and telling teenagers they don't know how lucky they are, are best left unsaid. Simply bite your tongue when thoughts like that cross your mind. I've drawn blood a few times myself, so I know what I'm talking about.

As for trusting and not trusting a teenager, you might say something like the following:

"Okay, tell you what, let me talk it over with Mom (or Dad), and I'll let you know tomorrow night at dinner." That kind of remark isn't a flat no. It gives you time to think about the teenager's request, and if his or her ideas are off the wall, the teenager will probably realize it and be more prepared to hear you say no if you must.

As for demanding that teenagers prove they are trustworthy, far better to say, "Listen, I think you can handle it, but I need a few more details before I can give my blessing."

I realize that thinking up just the right remark on the spur of the moment isn't always easy. In fact, I often challenge parents to memorize a few basic responses they can use in many different situations. For example, when the teenager comes with complaints about how unfair and tough life is, say sincerely, "I'm sure you can handle it."

When teenagers are pressing their case and you're not sure you agree, just say, "Well, you could be right."

And when a teenager has a minor war going with a sibling and wants you to get in the middle to play referee, say, "You know, you and your brother (or sister) will have to figure this one out. I'm sure you can do it fairly and sensibly."

I'm not saying remarks like these will always work. Sometimes there can be just too much tension in the air or too much pressure. Maybe you've had a hard day, and you're just not ready for what the teenager has in mind. The rule of thumb is to always try to give yourself an out and your teenager a way to save face. Diplomacy is always better than a shooting war. Any fool can start a war, but there's a real art to keeping an orderly peace in the family.

MEMORIES MIGHT BREAK THEIR SILENCE

Many parents complain about their "silent teenager." At worst, all they get are guttural sounds that would seem to belong better in the sound track of *80 Million Years B.C.* At best, they get short, terse answers and cool shrugs. As one parent put it, "It's like having a surly boarder in the house."[8] Perhaps you've been feeling as if you're trapped in playing the game of asking banal questions such as "How was school today?" that are always answered, "Fine" or "Okay." As the game goes on, you ask, "What did you do?" And the answer comes back, "Nothing much."

To take a different tack—and also possibly learn something valuable about your teenager—try asking your teenagers about their childhood memories. Wait for a relaxed time—possibly during dinner, when everybody's feeling full and fairly human—and just say, "What do you kids remember about when you were little, when you were very young?"

I'm not guaranteeing this question will suddenly turn your teenagers into fountains of communication. You may get back, "Nothing" or "Not much." On the other hand, your kids might perk up and respond to this different kind of question. And as they tell what they remember, you can learn a lot about how they see life today.

We Adlerian psychologists use childhood memories as a key counseling technique. In fact, I teamed up with Randy Carlson, a counseling colleague, to write a book in which we said: "Who you are today . . . your basic personality . . . your personal life philosophy . . . the secret to your entire outlook on life . . . is hidden within your earliest childhood memories."[9] The point is that our childhood memories are consistent with how we see life. And you don't have to be a psychologist to interpret what your teenagers remember. The key is to note if the memory is negative or positive.

One evening at dinner, I tried this concept on our three older children and asked them to recall a memory of when they were little. This is what they came up with.

Holly popped up first and said, "I remember when I was about three or four years old, and you gave me a red sweater, Mom. I hated that sweater and wouldn't wear it, but when a lady was coming for dinner, you really wanted me to wear that sweater and you offered me my favorite candy—Reese's peanut butter cups—if I'd wear the sweater."

"What happened?" Sande asked. "I'm not sure I remember myself."

"Well," Holly recalled, "I remember saying to myself, *I want those Reese's peanut butter cups so bad, but I'm not going to wear that dumb red sweater for anything.*"

Sande and I had no trouble seeing that this memory is consistent with how our firstborn daughter views life. She's tough-minded and has her convictions. She's the law-keeper in the family, reminding all of us when we go astray. And she sticks to her guns. Once she makes up her mind, only dynamite or the Lord Himself will get her to move off dead center.

Next it was Krissy's turn, and the first memory that leapt into her mind was of the time she was around six and Daddy was giving her a lesson on how to ride a bike.

"We were on this little hill," Krissy remembered. "Dad, you started out holding me as we went down the grade, but then I got going fast, and I guess you couldn't keep up, and you let me go. I rolled all the way to the bottom of the hill, lost control of the bike, and landed in a cactus bush."

This memory also fits Krissy to a T. To this day, she remains cautious, the kind of person who has to look before she leaps. She doesn't take chances and is not at all what you could call a risk-taker.

And what about Kevin's first memory?

"I remember when Holly and Krissy dressed me up for a play

they were putting on for the neighborhood kids. I really liked that—putting on the costume and being part of the play."

As you may recall, Kevin is the budding entertainer in our family. His childhood memory of getting dressed up for a neighborhood play fits perfectly with what he likes to do today—be an amateur magician with his sights set on taking over from David Copperfield!

If you ask your kids about their childhood memories, you may or may not be able to make some applications like those above, but if triggering your teenagers' memories works at all, you just may have fun talking together. Try it. You don't have a lot to lose, and you might just get a reading on how your teenagers view life. The more you understand your teenager, the more you can move from playing the role of disciplinarian, judge, and jury to being your teenager's friend and guide. We will look more closely at being your teenager's best friend in the next chapter.

Don't Forget . . .

- Reality Discipline can be used with teenagers if you remember they want to be treated like adults, not little kids.

- You can hold teenagers accountable for their actions, but don't spit in their soup or rub their nose in it when you do.

- When adolescents don't have the opportunity to have their adolescence, they may grow up too fast and wind up going through adolescence fifteen years later in bizarre and destructive ways.

- If using Reality Discipline sets off World War III with your teenagers, be calm, but stick to your guns. If you are consistently firm but fair, your teenagers will respect you.

- To communicate with your teenagers, try to do more listening and less talking. When listening to your teenagers, don't just hear their words; hear their feelings, too—what they are really trying to say.

• Any fool can start a war, especially with a teenager. It takes wisdom to keep the peace.

And Why Not Try . . .

• Talk with your spouse about your parenting style with your teenagers. Are you too authoritarian? Too permissive? Would your teenager call you "firm but fair"? What can you change to fall more in the firm but fair category? Do you need to do more sticking to your guns, or do you need to do more listening to your teenager's side and bending now and then?

• Try listening to your teenager more carefully. Give your teenager your full attention, and "actively listen" for feelings, not just facts. See if it doesn't make a difference.

• Go over the examples of "least favorite lines" parents use on teenagers (p. 255), and see if there are any you are guilty of. Make a pact with your spouse to delete these lines from your vocabulary or to change them to more positive statements. Then try to do so.

• Memorize some of the "basic responses" suggested on pages 255-56, and use them next time you get into a less-than-calm discussion with your teenager. Remember to always give yourself an out and your teenager a way to save face whenever possible.

• If you have silent teenagers, try the "childhood memories" approach to getting them to talk. Ask, "What do you remember about when you were very young? What are some of your first memories?"

• Talk to some other parents whose children are grown and have turned out well. Ask what key things they did to get their kids safely through adolescence.

Chapter 12

How to Be Your Teenager's Best Friend

---•---

Nine Tips That Can Pay Big Dividends

O NE OF THE MAJOR GOALS FOR ANY PARENT OF A TEENAGER IS TO MOVE toward being less of a "mommy" or "daddy" and more of a friend and guide. Yes, you will always be a parent, but you do want to try to become your teenager's best friend, not your teenager's buddy. As I define the two words, there's a big difference between being a true friend and a buddy.

- Friends tell you the truth. Buddies go along because they don't want to offend.
- Friends are always there for you. Buddies can fade faster than a Tucson sunset in a sandstorm.
- Friends want what is best for you. Buddies really want what's best—and most convenient—for them.

Following are nine Reality Discipline ways to be your teenager's best friend.

1. Be Real, Honest, and Transparent

A common mistake made by many parents is to try to maintain the aura of "perfection" they had carried when their children were small. To the small child, adults can do no wrong, but any teenagers will tell you their parents blew their cover long ago.

One mother brought in her seventeen-year-old daughter to see me because she had been in all kinds of trouble, including getting stopped by a traffic cop who found a six-pack of beer and a marijuana cigarette in her car. When they came in for their next appointment several days later, Mom was still steaming. As they sat with me in my office, I could see things weren't going all that well. Finally, the girl asked her mother, "Didn't you ever try pot or drive after having a beer?"

"Of course not," Mom snapped. "It's against the law!" I did a quadruple take on that one, because I knew that what the mother was saying was an absolute lie. In previous sessions, the woman had admitted she was an alcoholic, and surely more than once she had driven while drinking.

I asked the daughter to step outside for a few minutes, and then I turned to the mother and said a little incredulously, "With your history of alcoholism, are you saying you never operated a car while you were under the influence?"

"Of course I have," she snapped, "and I've used pot, too, but I certainly wouldn't admit that to her."

I tried to explain to this mother that she had made a tragic mistake. She had blown a tremendous opportunity to really communicate with her daughter—maybe for the first time. If she had been honest enough to admit her own mistakes, she might have been able to help her. At least she might have established some feelings of empathy and understanding between the two of them.

But it didn't happen because she refused to listen. The mother buried her head in the sand, and the daughter buried her head and heart in resentment. From then on, the daughter wouldn't listen to her or to me. There is nothing you can do with someone who simply isn't interested.

I know from personal experience with three teenagers of my own that being honest, open, and transparent is not easy. Sometimes things can get sticky, even for psychologists who supposedly know all the answers. I've had plenty of moments when I've had to admit I've blown it, when I've had to confirm what my kids already know—that I am light-years from being perfect. But every time I do, it's worth it, because I don't lose their respect. In fact, I gain their respect and friendship.

I recall, in particular, a scene at our breakfast table when I got into an animated discussion with Holly, which turned into an argument. The details of it have faded from my memory, but I'll never forget what Holly said after I had made a particularly cutting remark: "You know what you ought to do?" she demanded.

"No, what?" I responded, failing to see I was being set up.

"You—you ought to read your own books about how to be a parent, that's what!"

That stopped me. Whatever it was we were arguing about, it had gone too far. I can't tell you what started the argument, but I can tell you I ended it quickly by saying, "I'm sorry, honey. I apologize."

In the next few seconds, the glow of battle faded from Holly's eyes. "Okay" was all she said.

Later, as she left the table, she came over and gave me a hug good-bye. "See you, Daddy," she said. "I love you!"

"I love you, too, sweetheart," I answered. And then she was gone, leaving her dad to make a mental note to catch up on some important reading.

2. Be Firm But Flexible

I want to make one more point about being willing to say no to your teenager. Often, teenagers look to their parents to say no so they can go back to their friends and get off the hook. In other words, there are many occasions when teenagers don't want to go along with their friends, but at the same time, they don't have the courage to stand up to the peer group and tell them, "No, I just don't want to do that."

Instead, a teenager comes to her parents to ask permission to do whatever her friends have cooked up, and when the parents say no, she can go back and say something like, "I'm sorry, I can't go. You see, my parents are so antediluvian, they won't let me."

Then her friends nod understandingly and sympathetically because they, too, know what it's like to live with archaic beings who just aren't part of the twentieth century.

Not too long ago, I was fast asleep in my king-size trundle bed when a hand shook me awake. "Dad, it's Krissy. Can I take the car?"

I opened one eye and glanced at the clock radio. Its glowing orbs told me it was two o'clock in the morning. Although I wasn't quite awake, I was perfectly able to say, "No, you can't take the car. It's two o'clock. Go to bed."

That's all I remembered until morning. At breakfast, I told Krissy, "I'm not positive, but I think you were in my room last night, asking me if you could take the car."

Krissy looked up from her cereal and said, "Oh, yeah. Some of the kids who stayed over last night wanted to go into town for a pizza."

"You know you can't be running around at two o'clock in the morning looking for all-night pizza parlors," I said.

"Of course, Dad. I knew you wouldn't let me go. But I had to come and ask you so you could tell me no, and then I could tell them I couldn't."

"Anytime you need to get off the hook, I'll be happy to oblige," I told my daughter. "But try not to do it at two in the morning, okay?"

Not many days later, another incident occurred that illustrates that parents need to be able to say no, but also to bend a little when circumstances warrant it. Krissy had gone out for the evening with a girlfriend, and it was getting toward midnight when the telephone rang.

"Dad, it's Krissy. Can I spend the night with Becky?"

My initial response was no, because Krissy is well aware of the rule in our family: If you're going out and planning to spend the night somewhere, you arrange all that beforehand. But never bushwhack Dad by calling later in the evening with a "change of plans."

"No," I answered quickly. "You know the rule—you should be getting yourself home right now."

"But, Dad . . ."

"*What*, Krissy?"

"Well, while Becky and I were driving around in her car, some guys chased us and flashed their lights and scared her pretty bad. She's really shaky, and her mother said she'd feel better if I spent the night."

"Oh?" I answered after a few seconds' pause. "Well—now that you've explained things, that's a little different. I guess it will be okay to spend the night this time."

"Thanks, Dad," said Krissy, and hung up.

The next morning, Krissy was home by 7:30. I hadn't let her break our family rule, but I had let her bend it a bit for a good cause.

3. Hear Them Out, Then Decide

Being able to bend a little with family rules leads into our next way to be a best friend. Before making any snap judgments, it's always good to hear your teenagers out. Because Reality Discipline relies on action, not just words, there is always the temptation to act or speak too quickly, to make a snap judgment that really isn't the best approach. To put it another way, "Parents should think before they act."

With teenagers especially, it's imperative to think about the long-range—and even the short-range—consequences of any action you may take. Because they're at a sensitive age, the feelings of teenagers are like exposed raw nerves. They are not likely to forgive and forget if you run roughshod over them. Remember you're dealing with a not-quite-adult adolescent who can take offense and not be that quick to forgive. Furthermore, when it comes to slights and offenses, teenagers have the memory of an elephant.

Our daughter Holly has a congenital problem with her jaw that led to five surgeries during her teenage years to try to correct the defect and relieve the pain and discomfort. By the time she was a senior in high school, Holly had already had four jaw surgeries, two of which were botched so badly, they had to be done over. She had gone through incredible pain and discomfort, and while I knew her jaw wasn't perfect, I felt things had improved and that her pain had lessened. I was wrong.

One evening when I came home from the office, Holly and her mother greeted me with news that could easily be classified as a bombshell. As a matter of fact, it hit with the impact of a cruise missile.

"Dad," said Holly, "I'm going to have surgery again."

I gave Sande an if-looks-could-kill-I-would-be-a-widower glance as I thought of Holly going through all that pain again. Without hesitation (and without thinking), I said, "Holly, let me put it to you this way. No one—and I mean *no one*—is to touch your jaw."

As Holly left the room with tears flowing, Sande pulled me aside and said, "Listen, I know how you feel about this, but you'd better go easy this time. All day long today, Holly has been crying. Her jaw is still not right. She has been in constant pain every day, but she hasn't complained. Don't just say 'Absolutely no.' At least sit down and listen to what she has to say."

Later, I went to Holly's room to talk. "Holly," I began, "I guess I gave a knee-jerk reaction to the news about surgery. And I think you understand why I said what I said, after all you've been through. But tell me, what's going on? What do you think? I just want to sit back and listen to you. Tell me how you feel."

Tearfully, Holly explained how terrible she still felt, how she had pain every day.

"Dad, I'm going away to college in the fall, and I want to try to get this done now, before summer. It's my last chance, Dad."

I wasn't quite sure what Holly meant by her "last chance," but after discussing it further with Sande, I agreed that she should go ahead with the surgery. Ten days later, she underwent what the doctors call an *orthogmathic procedure.* So far, the results have been favorable. Holly is glad she had the surgery, and I'm glad I had the sense to hear her out before saying a flat no.

But what about situations where you hear the teenager out and still don't agree? When you're sure a teenager wants to do something that is not in his or her best interest, and certainly not in the family's best interest, that's when you say, "No, we've been over this thoroughly, and the answer is still a definite no."

Don't continue to hash the subject over. Don't be drawn into more debates. Say no, and that's it.

4. Forgive, Forget, and Trust

The mark of a true friend is the ability to forgive and at least try to forget. I'm not sure anyone ever completely forgets, but at least you don't have to dwell on things and keep nursing hurts and grudges.

I know of one fifteen-year-old who didn't want to go to a certain party because she knew there would be a lot of drinking. She finally knuckled under to peer pressure, but just as she got in the door, the police raided the place. The girl got picked up for breaking the local curfew law for teenagers, while the rest of the young people were arrested for drunkenness.

Going through the embarrassment of being hauled off to jail in a police car and then searched by a matron was bad enough, but her parents' response was even worse. Her father had to pick her up at the jail at four in the morning, and he never let her explain what had happened. Her parents berated her with what she had done over and over, and years later, they still hold that incident and other things she "did wrong" over her head.

This girl's story illustrates one of the firm rules I give to parents who are having trouble with their teenagers:

Don't be a bone-digger.

A bone-digger is someone who goes back and unearths old bones of contention. Bone-diggers dig up the old issues and never let them go. If you want to be a friend to your teenager, quit digging bones, and if you have never dug any, never start.

But suppose your teenager has blown it, and you feel you want to bury the bones for good. How do you trust your son or daughter again? First, *do not* say, "You've got to earn my trust." Whenever you tell the teenager "You've got to prove I can trust you," you only put your son or daughter in a vicious bind—what I call a cycle of distrust.

The cycle of distrust works like this: The teenager blows it and makes a bad mistake, breaks a cardinal rule, or acts irresponsibly. Instead of forgiving the teenager, the parent says, "I'm not trusting you until you *prove* you can be trusted."

But how can the teenager prove he's worthy of being trusted if the parent isn't going to trust him? Whenever the parent says "Prove I can trust you," all the parent is communicating is distrust. In many cases, I have dealt with teenagers who went ahead and got in trouble because "my parents don't trust me anyway, so what's the difference?"

Trust and forgiveness go hand in hand. Both need to be given again and again. Besides, you might as well trust your teenager. You really don't have any other choice (unless you plan to ride around in the backseat with her wherever she goes).

Am I suggesting you play the ostrich and look the other way if your teenager is really off-base, doing things you know are wrong, and undermining the family unit? Of course not. It's then that you have to confront the problem. More to the point, confront your teenager and talk about what's going on. The word *trust* doesn't even have to come up. Deal with the problem and how you can resolve it. Make it clear what the consequences will be if the teenager continues with this kind of behavior.

5. Be Willing to Do the Right Thing

The other side of the trust coin reads, "Be willing to do the right, and sometimes the very tough, thing for your teenager's own good." For example, it's important to know who your teenager's friends are. If possible, have them over and really get to know them as more than voices on the phone or faces you see zooming away in a car that has just picked up your son or daughter.

If you and your spouse both have to work, do all you can to be sure younger children have supervision of some kind. A survey by a team of scientists reported that eighth graders who were latchkey kids and spent more than two hours a day unsupervised were twice as likely to get into drug use as kids under supervision.

Five thousand eighth graders in California schools were asked about their family situation, their after-school activities, and their use of alcohol, cigarettes, and marijuana.

Fourteen percent of the supervised kids and 24 percent of the unsupervised teenagers said they had tried pot at least once.

Eleven percent of supervised eighth graders and 23 percent of the unsupervised students reported they had consumed more than eleven alcoholic drinks in their lives.[1]

Just a generation or two ago, the parents in a community automatically knew what was happening, because they communicated with one another. Everyone knew everyone else in town and what was going on. But today, that won't happen unless parents are willing to band together for their kids' own good.

I read recently about some parents who were cleaning up following their daughter's thirteenth birthday party, only to find the backyard littered with beer cans, wine bottles, and marijuana cigarette butts. Their answer was to invite all the parents of the party guests over to their home to discuss the problem they all had in common. Out of that meeting came an 11:00 P.M. curfew for the junior high students who had been involved in the party. Rock concerts were off limits, and there was to be parental supervision at all social functions held by these young teenagers.

Did the kids scream, "You don't trust us!"? I'm sure some did, but six months after those parents met, all their children were drug-free, and they remained that way.

The first meeting by that group of parents was the beginning of what are now known as Peer Parent Groups (PPGs). Today there are nine thousand such groups in cities and towns across the nation. The parents who are in PPGs are convinced there is strength in getting together and organizing to protect children from the dangers of alcohol and drug abuse.[2]

Sometimes parents have to take even stronger measures. A couple I worked with suspected their seventeen-year-old not only of using drugs, but even of dealing them. They literally put a private investigator on his trail, and soon the investigator discovered the boy was, indeed, mixed up in drug trafficking.

Instead of turning him in to the police, they confronted the boy and made him a proposition. They sent him several states away to the home of his aunt, where he was tightly supervised. Once he was away from the influence of the group he had been running with back home, he cleaned up his life and was doing well.

6. Take Them Seriously

Take them seriously—in other words, show your teenagers the same kind of respect you want them to show to you. You can do this in several practical ways.

Respect their privacy. I've heard more than one horror story from teenagers in my office who tell me their parents open their mail, go into their room and read their diary, and even listen in to telephone conversations on an extension phone. Granted, if parents have strong reason to believe their teenager is doing something like dealing drugs (see point 5 above), that's one thing. Invasion of privacy may be necessary then. But in the vast majority of cases, parents should honor a teenager's privacy whenever possible. The questions for the parent to always ask are, "Would I violate the privacy of a friend?" and "Would I want my friend to violate my privacy?"

Respect their opinions. This may well mean allowing for disagreement and having to listen to ideas you think are totally ridiculous, if not insane. Remember that teenagers are groping and grappling with becoming adults. They can't learn if they're not given the opportunity to express themselves. You don't have to agree with their ideas—you only have to allow your teenagers to express them.

Respect their feelings. The teenage years are times of puppy love, of exploring and learning about one's sexuality and how to deal with the opposite sex. The teenage years can also mean getting cut from the basketball team, failing an important exam, and being ostracized by the "in" group. All these things and many others can be devastating to a teenager, and the last thing the teenager needs to hear from you is, "Oh, you'll get over it. It's no big deal."

To the teenager, it *is* a big deal, and when you let your teenager know you understand and care, you will be acting like a true friend, indeed.

7. Expect—Then Back Off

One of the cardinal rules you find in books discussing teenagers is that parents must "learn to let them go." If there's anything teenagers hate, it's being smothered by too much love and supervision and being told what to do about every move they make in life.

Balanced against letting your teenagers go is the fact that you aren't always sure what they'll do. How does Mom or Dad use Reality Discipline and stay on comfortable middle ground?

I mentioned earlier that the Leman family spends every summer on Chautauqua Lake in western New York State. There is a summer campground nearby, where our children have been enrolled over the years and where our two older girls, Holly and Krissy, have served as counselors. The summer when Krissy was sixteen, she was invited to attend a reunion of the teenage camp staff, which would include having the whole group stay overnight at the camp for a special party—all carefully supervised by adult counselors.

It looked like a nice, wholesome evening to Sande and me—until Krissy announced she really wasn't planning to stay all night at the camp because she had "made plans." Her boyfriend lived about ten miles away in Jamestown, and because she and Holly would be driving the car over to the camp reunion, Krissy saw no problem with leaving the festivities later in the evening and running over to see him. Not only that, but she also planned to stay the night with a girlfriend who lived in Jamestown.

Krissy's announcement left me feeling a bit between a rock and a hard place. I much preferred she stay for the entire party, then sleep at the camp along with all her other friends and the adult counselors. Her idea wasn't a good option at all, in my opinion.

And so there I was with my own Reality Discipline principles staring me in the face. I wanted to use guidance and not force; I wanted to be consistent and decisive, yet respectful of my teenager as a person.

My personal style as a father is to always tell my children exactly how I feel about things. In fact, in some situations I tell them what I think they ought to do, then back off and wait to see what happens.

I told Krissy I preferred she stay at the camp and at the camp staff reunion party throughout the evening and then spend the night there with the rest of the group.

Krissy didn't see it that way. She didn't want to spend the night there. She wanted to go see her boyfriend, then stay at her girlfriend's house.

"I think it would be a real insult to your camp staff friends and the counselors if you left the party," I told her. "There will be plenty of other opportunities to see your boyfriend, and this is one time when I think your responsibility lies with the other kids."

We left it at that, and Krissy drove off to the camp staff reunion party. The next morning when we got up, I told Sande, "It's twenty minutes to nine. I know the camp staff planned to have breakfast this morning at 8:30. I think I'll call Krissy and say hi."

I dialed the number, got the camp switchboard, and eventually Krissy came to the phone. "Krissy, this is Daddy. I just want to let you know that if you want to use the car today, you're welcome to it, because Mom and I won't need it."

I didn't say a word about whether she had stayed at camp or not. I simply assumed she had done so. The unspoken message was, "I'm calling to let you know I know you're there. I know you didn't leave the party to go see your boyfriend, and you didn't stay overnight at your girlfriend's house in Jamestown. You stayed the course, and you did the right thing."

You see, I hadn't flatly forbidden Krissy to leave the party. I had let her know exactly where I stood, and then I had backed off to let her make her own decision.

Reality Discipline tries to use guidance, not force. I could have threatened to take away the car keys and make both Holly and Krissy stay home that night. But that wouldn't have been Reality Discipline—that would have been authoritarian stupidity. On the other hand, Reality Discipline doesn't mean using clever manipulation or the flawless use of active listening and unconditional positive regard. I believe in actively listening to my children, and I do all in my power to treat them with unconditional love, but there are times, when the chips are down, when, like any other parent, I have to say it like it is: "Look, I really prefer you do *this*."

And what if Krissy had not been there when I called that morning?

I would have lived with it. After all, I gave her the choice. At an opportune time, however, I would have told her, "I just want you to know that I realize I gave you the right to decide what to do the other night about the camp party and going over to Jamestown. You did what you wanted, but I still believe it was not the best choice for reasons I already spelled out. I want you to know I'm not happy with your choice, because I think it was not in your best interests or anybody else's."

I always try to tell my teenagers where I stand and where they stand with me, even if it means bumping heads. But I always try to do it in a way that confronts them with being responsible and accountable. Teenagers won't always agree with you, but if you can at least get them to think about *What is the responsible thing to do here?* you will go a long way in helping them prepare for life as adults in the real world.

8. Be There for Them

To hear many teenagers tell it, they would rather "just die" than be seen with their parents anywhere in public. To a great extent, that is true. Teenagers are trying to break away, to become independent, and the last thing they want is to project even the slightest image of "having to depend on Mommy and Daddy."

Nonetheless, that doesn't say parents should simply ignore their teenagers and not try to spend time with them. On the outside, they may claim they're embarrassed when you're around, but on the inside, they want and need your interest and support.

Our daughter Krissy was a starting guard on her high school basketball team, and we tried to make every game we could. We once drove what seemed to be at least one hundred miles out into the desert southwest of Tucson to some little town where Krissy was playing. I got there a little late, and the game was under way by the time I entered the gym.

Krissy acted as if she had never seen me come in, even though it was a crackerbox gymnasium and not many people were there. As the game went on, she got fouled and was awarded two free throws. As she stood at the line, waiting for the referee to toss her the ball, she put her hands on her hips to draw some deep breaths. She was directly in line with my seat in the bleachers, and while she never looked at me, I saw her pinky finger do a little "wave" as if to say, "Hi, I'm glad you're here."

Granted, that wasn't much recognition for driving one hundred miles to watch a girls' basketball game in a drafty gym with hard bleachers. But it was all I needed, and I'll continue to drive one hundred miles—or more—to show her I'm interested in what she's doing.

When Kevin was to turn thirteen, I noted that I'd be on the road doing a book tour when the magic date of February 8 arrived.

"Put Kevin's birthday in my appointment book," I asked Gwen, my office assistant. "No matter where I am on that book tour, I'll be flying home the night of February 7 so I can spend the next day with Kevin for his birthday."

And that's what I did. As I recall, it required two or three plane changes and getting in late, but I was there on the day my son turned thirteen. It would have been easy enough to call and tell him, "Sorry, Kevin, I can't get home. We'll celebrate your birthday later." But I knew that when you're a kid, birthdays are important—especially the one when you officially enter the ranks of the hormone group.

But the birthday celebrating didn't stop on February 8. Two days later, Kevin and I boarded a plane and flew from Tucson to Ontario, California, so he could attend a Christian magicians' convention being held in Riverside. Frankly, the last thing I wanted to do right after getting home from almost two weeks on the road was to get right back on an airplane, but I was glad to go and spend time with my son as he enjoyed his favorite pastime—magic.

We had a great weekend together and some good talks, including some fine-tuned conversations about the birds and the bees. Come to think of it, it was a magic time, indeed, in more ways than one.

For Kevin's birthday, I was able to plan ahead and come home in time to celebrate with him. Sometimes, however, a parent is on the road and can't be back for a special occasion. Nonetheless, there are ways to be there that can be even more effective than being present in person.

While I was on an extended trip, I called home a day or so before Valentine's Day and was talking with Sande when she said excitedly, "Oh, I almost forgot. Holly got a letter of acceptance today from the college she wants to attend next fall."

I was as thrilled as Sande was, if not more so. I knew how important it was to Holly to get into this particular college, a liberal arts school in Pennsylvania with the highest academic standards and rankings.

After hanging up, I couldn't get to sleep for a while because of the wonderful news. The next morning, I called a florist and ordered a dozen pink sweetheart roses to be sent to Holly. The enclosed card said:

Congratulations! I'll bet you're really proud of yourself!
Love, Daddy

The next night, I called home, and Holly got on the phone. "Oh, Daddy," she said. "Thank you for the roses. When I saw the man from the florist shop at the door, I knew they had to be for Mom for Valentine's Day. But then I saw my own name on them, and I thought, *My goodness, they must be from Lincoln,*" her boyfriend.

"But Daddy," Holly went on quickly, "the flowers were from *you,* and that's even *better!*"

I treasure Holly's words. When a father's flowers can rate "even better" than flowers from a daughter's steady boyfriend, it doesn't get any better than that!

I don't know the makeup of your family, but if you have children, especially teenagers, I urge you to take time to be there for them in whatever ways you can. Go to their games, their recitals, their back-to-school nights. Even offer to take your teenagers on outings. They may be far more willing to go than you think, if they can be sure their friends won't see them with you! And in some cases, they'll be willing to go with you if they can invite one special friend along.

And if push comes to shove, you can always send your teenage daughter flowers. She may like the flowers better than having you there in person!

It doesn't have to cost a lot of money. It does take some time and some energy, but everything you spend on your teenagers will be well worth it and will come back to you tenfold.

When Krissy turned sixteen, she wrote the following notes to her mother and me:

> Mom—
> where do I begin? you've kissed me knees & elbows when I fell, stayed up with me when I was sick, plus, gave birth to me! mom, you are _so_, _so_ dear to me, I don't say this enough but you _are_ the best mom & I love you so much!! thanks mom!!
> Krissy

> Daddy,
> you've been such a special father over the last 16 years, thanks for encouraging me to do my very best! you've helped me to get this far and I'm sure I'll continue to succeed thanks to you! I love you Dad!
> Kristin

9. Hold Them Tight, But Let Them Go

This enigmatic statement contains a big key to parenting teenagers. You always want them to feel your love and concern, but you've got to balance that by letting them test their wings, even when you're not quite sure they're ready.

As for "holding them tight," be a toucher. I don't necessarily mean big, full-fledged hugs, because teenagers usually don't appreciate being locked in parental bear hugs. But there are ways to just touch them on the arm or the shoulder and tell them every day in one way or another, "Hey, I love you. You're really special, and I'm glad I'm your dad (or mom)."

As you keep a rein on your teenagers, make sure it's a long rein. Give them room enough to operate, but don't fail to know what they're doing or who they're with. Giving a teenager a long rein doesn't mean looking the other way; it doesn't mean turning your teenager loose to do whatever he or she feels like doing with anyone who comes along. Showing them your love and concern while giving them the freedom to explore and experiment is an ongoing process that happens every day, week, and month.

Unfortunately, some parents don't bother. Out of permissiveness or blasé neglect, they look the other way, excusing themselves by saying, "Our teenagers are old enough to take care of themselves." Tragic accounts of teenagers who were "old enough to take care of themselves" abound in newspapers and on television. One such tale of horror involves a wealthy girl of seventeen who was allowed the run of her parents' mansionlike home. The parents spent a lot of time out of town and let the girl "take care of herself."

One day the girl had friends over—two other girls and three boys. The group drank whiskey and beer, smoked marijuana, and took LSD. As the party wore on into the night, things went sour. One of the boys—a sixteen-year-old—found a shotgun somewhere in the house and killed the girl who had given the party. Then he handed the gun to his seventeen-year-old friend, and he killed the other two girls. The third boy, a sixteen-year-old, just watched in horror. Then all three of them fled, only to be apprehended a few days later.[3]

The teenagers involved in this senseless tragedy were living without any kind of rein at all. In this case, parental permissiveness had turned into neglect, and three young women paid the ultimate price.

At the other end of the spectrum, a parent can hold too tight a rein. Not long ago, the subject on our "Parent Talk" radio call-in show was dating—specifically, "How old should teenagers be before they are allowed to date?" One mother called in to say, "My husband and I have decided not to let our daughters date as long as they are living under our roof."

Not quite sure I was hearing what I thought I was hearing, I asked, "You mean your daughters will not be able to date even when they're juniors and seniors in high school?"

"That's right—as long they live under our roof, we're not going to let them go on dates. There's just too much chance of getting into trouble."

"I appreciate your concern for your daughters," I told the woman over the phone, "but I'm afraid you're setting your kids up for rebellion. This approach is simply not realistic."

The woman would not budge from her position, and a few minutes later, we went on to another caller. A man was on the line, and he said, "I know the woman who just called and told you she will never let her daughters date. Her children are already rebelling, but she doesn't know it."

I told the caller I was not surprised. Dating is one of the most volatile areas in families with teenagers. When it comes to dating, I suggest a few ground rules—but the fewer the better.

Rule No. 1 is not to get uptight. The more laid back you are about the subject, the better.

Rule No. 2 is to be very open in allowing your children to do things with their friends as a group. This is especially important as children move into the junior high years and they start to become more social. Young teenagers of thirteen and fourteen are probably not ready to date one-on-one, but they can enjoy learning how to act with the opposite sex in group events and activities like parties, socials, going to ball games, and the like.

Rule No. 3—and this is only if you absolutely *must* have an age limit to start dating—is to let your teenagers begin dating at age sixteen. I give this number reluctantly, because I know some teenagers are ready to date earlier than that. In fact, our daughter Holly had one or two dates late in her fifteenth year. Krissy began dating at sixteen, although we had never really laid down any rule of our own for our family. It just seemed to happen that way.

The important thing is to make the age for dating a rule of thumb, not something hard and fast, like the age for acquiring a driver's license. A lot depends on who and what is involved in the date or the outing the teenager has planned. The key is to hear your teenager out and be willing to work with him or her.

Last summer, while we were spending our vacation at Chautauqua Lake in New York, near the Canadian border, Holly came to me with a request to allow her to drive with a girlfriend into Canada. It would be a trip of some one hundred miles, farther than Holly had ever driven before at one time. It would mean going through Buffalo, across a bridge, through Canadian customs, and on into Canada—all unfamiliar to Holly and her friend, who hadn't made the trip before either.

"Honey, it sounds a little bit much to me. I'd like to think on it for a while," I said.

"Well, Dad, if you're ever going up to Buffalo, do you think you could take me along and sort of show me the route?"

"Well, maybe I'll do that" was all I said, and we dropped it.

About a week later, I had some errands to do in Buffalo, and I took Holly along. I showed her the exact route, all the way from our cottage on Chautauqua Lake right up to the Canadian border. We talked about getting through customs and what was involved. I also cautioned her about driving in Canada, where the Mounties are strict about speeding laws.

We went back home to the cottage, and I talked with Sande about what would be involved if Holly actually made the trip with her friend. Two weeks later, we allowed her to go, and it all came off without a hitch.

It was never a question of whether Holly would be responsible. I wasn't worried at all about what she might do, but I do confess I did worry about what other people out there on the highway might do.

I tell you this homey little story of a doting dad to point out that it's hard to give responsibility to your teenager, who, by the way, no longer thinks she is a child. And she isn't. In many respects she's an adult, but she lacks an adult's experience, and there's the rub. And so dads and moms worry. It's the parental prerogative. My advice to all parents is, "Go ahead and worry, but keep the reins loose and long. Trust your teenagers to act responsibly—and they will."

Being your teenager's best friend is a hard and sometimes thankless job, but keep at it, because every effort you make will pay off somewhere down the line. And sometimes you just may receive a bonus. Sande and I got the following note from Holly, penned on December 6, just before one of her several jaw surgeries. It wasn't her birthday, and maybe she was setting us up for Christmas—I'm not sure. But I treasure what she said:

Dear mom & Dad~   Dec. 6, 1987

Hello! I'll bet you're wondering why I'm writing to you. Well, I just wanted to thank you for everything you've ever given me. I realize how lucky I've been to be blessed with so many things & such great parents. I truely love you both & I'm proud that you guys are my parents. Thank you for always encouraging me to be the best I can possably be, to follow my dreams and to stick up for what I think is right. I'm so lucky that you're allowing me to have this operation & I know you'll both be beside me all the way. Thank you for all your work to make this family a family. God Bless! love in Him, Holly

Don't Forget . . .

- There's a big difference between being a buddy and being a best friend to your teenager.
- It's not always easy to be open, honest, and transparent with your teenager, but it is always worthwhile.
- Sometimes teenagers depend on their parents to say no to help them stand up to their peer group.
- There are times to bend the rules. A good rule of thumb is, if a rule can't bend, it isn't a good rule.
- It's always better to hear your teenager out first and then give your opinion.
- When your teenager blows it, forgive, forget, and continue to trust. *Don't be a bone-digger.*
- Contrary to their opinion, teenagers are not ready to run their own lives without guidance and supervision. When it's time to intervene, do not back off—stick to your guns.
- One of the biggest needs among teenagers is to be taken seriously. Many of them feel like Rodney Dangerfield—"I just don't get no respect!"
- Let your teenagers know what you expect, then back off and give them a chance to make their own decision.
- Invest time in being there for your teenager; you will be repaid a hundredfold and more.
- If you love your teenager, you will be willing to let him or her go (and it's okay to worry a little bit).

And Why Not Try . . .

- If "I was wrong" and "Forgive me" are hard for you to say, try taking tiny steps in that direction the next time you have the opportunity. (You shouldn't have to wait long.)
- The next time your teenager comes up with what sounds like a harebrained idea, hear your teenager out

before voicing your opinion. It might even lead to communication.

- Talk with your spouse about how well both of you forgive and forget when your teenagers blow it and how easily you trust them again. Ask each other, "Am I a bone-digger? If you think I am, give me some examples."
- Try to become better acquainted with your teenagers' friends. Let your teenagers know their friends are welcome in your home.
- Talk with your spouse about how well both of you are doing at voicing your expectations and then backing off to let your teenagers make their own decisions. Is anything coming up where you will have opportunity to do this?
- Check your calendar or appointment book. Are your teenagers penciled in? If not, why not? If your teenagers are getting toward the age for dating, what are your policies? Have you sat down with your teenagers to talk about this? If not, why not do it soon?

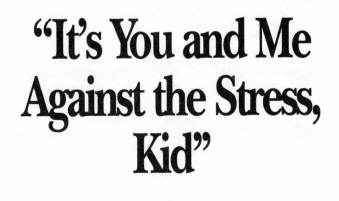

Chapter 13

"It's You and Me Against the Stress, Kid"

Reality Discipline and the Single Mom

THIS CHAPTER IS DEDICATED TO THE PERSON WITH THE TOUGHEST JOB on the face of the earth:

the single mom.

According to statistics, half the children in the current generation are likely to live in a home headed by a single parent. I know single dads have it tough, too, but from what I see in my office, by far the majority of single parents who are coping with being the full-time custodian of children are women. Now I want to speak especially to them.

If there is one word that describes the major challenge facing single mothers, it's *stress*. According to David Elkind, separation and divorce are perhaps the "most pervasive and endemic source of stress in America today," affecting one out of three marriages.[1] Obviously, separation and divorce are stressful to everyone in the family, but they're particularly hard on the woman. Not only does she go through the stress of a failed marriage and the trauma of the divorce, which is often a nasty, drag-out fight, but she also has to grapple with how to survive economically and emotionally.

Single mothers who come to see me are practically in a state of shock and panic. They are trying to be both mother and father, along with trying to earn a living. Even if they do get child support, it's not even close to being enough to pay all the bills. In many cases, they lack the skills they need to earn a reasonable living.

And what, pray tell, might happen if the single mom got sick? She tells herself, *I can't get sick—at least not too sick to work.* When the colds, sore throats, and sinus infections that are part of life come along, most single moms suck it up and go out the door. They don't feel all that well, but they have no choice but to go to work.

The stress doesn't stop there, either. When you're single, it's hard to fit in with your former friends, most of whom are married. Operating alone is difficult. Does a single mother want to go to a play or movie by herself? If she can't find a friend who is willing to accompany her, she just may opt to stay home.

And then there's the question of male friends. Is the single mom still attractive to men? She may not be sure she is. How should she go about trying to meet another man, and how long should she wait after the divorce to begin dating? More on that later in this chapter.

These are just a few of the stress-filled questions that face the single mothers I see. But the biggest stress of all is perhaps that word *single.* She has to do everything alone, with no daily and hourly help. Her family may live nearby and give her some support, but it's still a very partial solution to her problem of aloneness. As Elkind points out, "To support children financially and emotionally, without herself enjoying those kinds of support, is perhaps the most severe stress encountered by a female in our society."[2]

A few years ago, I wrote a book entitled *Bonkers: Why Women Get Stressed Out and What They Can Do About It.*[3] As part of my research, I asked several hundred women, "What causes stress in your life?" I got a lot of answers, but six of them stood out as the biggest stressors of all. Not surprisingly, the number-one stressor was the children. Number two was lack of time—a schedule packed with too much to do and too few hours to do it in. As one single mother told me, one of her goals for the coming year was to read the newspaper on the day it was published.

The third-ranking source of stress was their former husbands. I haven't done any extensive survey of single moms, but it's my guess that confrontations with their ex cause them no end of stress, whether it's over money (the support check didn't come again) or his failure to come when he said he would and disappointing the children—again.

WHY STRESS IS SO DANGEROUS

Before we go any further, we need to define just what stress is and why it can be so dangerous, particularly for a single parent who is carrying a load that is double and even triple what it used to be. The best definition of stress I've seen is: "The wear and tear on our bodies produced by the very process of living."[4] The term *stress* was introduced to the general public by Dr. Hans Selye back in the 1950s, when he wrote *The Stress of Life.*[5] According to Selye, stress happens when your body has an extraspecial demand put upon it physically, emotionally, or intellectually. Whatever makes that kind of demand is called a *stressor.*[6]

Stressors can be anything—from something good like watching your favorite team win a game in the last seconds, to something bad like getting rear-ended in morning rush-hour traffic. Whatever happens, the stress causes your body to make an "adaptation" to what's going on. According to Selye, we all adapt to stress by going through three steps: alarm, resistance, and exhaustion.

When you're handling stress fairly well, you will only go through alarm and resistance. But if the stress continues for many days and even weeks, the pressure mounts, and you wind up in the exhaustion stage, where you are dangerously low on what Selye referred to as "adaptation energy."[7] It's not hard to guess that by the time a single mom comes to see me, she is near or in a state of exhaustion after trying to do it all. It reminds me of buying the best DieHard battery you can find, but if you have a habit of leaving the lights on, even a DieHard finally runs down.

BETTY HAD BURNOUT IN HER EYES

When Betty, a single mom with three children, walked in, I could see burnout in her eyes. She had come to get help with controlling her kids, who were in various stages of rebellion.

Most serious was ten-year-old Christopher, who refused to cooperate on much of anything, screaming that he hated his mother and wanted to go live with his dad. His latest and most serious act of defiance was to "run away" for several hours. He didn't return home until about eleven o'clock, two hours after Betty had frantically gotten the police involved in looking for him.

As Betty's story poured out, I could see she was making a typical mistake: being too permissive with her children in order to keep their allegiance. Her ex-husband, Joe, was giving the kids the "Disneyland treatment" on the weekends he took them, and Betty was afraid he might win the children away from her.

"Every time the kids go to see their dad on weekends, he throws a big party, and it always takes them several days to settle down after they get back with me. Joe has different rules—he lets them eat a lot of sugar, for example, and by the time I get them back, they're wired. Sometimes they even come home rebellious and accuse me of being an old witch when I try to reestablish any kind of discipline," Betty complained.

"And so you're backing off on the discipline in order to stay in their favor, and it's backfiring on you," I commented. "When parents are too permissive, it can make children very insecure, and they take that insecurity out on the parent. Your children, particularly Christopher, resent the divorce, and you're getting the brunt of their anger."

"I don't know why they want to do that," Betty replied. "Their dad didn't pay much attention to them when we lived together, and when he did, it was usually to go overboard on punishing them."

"I know it sounds crazy, but nonetheless it happens all the time," I tried to explain. "You've got to remember your entire family has been through a terrible trauma with the divorce. Even when a father isn't doing a great job, he gives kids a tremendous feeling of security, and they don't want him to be gone. And now that he's gone and suddenly giving the kids the Disneyland treatment on weekends, they're really confused. Joe has you in the classic dilemma: having to be their custodial parent and responsible to give them discipline, while all he has to do is show them a good time and spoil them while they're with him."

"That pretty well describes it," Betty admitted. "So now what do I do? Something has to change or I'm just going to go totally bonkers."

"Well, the one thing I don't want you to do is suddenly become the Gestapo. Don't crack down on the kids to show them who's really boss. Instead, move in on them gently with firmer rules and a little more structure. I call it the firm but fair approach."

"Sounds good, but I'm not sure I'm up to it. The kids will resent me even more. What if I lose them to Joe?"

"That's exactly what's wrong. Right now you're worried about losing them, and they're interpreting it as you're not really caring about them. You're letting them run roughshod in many ways. You're a paper tiger, when they're looking for a mama lion who will give them a gentle cuff now and then but still be someone they know they can count on."

"Well, I'm willing to try," Betty said dubiously, "but I don't even know how to start."

"Most mothers in your situation think they have to start with their kids because their kids are giving them the problem," I said. "But actually, you need to start with yourself. You have to do a little shoring up of your own feelings and self-esteem in order to be in better shape to handle your children and do what's best for them right now."

DON'T NEGLECT YOURSELF TO NURTURE YOUR KIDS

What I tell all single mothers is that the most common trap they can fall into is to try to cover all the bases and juggle all the responsibilities, and in so doing forget to take proper care of themselves. The inevitable result is that they tire out, wear down, and finally burn out. By the time Betty got to me, she was right on the edge of burnout. She had been trying to do it all for a year, and when we probed into why, her feelings of failure—"I feel like such a loser"— came out.

Because Betty's marriage had failed, she was sure she was a failure, and she was trying to make it up to her kids in every way she could. But where she was breaking down was in failing to give them enough discipline. Obviously, she needed the firm but fair approach described in chapters 8, 9, and 10, but that's much easier said than done. Frankly, it's hard enough for two parents to use Reality Discipline on their children, even though they have each other to lean on and can draw support from each other.

Of the ten Reality Discipline principles we've already discussed, the first three apply especially to the single mom, but with a few qualifications and amendments:

1. Now that Mom is single and caring for the children, the whole is even more important than the parts. The family has to pull together as they never have before.

2. Having values and living by them is also more important than ever. Indeed, now values are like a compass,
   and unless a single parent has values she will not compromise, her family ship can sail onto the rocks.
3. Principle No. 3—Always put your spouse first—has to
   change. Now the single mom has no spouse, so the new
   principle is:

> Sometimes you must put yourself first.

The first thing I suggested that Betty do was start thinking
about how important she is to her family, especially now. Does she
feel as important as her children? She should, because unless she
functions well, they face a hard time.

"Do you make time to do things you enjoy?" I asked Betty.

"Not really. Usually I get home from work, feed the kids, clean
up the kitchen, and get everybody bathed and into bed. Then I
usually pop some corn and watch something on TV. Sometimes I
just drop off to sleep after nibbling on a bowl of popcorn."

"I know it sounds crazy," I interrupted, "but have you thought
about getting any exercise? Joining a gym or some kind of fitness
program? I know you're tired, but a lot of that is a mental tired-
ness, and getting even a brief, brisk physical workout can do wonders to give you a little more energy and make you have a completely different outlook on life."

Betty admitted she had done little exercising and was concerned about the several extra pounds she had put on while sitting
around at home, nibbling popcorn. Joining a gym was not possible
for Betty at the moment because she was short of money, but I gave
her a couple of alternatives:

1. She could make arrangements with her child-care service to keep the children an extra hour three times a

week so she could do some brisk walking in a pleasant
and safe spot not far from where she worked.

2. She could buy or borrow an aerobics workout videotape
and get her kids to exercise with her to have a little family fun together.

CONCENTRATE ON YOUR GOOD QUALITIES

Another thing I wanted Betty to work on was making a list of the
qualities she has that make her feel good about herself. At the
same time, I wanted her to write down negative things that made
her feel discouraged. On her first try, the negative list far out-
weighed the positive, which is only natural. Even when people are
in a fairly good situation, they will find more things wrong with
themselves than what they can see is right.

In Betty's case, coming off a traumatic divorce and adjusting to
being a single parent, she found plenty of negatives and not many
positives. I worked with her to help her see that many of the negatives were self-inflicted judgments she had made out of feelings of
guilt and failure. I had her concentrate on what she was doing
right, beginning with the terrific job she was doing loving and sup-
porting her children. I also pointed out that she tended to bite off
more than she could possibly chew. She had a lot of expectations
she wasn't always able to fulfill.

"What you need to do is reexamine your goals and what you
expect of yourself," I said. "Instead of labeling yourself a failure, reset
some of your goals, and lower your sights a little. For example, I
believe you told me you're still trying to do some PTA activities at
the kids' school. I don't see how you can work full-time and have
energy for that as well. I'd quit all that, or at least cut it way back."

I wanted Betty to start taking control of her life rather than
continuing to feel she was a tiny boat being swept toward the
waterfall. "You need to schedule some 'alone time' every day," I
continued. "I'm not sure when it would be best for you. Some

people get up early, before the kids are awake, for time alone to take a nice, hot shower, have a long cup of coffee, read the paper, and most of all, just sit and sort out feelings."

One way to take more control of your life is to give yourself something to look forward to each day—some small pleasure that will help you take your mind off your tremendous load of responsibilities. Because a single mom seldom has much time, these "small pleasures" are usually just that—very small. But it all comes back to taking time for yourself, nurturing yourself, and strengthening yourself for the ongoing war you're fighting with life's list of daily duties.

Maybe it's time you looked into picking up that hobby you gave up years ago. How about needlepoint or taking time to read just for pleasure—a novel, a magazine, or a short story? Maybe you should take a walk—not for exercise, but for relaxation, a stroll in a spot you find relaxing and beautiful.

Try making a "pleasure list" of things you can do even just a few minutes a day, and then take time to do them. Don't let the day go by without making a real effort to do this. It's so easy to get enveloped in all the urgent activities that you forget the really important things. And the really important things include nurturing your own emotions, your own body, and your own soul.

I've already mentioned the importance of the spiritual element in anyone's life. In the case of the single mother, I feel the spiritual is crucial. Questions I often ask single moms include, "How do you relate to your Creator? Is God someone Who is loving, or is He judging you for what happened?"

Passages like Psalm 68:5 make it clear that God has a special compassion for single moms (and their kids): "A father to the fatherless, a defender of widows, is God in his holy dwelling." Be assured that He loves you, accepts you, and wants to be your provider.

In Betty's case, she admitted she and Joe had started out their marriage by attending church, but Joe had decided it was boring, and they had eventually stopped going altogether. I urged her to get established again in a church where the pastor and people were not judgmental. She had to try several before she happened on a little neighborhood church, not far from her home, where she felt loved and accepted.

And a real bonus were the programs the church offered for the children. Two nights a week, Betty could drop them off at church and have two or three hours for herself, knowing they were engaged in wholesome, character-building activities and not just hanging around the neighborhood.

PICK THE RIGHT KIND OF FRIENDS

Another important area to work on is friendships. While the divorced woman should go slow in developing new relationships with men (more on that shortly), I think it's important that she maintain strong friendships with other women.

Don't become a recluse. Fight the desire to simply go to work, come home, cover the bases, and crash into bed, only to get up and do it all over again the next day. Get out to see friends for lunch, for a cup of coffee, or for a walk together where you can talk, laugh, and even cry.

Be sure to spend time with friends who can nurture you, not nibble at you. Flaw-pickers of any kind you do not need. Make it a point to see little or nothing of people who make you feel anxious, angry, or depressed.

FIND HAPPINESS IN HELPING OTHERS

Another excellent approach to self-nurture (not self-indulgence) is to remember that "busy hands are happy hands." A lot of single moms—and Betty was among them—look at me as if I've "lost it" when I mention my little slogan about "busy hands." Their hands are *very* busy, they tell me. How can dwelling on being busy make you happy?

I explain that I'm not talking about the regular routine of busyness, which is bound to wear anyone down. Anybody can get depressed while doing what they have to do day after day, hour after hour. I'm talking about choosing to be busy helping someone else just for the sheer joy of helping.

For example, is there an older person in your apartment complex that you could take out once a week for groceries? A lot of people have no way of getting out because they don't drive, they don't walk that well, or whatever the case may be. To help someone like this can do a great deal to take your focus off your own problems, and you can realize there are many people who are much worse off than you are. As Jesus put it, "It is more blessed to give than to receive."[8]

Again, there is a possible bonus for your children when you help others. You teach them the value of helping someone less fortunate, and it's also a great opportunity to have the kids learn, through hands-on experience, how good they have it. They'll see firsthand that despite any problems you've had as a single-parent family, there are always people who have a much more difficult time of it.

As for being too tired, let me repeat that you'll find new energy in doing something that differs from the routine. It's also a great way to fight stress. Hans Selye once listed for some colleagues his three main approaches to coping with the stresses of life. First, you should know your own limits. Next, you should set proper goals that fit you and not somebody else. Finally, develop the strategy of "altruistic egotism," or looking out for yourself by being necessary to others and earning their goodwill.[9]

Selye called altruistic egotism his "secret seasoning" of life. His term suggests you need balance. If you become too altruistic, you turn into a superpleaser, working yourself to death trying to cover all the bases to make everyone else happy. Emphasize egotism, and all you do is join Robert Ringer and his ilk as you look out for Number One. What Selye suggests points to the well-known biblical saying: "Do to others as you would have them do to you."[10] Follow this advice and you land in the perfect middle ground where you are neither indulging your own ego nor wallowing in false humility and self-deprecation.

He Won't Change, So Why Get Upset?

Next to weariness, the most prevalent feeling I find in single moms is anger, and there's plenty for them to be angry about. One of their most common causes for anger is encounters with the ex-husband over money or the children. Or perhaps the ex-husband fails to come through on time with the support check, or he fails to show up on visitation day and thereby disappoints the children.

Sometimes when an ex-spouse starts dating someone else, it can make the other ex-spouse sad, feeling left behind or like a failure. And if your ex-husband starts living with someone else, it can cause all kinds of angry responses, including not wanting to allow the children to visit their father because you don't want your kids in that kind of environment.

Another source of anger is the children themselves. Their incessant needs and demands (what sometimes seems to be their incessant selfishness) can wear the single mom down.

When other family members or friends are critical or unsupportive, that can prompt anger, too. And because more single moms have to go into the work force, they can also be angered by what happens on the job—with their boss or fellow employees.

A lot of things can make the single mother angry and upset, but the two that seem to come up the most often are the children and the ex-husband. We'll look first at dealing with the ex-husband; then we'll talk about handling the children in a loving but firm manner.

Some single moms get along fairly well with their ex, particularly if he keeps up support payments and treats the children decently. Unfortunately, those mothers are in the minority. The typical scenario is much like Betty's: tense encounters with the ex-husband when he did come over to see the children, and frequent cancellations without bothering to call and explain why.

"And yet Joe has the gall to keep criticizing me about how I'm raising the children and how much money I'm spending," Betty complained. "I gave each child only one Christmas gift and held the price of each gift below twenty-five dollars, but he was still upset and accused me of spending his hard-earned money as if it were going out of style."

"It sounds like Joe is a flaw-picker," I observed. "Life is tough enough, and if your ex-husband could be less critical, that would at least help, wouldn't it? But that isn't happening. Life is kicking you squarely in the teeth, so the question isn't whether it's fair or not—the question is, what are you going to do about it?"

"What do you mean, 'What am I going to do about it?'" Betty wondered.

"Whenever life treats us unfairly, it's easy to blame someone else—our parents, our sister-in-law, our ex-husband. But that's pointless and fruitless. Better to make the best of what you've got. That always separates the winners from the losers."

"But I'd really like to tell him what I think," Betty said.

"Then do it. Articulate your anger, ventilate it in a proper way—and then get on with living. One of the things I often suggest to people in your position is to write the ex-husband a letter. Tell him exactly how you feel. It probably won't change much, but it can help you come to terms with what's been going on, and then you can work on letting it go. If he keeps flaw-picking, all you have to do is 'consider the source.'"

"Well, I suppose I can handle his criticism. He isn't around that much anyway," Betty said. "But it really can be a problem when he doesn't show up to take Christopher to the park or whatever he said he would do."

"The thing you want to avoid at all costs is what I call triangles," I told Betty. "When Joe disappoints your son, you stay out of it. When his little nose is pressed to the window and his little lip is quivering, and your ex-husband hasn't shown up, and he's two hours late, you simply tell Christopher, 'You know Daddy's phone number, honey. You call him and ask why he hasn't come.'"

DON'T POUR GAS ON THE FLAMES

As inconsiderate and bullheaded as some ex-husbands can be, it's important that the single mom who has custody of the children not cut him off from seeing his own kids. In another case, a single mom I'll call Teresa told me her mother wanted her to change her children's last name now that the divorce was final. The mother wanted the children's last name to be the same as hers—that is, her daughter's maiden name. In this case, the former mother-in-law truly hated the former son-in-law and couldn't stand the fact that her grandchildren carried his name.

I told Teresa, "Wait a minute. These two little boys are your former husband's sons. You cannot change their names. It would be like pouring gasoline on the flames. It will enrage your ex-husband, and he'll fight you tooth and nail."

But Teresa seemed determined to go ahead with the name change. I spent almost an entire session suggesting alternatives and what would be the wisest thing to do.

"Like it or not, your children carry your ex-husband's name," I pointed out. "And he does have a right to see them, even if he doesn't always show up and sometimes breaks their hearts. Your ex-husband may act at times like a real jerk, but rather than letting all this eat at you, accept him for who and what he is. Don't expect too much from him, and then you won't be so disappointed. After all, he's only acting just as he did while you were married. Did you really expect him to change once the divorce was final?"

I also advised Teresa never to criticize her ex-husband to the children. She may have her own thoughts about him, but it's better to say little or nothing. She must keep in mind that her children have to build a relationship with their father as well as with their mother.

FORGIVE—AND REMEMBER

The old cliché says, "Forgive and forget," but the truth is, we never forget. It's much better if you can come to the place where you can forgive and remember. Remember what your ex-husband is like. Remember that he isn't going to change, so why waste energy criticizing, analyzing, and complaining about him?

Once the die is cast and you split the blanket, stop trying to change the very things that caused the split in the first place.

Make a conscious effort to forgive your ex-husband for the past and go on to the future to build a new life for yourself and your family. If hassles do come up, you have two excellent allies: your attorney and the legal agreement that was part of the divorce. For example, a single mom complained to me that her support payments had arrived late twice in a row. At my urging, she contacted her attorney, who talked to her ex-husband's lawyer. That's all that was necessary. From that point on, every support check arrived on time, sent from the office of her ex-husband's attorney.

In another case, the ex-husband moved away from Tucson to California, then requested that his children—ages seven and eight—fly over to see him for weekend visits.

The children's mother told her ex: "The kids aren't flying over to see you by themselves for any weekend visits. Our agreement says you have the right to visit the children every other weekend, and you can fly over here to do that. If you want to take the children to California sometime for a long weekend, that's okay—*if* you fly over to Tucson, accompany the children back to California on the plane, and then accompany them back here at the end of their stay."

Using this approach, the single mother was able to deal with her ex in a reasonable way and avoid a big hassle. It turned out her ex wasn't that interested in having the children come to California if it meant double plane fare for him, so he only did it once or twice a year. The rest of the time, he flew into Tucson to see his children, as per the every-other-week agreement.

In this way, the single mom stayed in control and did not let her ex-husband's circumstances dictate altering the legal agreement.

TAKE YOUR TIME FINDING A NEW MAN

Regarding new relationships with men that could lead to remarriage, I offer single moms the following short course in How to Find a Good One.

Take your time. I always advise a woman whose marriage has broken up to wait four years before even thinking about a new relationship. I suggest four years, hoping she will wait at least two.

I repeat, go slow. A divorce is an extremely traumatic experience, and your feelings are so tender that they could easily sway your better judgment. And if you do plan to remarry, you need all the good judgment you can muster to avoid making the same mistakes again.

Swim in safe waters. In other words, stay out of singles bars and other places of bad ilk. The reason is obvious. Men worth marrying are seldom—if ever—found in singles bars. As a rule, predators, losers, and lonely neurotics hang out there.

The next question is, where can you find a decent man? There are many possibilities, including where you work and any number of clubs, from gardening to hot-air balloons. There are also library programs and activities, co-ed fitness and workout gyms, dance classes, and bowling leagues, to name a few.

If you get involved in a church, there are often singles ministries where eligible men can be found. But don't automatically assume that if you find him in a house of worship, he will be great husband material. Clinkers can be found in churches, too, but your odds of finding a gem should be improved.

When you do start dating, read the man carefully. Discover answers to such questions as:

- Does he have a good relationship with his mother? Does he treat her well? Does he respect her, and does she respect him, or has she always dominated him? If the relationship between a man and his mother is not healthy, it does not bode well for you.
- Does he have a temper? If he shows flashes of real temper or even capability of violence, back off fast. I have counseled many an abused wife who ignored the signs of temper and paid the price with years of beatings and other abuse.
- Is he a controller? Violent men with tempers are usually controllers, but there are other kinds, too. Controlling men are just that—they want you under their thumb. They want to dominate you and have you do nothing but spend your life pleasing them.
- That leads to the other question: Are you a pleaser? Perhaps that's what led to the problems last time. What have you done to try to become a more *positive* pleaser? For specifics on how to go about that, see my book *The Pleasers: Women Who Can't Say No and the Men Who Control Them.*[11]
- Keep your pants on. This is especially good advice for the woman who thinks she has found Mr. Right. The bells and whistles are going off again. Her heart flutters when he calls. Go extra slow at this point. If the phrase *keep your pants on* is offensive, I apologize, but I use those very words when counseling the divorced woman—not for shock value, but because I want her full attention. Many divorcées say I am absolutely right. They know from bitter

experience that hopping into the sack with a man because he expects it and society condones it is stupid. If he really loves you, he'll want you to be different, and he'll want to treat you differently.

- Don't be trigger-happy and write off the man who, during your first encounter, appears to be a bit boring. Give the "dull" ones another look, particularly if you're prone to be attracted to Mr. Excitement, who usually winds up providing the kind of excitement you don't need. This is especially true for the woman who has had a poor relationship with her father. Ironically, she is drawn to the kind of loser who treats her badly but still "turns her on." I've talked with many happily married women who tell me, "The funny thing is, when I first met my husband, I thought he was a real nerd. A friend of mine fixed us up, and there just wasn't any chemistry—at first. But he wouldn't give up, and eventually we fell in love."

Finding a good one is difficult, but if you're patient and stick to values and standards you know are best for you, you will be rewarded. There *are* good men out there, and they are well worth the search.

ACCEPT BUT DON'T LEAN ON YOUR KIDS

Strong feelings are part of every divorce, and those feelings run through the entire family. Sometimes they're hidden, and in other cases they're apparent. Betty's children had a lot of feelings, and they were letting them show by being rebellious, openly angry, and even hostile. A cardinal rule for the single mom is to accept her children's feelings. I'm *not* saying you should accept disrespect or physical abuse from them, which is what Betty was doing in the belief that she could hold their love.

"I understand why you're letting your kids get by with what

they're doing and saying to you," I told Betty, "but it won't work. Permissiveness is a cop-out. Yes, they're hurting, and they have a right to feel hurt, but that doesn't preclude their need to learn to be responsible and accountable. Your family has been dealt a tremendous blow, but if you're going to survive as a family, you've all got to pull together to make it happen."

I went on to explain to Betty that Reality Discipline is the best approach to pulling together as a family. Even the smallest child can be a help if the single parent faithfully follows the principles of Reality Discipline.

You use Reality Discipline with children in a divorced home the way you use it in a home where both parents are present. You're firm but fair. You try to be accountable to your kids and in that way model what accountability is all about, in the hope that they will be accountable as well.

Accept their feelings. Tell them it's okay to feel sad and even angry. Teach them how to express their anger in acceptable ways (assuming, of course, that you've learned how to do the same).

It's vital that the single mom not try to be her children's problem-solver. When a child tells Mom how he feels, she shouldn't deny those feeling with remarks like, "Now, honey, you don't really mean that" or "Don't say that; you shouldn't feel that way."

It's important to never "should on" your kids, and that goes double in the home where only one parent is present. When you "should on" your kids, you tell them in one way or another, "You should do this" or "You shouldn't do that." Another term for this well-known practice is *nagging*. To "should on" your kids only implies they must jump higher and perform better. Frankly, right now they don't need that. They have enough to deal with.

Research polls show that children's number-one fear is not getting AIDS or nuclear war. It's the fear that "my parents will get a divorce." When that fear is realized, your children see one parent leaving the home—usually the father. Accompanying the fear of divorce is the fear of abandonment. When divorce actually happens and Dad leaves, the children's fear grows even stronger. What kids need, particularly in the first year or two following a divorce, is assurance that "Mom isn't going to leave you. You're okay—everything's going to be okay."

To women who are in a divorce situation and facing the single-mom challenge, my advice is to keep things as much the same as you can. Don't move unless the divorce settlement requires sale of the house. If you do move, try to stay in the same school district or at least as near to as many of the children's friends as possible.

And if you must move to a new place, decorate it as much like the old house as possible, particularly the children's rooms. Do anything you can to make your children feel their whole world hasn't changed completely. Change is hard on kids, and the rule of thumb is to keep things the same if you can.

GOOD CHILD CARE IS A MUST

Getting decent care for the children is the first problem that must be solved if the single mother's life is to have any semblance of order. She must know her children are safe and well-supervised while she's away at work. I realize some single mothers believe they have no choice and must allow their children to be latchkey kids. Some latchkey situations are tolerable, but many are not. My general advice is to make any latchkey situation as temporary as possible. Also, as a general rule, don't ask any child under the age of eleven to be in latchkey situations for longer than a few minutes.

Latchkey situations are never ideal, and sometimes they can border on dangerous neglect. One single mother called our "Parent Talk" program to see what we thought of how she was dealing with her schedule. She was working at an assembly plant, and the bosses had transferred her to the graveyard shift. That meant leaving her two children, ages fourteen and ten, home alone through the night until she would get back at 7:30 in the morning.

"I know it's not the best, but it does pay an extra $160 a month, which we really need right now," the mother said to help justify what she was doing. "My fourteen-year-old daughter is very responsible and takes good care of her younger brother."

"I can appreciate your problem, and I know the extra money is tempting," I told this mother. "But I believe you're putting your children in real jeopardy, and you should change the situation as soon as you can. If necessary, find another job." As we completed our call with this mother, we had the distinct feeling she wasn't going to quit her night shift—at least not right away. We could only hope she would think about it and change her mind. Two children, fourteen and ten, should not remain at home alone all night on a regular basis.

The same "Parent Talk" program revealed another case that was even worse. A flight attendant called to say she had a thirteen-year-old son whom she left home alone while she flew three-day schedules that took her out of town. Again, my advice was to get some kind of supervision for the boy. There are just too many things that can go wrong, too many temptations a youngster cannot resist.

With very young children, having some kind of child care is imperative, and the first (and in some cases only) choice is a child-care service or agency such as a preschool. While many of these agencies are staffed by dedicated, hardworking people, they're often so crowded that your child does not get the individual attention he or she might need. I know there are outstanding examples of good preschools here and there throughout the country, but from what I've seen and heard from clients, many of them fall into the category of what I call a "kiddy kennel." I always advise single mothers to try to find something better if at all possible.

The ideal situation, in my opinion, is a private home where a licensed person takes care of no more than three or four children. You don't want to put your child in a private home where a mother is trying to pick up a few extra dollars by frantically trying to keep track of nine, ten, or more kids as they rampage through her three-bedroom house. This is really no better than the kiddy kennel, and in most cases the kiddy kennel would provide better care and better facilities.

Another avenue to explore is getting a grandmotherly person to care for your children in your own home. Some single moms are fortunate enough to have their own mothers who live nearby and are available for regular child care—for example, from when the children get home after school until dinnertime. If that's your situation, thank the Lord and your lucky stars, and let your mother know often how much you appreciate what she's doing for you.

If your own mother is not available, you might look for an older woman who has reared children of her own and is willing to care for young ones simply because she loves kids. This kind of woman has usually been a "giver" all her life and has a track record of sacrificial service to her family. Now, with her children grown and living in other parts of the country, she seldom sees her own grandchildren and has no one to give to.

Finding an older person who is competent, healthy, and tuned in to small children is no easy task. One possible source is a church where a single mom might become involved. There is, of course, always the option of placing an ad in the paper, but be sure to check references carefully.

THE HURRIED CHILDREN OF DIVORCE

In chapter 10, I mentioned how many parents hurry their children into growing up too fast too soon. When divorce hits a family, this hurrying-up process is often accelerated. The strong temptation for the custodial parent—particularly the single mom—is to depend too much on the children for emotional and even physical support.

In the family where husband and wife work together to parent the children, there's always someone for one spouse to talk to, to discuss options with. Husbands and wives can turn to each other for ideas and advice when they're making decisions. The single mom, however, has no other suitable adult to whom to turn. Yes, her parents may be available, but going to parents to ask for advice is usually not something the single mother wants to do—at least, not on a frequent and regular basis. Because she is so alone, it's natural for her to make one or more of her children into a confidant, particularly the firstborn child who is eight or older.

For example, it's easy for Mom to confide in an eight-year-old daughter and tell her about what happens at work, or even to describe what happens on dates if she's seeing another man. Another common problem is finances. Again, it's possible to let a child know too much about pending financial problems or even the possibility of a layoff at work.

All this sharing may make Mom feel better, but it puts her children under tremendous stress. The children may even resent having to listen to her talk about work, men, money, and the many other adult concerns with which she must deal daily.

Also, be aware that separation from their father is no small thing to the children. As David Elkind points out, "Divorce hurries children because it forces them to deal with separations that, in the usual course of events, they would not have to deal with until adolescence or young adulthood."[12]

Elkind goes on to say that the consequences of the absence of the father from the home have come to be understood more fully in the last fifteen years or so. There was a time when the father was not considered that important in the child's upbringing. In recent years, however, the attachment that young children, especially, have to their fathers is much better understood. When Dad moves out of the home, it can cause an emotional overload for the children. As Elkind says, "Parents are the most important people in the world to their children, and separation is a very powerful stressor."[13]

It's important that a single mom not overestimate her children or share too many concerns with them that they simply can't handle or even understand. At the same time, however, I often tell the single mom she should not try to play the role of Supermom, never even letting her children know she's tired or has had a hard week at work.

Many single mothers feel guilt-ridden. They feel as if they have to be strong and never show any sign of weakness. I believe that's a serious mistake. There's nothing wrong with letting your children know when you've had a bad day at work, when you're not feeling well, or when you're concerned about a certain choice you have to make. Your children can profit from giving you comfort.

Remember, if you want your child to talk with you, you need to talk with your child. How much you say is always a judgment call, and it's the old story of the need for balance. Just don't make sharing your weaknesses a daily occurrence or a constant barrage.

You want to do all you can to shield the children from the nastier elements of the divorce, but in a sense, reality will dictate that they grow up a little faster than you would have liked. They will have to be "hurried" in their process of growing up. The divorce is final. The home they had before is gone. Life has kicked your children in the teeth, and they must deal with that.

By giving your children small tastes of dealing with the stresses you face, you can help strengthen their psychological muscles. The trick is to not pour on too much. Every home is different, and every family is different. The key is balance. Don't dump everything on the children, but if you have those moments when you're teary and anxious or exhausted, and you let your kids know it, don't feel guilty. Children are certainly not invulnerable, but they're not made of china, either.

What's important is to always help your children feel you're there for them and you aren't going anywhere.

Suppose, for example, Tom and Mary break up and the divorce is final. Little Ryan, age ten, goes to a private school not far from their nice home in the suburbs. Every morning, he was able to get a ride with one of his parents in their comfortable car.

Now the divorce makes it necessary to move to an apartment nearer town, and Ryan has to ride to public school on the bus. But Ryan's problems are only beginning. Because he's the new kid on the block, the class bullies pick on him, and he comes home with a bloody nose. Mom comes home from work to find Ryan crying, and she sits down for a talk.

"Honey, I'm sorry the divorce happened, and I'm sorry we had to move here and that you have to ride the bus, and that school isn't much fun right now," Mom says. "But it's going to be okay, I promise you."

Quietly, without telling Ryan, Mom calls the school and gets the principal on the line. He assures her he will pass the word along to the bullies who have beaten up her son and let them know this kind of thing will not be tolerated. The boys do back off, although they still tend to tease Ryan whenever they can. Three months after transferring to the school, Ryan makes several new friends, including one of the bullies, who has decided, *He isn't such a bad kid after all.*

The point to this little story is that even though reality has a way of looking hopeless at the moment, *reality always has a way of working out.* What a single mom has to do is have faith—in herself, in her children, and as I've said elsewhere, in God.

In this chapter, we have only touched on what I meant when I said the single mom has the toughest job in the world. Many single mothers feel as if they're adrift on the sea of life, the barometer is dropping, and the compass has gone haywire. Their good ship *Family* is about to be swamped, and the single mom cries out, "Why doesn't the captain *do* something?" Then she realizes, "Wait a minute—*I'm* the captain."

That is the moment of truth. The single mom takes the helm, steadies the ship, and chooses a port o' call for her and her children. The voyage will be hard, but with Reality Discipline, she and her crew will make port.

Don't Forget . . .

- Stress is the constant and dangerous enemy, particularly for the single mom. She must conserve her energy when at all possible.
- Sometimes the single mom must put herself first for the good of the family.
- Make it a point to schedule some time for yourself, even if it has to be brief.
- Single moms do not need flaw-pickers, and you should try to avoid them if at all possible.
- Helping others can take the focus off your own problems and give you energy you didn't think you had.
- Getting upset by an ex-husband who continues to be unreasonable is a waste of energy.
- If you have custody of your children, don't cut your ex-husband off, but also try to avoid triangles. As much as possible, stay out of problems he has with the children.
- Forgive your ex-husband, but remember what caused the divorce. Don't put demands on him that he cannot fulfill.
- Regarding relationships with men and possible remarriage, the cardinal rule is to take your time, swim in safe waters, and give "dull" men a second look. Many happily married women thought their husbands were dull on first sight, but they later changed their minds when they got to know them.
- Avoid "shoulding on" your children—they have enough to cope with as it is.
- Following a divorce, it's best for your children if you keep everything as much the same as possible.
- Do everything in your power to avoid asking your child to become a latchkey kid. If you have no choice, do all you can to prepare your child for emergencies and to let your child know you care.

- Try to find a balance between telling your child too much about your adult problems and letting him or her know you're not perfect or invincible, you do get tired, and you do need your child's support.
- If you want your child to talk with you, you must talk with your child.
- No matter how difficult or even impossible a situation may seem at this time, remember that reality always has a way of working out.
- You are captain of your family's ship. You *can* and *will* make it.

And Why Not Try . . .

- Analyze the amount of stress you feel you're under. List some ways you can try to preserve your adaptation energy.
- List some ways you can try to "put yourself first," with the goal of being able to give more to your children in the long run.
- If you have no time for yourself, consider getting up an hour early, before the children are up, to do things you enjoy.
- If you lack energy, set aside time for exercise. Ironically, exercise will *increase* your energy.
- Postpone making new male friends, but get in touch with women who can give you a listening ear. If you've been neglecting such friendships, contact someone for lunch this week.
- If possible, try helping someone who is less fortunate than you are. It can become a morale and energy booster.
- If your ex-husband is constantly inconsiderate and unreasonable, try writing him a letter to tell him how you feel.
- In developing any new relationships with men, keep the questions on page 301 in mind, and ask them often in different ways. Don't write off a man because he appears to

be dull upon first contact. Give a mature relationship a chance to develop.

- Talk with your children about how they're doing. Keep in mind that in a real sense, they are "divorced," too. If they feel you're demanding too much, what can you change to make them feel better?

- Take a few quiet minutes each day to be with God. Pour your heart out to Him, and let His love surround, encourage, and strengthen you.

There's Just One More Thing

W E HAVE SPENT THIRTEEN CHAPTERS LOOKING AT HOW THE PRINCIPLES of Reality Discipline can hold your family together when the world seems to be falling apart around you. If you're a firstborn or only child, you probably have all ten principles memorized. (Other, less-achievement-oriented birth orders can review the ten principles on p. 320.) All ten are important, but there is one I believe is most important of all, and I want to tell you one final story to show you why.

As usual, we were spending the summer near Chautauqua Lake in western New York State. It was around noon, and because nobody wanted to fix any lunch, I was nominated to go across the lake to a restaurant to pick up something to go for the children. As I was waiting for the order, a man stepped into the dining-room area and yelled, "Is there a Leman back here?"

With a knee-jerk reaction I raised my hand, and the man said, "Telephone."

It was Krissy, who said frantically, "Dad, Dad—do you know where you're supposed to be right now?"

"Krissy, you know where I am—I'm here at the restaurant, trying to get everybody's food. Your order's almost ready, and I'll be back in a few minutes. Why are you calling me?"

"Dad, you didn't quite hear what I said. Do you know where you're *supposed* to be *right now?*"

"Krissy, I don't know what you're talking about."

"You're supposed to be at the Holiday Inn to speak to this luncheon. The man on the phone said it's a 'standing room only' crowd, and he wants to know where you are and if you're coming."

"Oh, no," I groaned. I had forgotten completely!

"Dad," Krissy's voice broke into my thoughts, "Dad, you're supposed to call this attorney right away."

"Attorney? I miss a speaking appointment, and already they've got an attorney?"

Krissy gave me the number, and as I dialed, the thought kept occurring: *This is silly. How can they be suing me? They haven't paid me yet.*

An attorney did come to the phone, and it turned out he was the man who had arranged the speaking engagement with me.

"Where are you?" he said. "We're all waiting to hear you speak."

"I can't believe it," I stammered. "I can't believe it, but I completely forgot. I can't believe I did it, but I did it."

"Well, could you come right over?" he wanted to know.

"Well, I'm in grubby shorts, a T-shirt, tennis shoes, and an Arizona Wildcats baseball cap. I guess I could come. It won't embarrass me if it won't embarrass you."

But as we talked about it, we realized it just wouldn't work. My to-go orders weren't quite ready, and I had to take them back across the lake and over the bridge to the cottage, then turn around and try to get to the Holiday Inn. We both decided that by then the crowd would be just too restless, with people having to get back to work and to other appointments.

We ended up scrubbing the whole thing. I apologized profusely to the attorney. He said not to worry about it because it happens to everyone. I picked up the food to go and went back to the cottage, where I was razzed by my teenagers for getting too old to remember where I was supposed to be and when I was supposed to be there.

Now for part two of the story—the much more interesting part.

It's one week later, and we're trying to get Holly to the Buffalo airport because she's going home to Arizona early from her summer vacation at Chautauqua Lake. All of us are making the trip out to the airport to say good-bye, and so we face the logistical challenge of getting six people up—one of whom is a three-year-old—getting dressed, using bathrooms, gulping down breakfast, and getting loaded into the car.

I was playing my part. My role as the father in the family has always been to be out in the car before everyone else and then frantically beep the horn to let the rest of the family know they're late. This has always been one of my functions in life, and I have performed it to perfection!

And so I was out there in the car, doing what I was supposed to be doing, but the family wasn't cooperating, because they just didn't come.

Finally, as the clock ticked ever closer to take-off hour for Holly's plane, they straggled out. Sande was first, coffee cup and three-year-old Hannah in hand. Next, Krissy swaggered down the path, wearing her ever-present Walkman headphones. Kevin followed, carrying several magic tricks to amuse himself as well as anyone else who would pay attention. Last to appear was Holly, as bleary-eyed as her mother, pulling her suitcase as if it weighed four hundred pounds.

"Holly, you're going to miss your plane," I reminded her crossly. I must admit, I wasn't in a real good mood. We finally got everybody in the car and buckled up, and off we went, headed for the Buffalo airport some eighty-five miles away.

As I glanced at my watch, I could see we barely had enough time to get there. I had made the run many times to catch planes of my own, and I could see we were already past "cutting it close." At an intersection about eighteen miles from our cottage, I heard a voice from the backseat. It was Holly, and I thought she was say-ing, "Dad, I forgot my purse."

"You what?" Then I added, "Don't worry about your purse. I'll send you your purse in the overnight mail."

"But Dad . . ."

"What?"

"It's got my keys in it."

"What keys?"

"The keys to the car in Tucson."

"Do you have keys for the car she's going to be using back in Tucson?" I asked Sande, who was sitting beside me in the front seat.

Sande shook her head no, and that did it. Now I was really upset, because we would have to turn around and go back and get those keys. Holly would miss her plane for sure. At this point, I was not the confident psychologist who loves to charm people with his humor doing talk shows. I was a frustrated father whose family had been poky getting ready to leave, and now it looked as if my daughter would miss her plane. And she had a nonrefund-able ticket to boot!

I'm afraid I started talking a little loudly. I suppose some people would say it was more like screaming and yelling.

"Holly, how can you be seventeen years old and be so irrespon-sible? You can drive a car, but you can't remember your purse?"

I was really ripping into Holly as I made a quick U-turn and roared back toward the cottage, thinking at the same time, *How can I shortcut this? How can I save some time?*

I spotted a phone booth at a gas station and pulled up in a cloud of dust, stopped the car, and called the cottage. My cousin Gordy was there, and almost shouting, I asked, "Gordy, do you see a purse anywhere there? Holly's purse."

"A little, round one?" Gordy wanted to know.

"That's it! Grab it, get in your car, and drive as fast as you can up the lake road. I'll meet you about halfway."

I didn't even bother to say good-bye. I hung up the phone, jumped back in the car, and started driving down the lake road toward the cottage. Meanwhile, Gordy jumped in his car and came up the lake road in my direction. I spotted him coming and flashed my lights so he would be sure to spot me.

We stopped side by side and didn't even get out of the car. He simply handed me the purse as if it were the commercial where somebody had asked for a jar of Grey Poupon. I flipped another U-turn and roared back down the lake road. But now I was really unhinged.

"I can't believe this. Holly, you're going to miss your plane. Do you know what kind of ticket you've got? You've got the kind that can't be changed. You have to fly today. If you miss this plane, you have to take a later one and wait around two hours for the next one. That will make you late for your connection out of Chicago to Tucson, and you're going to have to spend a night in Chicago alone."

I was pouring it on, making it sound just as bad as I could to let my daughter know she had really caused a big problem. Sande sat quietly, never saying boo. But I knew what she was thinking: *Bury yourself, sucker, all the deeper. Just keep digging your own grave.*

But I kept ripping away at Holly, criticizing her and wondering how she could be so irresponsible. After a few miles, I could hear sobbing from the backseat. She was in tears, and in less than a minute I felt like a total schmuck. The guilties rolled over me, and then came the clincher. "At least"—Holly sniffed—"at least I don't forget *luncheons!*"

I remember realizing, *Oh, she got you, Leman. She got you good!*

Cut off at the knees, I started thinking, maybe for the first time that morning, *What are you doing? Why are you saying all these things? Why are you beating up on your daughter emotionally when she feels bad enough already?*

Suddenly my concerns with moving fast, getting there quickly, and making the plane vanished. I put on the brakes, looking for a

318 • KEEPING YOUR FAMILY TOGETHER

place to pull over. I didn't care if we missed the plane anymore. The car was stopping because there was something I had to do. I stopped the car, went around, and opened the back door on Holly's side. Gently I pulled her out of the car, stood her up, and hugged her tightly, saying, "Holly, I am so sorry, honey. Can you forgive me?"

Holly, with her big, brown eyes still filled with tears, looked up at me and said, "No, Daddy, I'm the one who should be sorry."

"No, honey. It's okay. I am sorry. It was Daddy's mistake because I made a mountain out of a molehill."

Finally we managed to get back into the car and proceeded at a more normal speed to the airport. At least three more times, Holly said from the backseat, "Daddy, I'm sorry." At least three more times, I told her it was okay, that I was sorry, that I was the one who had blown it and needed forgiveness.

As fortuitous fate would have it, the plane was late taking off. Holly made the plane, and the Leman family returned to their cottage at Chautauqua Lake.

Dr. Leman drove much more slowly on the trip back, because he had a lot to think about. Mrs. Leman, who is not only smarter but wiser, said nothing. She had seen Dr. Leman dig his own grave before, and she knew words were not necessary.

As I contemplated what had happened, I realized I had really blown it. As the kids would say, I had blown it "big time." Of course, the irony of the situation was not lost on me. Here was Dr. Leman, the Reality Discipline specialist who believes in holding children accountable for their actions and helping them learn from their experience. I'd held Holly accountable, all right, but what about treating her as a person and not a thing?

Some role model you are, Leman, I told myself. *You lecture your daughter about being responsible, and she nails you with your own irresponsibility.*

And then Reality Discipline Principle No. 4 crept into the back of my mind. What was that about balancing responsibility with forgiveness and love? That's what must always be done, or Reality Discipline becomes so much noise beating on everyone's ears and meaning nothing. As the apostle Paul put it so eloquently in 1 Corinthians 13:1, "If I speak in the tongues of men and of angels, but have not love, I am only a resounding gong or a clanging cymbal."

It's not easy to tell you this story, because obviously it doesn't make me look good. But I tell the story anyway, because I don't want anyone to put this book down thinking he or she can use Reality Discipline to become the perfect spouse and parent in ten easy principles. You will blow it, too, maybe not as "big time" as I did, but we all blow it because we're all human. The real strides we make with our spouse or our children happen when we're humble enough to say, "Honey, I'm sorry. I was wrong. Will you forgive me?"

One of the classic Christmas films of all time is *It's a Wonderful Life*, starring Jimmy Stewart as George Bailey, a small-town banker. While the story in the film happens during the Christmas season, its message is good all year long. At the end of the film, the townspeople gather in George's living room to rescue him from financial ruin. George's brother, who has come a great distance from out of town to help, raises a toast and says, "To my brother, George, the richest man alive!"

How could George Bailey be rich? Less than an hour before, he had stood at the railing of a bridge contemplating suicide. But George *was* rich, and not because people came forward to put whatever they could in the pot. He was rich because he had family and friends who loved him and cared for him.

That is what Reality Discipline is all about. It's not a list of rules to obey. It's a way of living that will make the difference in the daily headaches and hassles of life, and above all, it will make a difference way down the line, when your children are grown and have kids of their own.

When they're grown, will you think back to what you should

have done differently? Will you wish you could turn back the clock and the calendar to relive part of your life? As Harry Chapin's song puts it, they do grow up, just like us, and what we sow we always reap.

As I said way back in the beginning, Reality Discipline seems almost too simple. But why not try it? You have nothing to lose but some bad habits, and you have only your family's success and security, along with their love and respect, to gain.

The Ten Principles of Reality Discipline

1. The whole is always more important than the parts.
2. Have values, and live by them.
3. Always put your spouse (not the kids) first. (For single moms, sometimes put yourself first.)
4. Balance responsibility with forgiveness and love.
5. Stick to your guns.
6. Keep responsibility where it belongs.
7. Treat people like persons, not things.
8. Use guidance, not force; action, not just words.
9. Be consistent, decisive, and respectful of your children as persons.
10. Hold your children accountable for their actions, and help them learn from experience.

Worthwhile Reading

———●———

Robert Hemfelt, Frank Minirth, Paul Meier, *Love Is a Choice: Recovery or Co-dependent Relationships* (Nashville: Thomas Nelson, 1980). A very readable explanation of co-dependency and dysfunctionalism, with many practical illustrations and suggestions of what to do if you have been in this kind of family.

M. Scott Peck, *The Road Less Traveled* (New York: Simon and Schuster, a Touchstone Book, 1978). Excellent insights into what Reality Discipline is all about. Profound, but still easy to read for the most part.

Dr. Kevin Leman, *Making Children Mind Without Losing Yours* (New York: Dell Publishing, 1984). A comprehensive application of Reality Discipline to childrearing, with dozens of specific examples of what to do in certain situations.

Dr. Kevin Leman, *Bonkers: Why Women Get Stressed Out and What They Can Do About It* (New York: Dell Publishing, 1987). Practical help for any woman who is feeling burned out from mother-stress or any other kind of stress in her life.

Dr. Kevin Leman, *Sex Begins in the Kitchen* (New York: Dell Publishing, revised 1992). Practical advice on putting intimacy into your marriage by working at it all day, not squeezing it in after the late news and before Jay Leno.

Dr. Kevin Leman, *The Pleasers: Women Who Can't Say No and the Men Who Control Them* (New York: Dell Publishing, 1988). Candid advice to the woman who is killing herself trying to make things right for others and hoping everyone will always like her. Specific help on how to move toward becoming a "positive pleaser."

Dr. Kevin Leman, *Were You Born for Each Other?* (New York: Delacorte Press, 1991). Using practical knowledge of birth order to find, catch, and keep the love of your life.

Dr. Willard F. Harley, Jr., *His Needs, Her Needs* (Old Tappan, N.J.: Fleming H. Revell Company, 1986). A commonsense discussion of the five most important needs in men and the five most important needs in women. Practical advice on how to affair-proof your marriage and build a happier relationship with your spouse. One of the best books on marriage in print today.

Linda Albert, *Linda Albert's Advice for Coping with Kids* (New York: E. P. Dutton, Inc., 1982). By the director of the Family Education Center of Florida, who is trained in Adlerian psychology and believes in using Reality Discipline with children. Loaded with many practical examples of what to do in various situations.

Dr. Kevin Leman, *Smart Kids, Stupid Choices* (New York: Dell Publishing, revised 1992). A survival guide for parents of teenagers. Practical help for the problems of the nineties: drugs, sex, venereal disease, teenage pregnancy, peer pressure, and much more.

David Elkind, *The Hurried Child: Growing Up Too Fast Too Soon* (Reading, Mass.: Addison-Wesley Publishing Co., Inc., 1988). The best book available on how parents are making the serious error of overestimating their children's competence and ability. After reading this book, you will have new insights on how to let your kid be a kid.

Kathleen McCoy, *Coping with Single Parenting, Your Essential Guide: How to Find the Balance Between Parenthood and Personhood* (New York: A Signet Book, New American Library: first Signet printing 1988). A gold mine of help for the single mom or dad, but with emphasis on single motherhood. The author talked with over one hundred solo parents as well as dozens of professionals to put together sound, supportive strategies for being a loving single parent. Also includes dozens of names, addresses, and phone numbers of counseling services, hot lines, and other supportive organizations for single parents.

Nicky Marone, *How to Father a Successful Daughter* (New York: Fawcett Press Books, published by Ballantine Books, 1988). A junior high teacher's step-by-compassionate-step guide for fathers who want to give their daughters good self-esteem and the confidence they need to be in the real world.

Keith W. Sehnert, *Stress/Unstress: How You Can Control Stress at Home and on the Job* (Minneapolis: Augsburg Publishing House, 1981). A practical and readable explanation of what stress is and how to deal with it by a disciple of Dr. Hans Selye, the man who made *stress* a common word in today's vocabulary.

Dr. James Dobson, *What Wives Wish Their Husbands Knew About Women* (Wheaton, Ill.: Tyndale House Publishers, 1977).

Robert Hemfelt, Frank Minirth, Paul Meier, *Passages of Marriage* (Nashville: Thomas Nelson, 1991).

Robert Hemfelt, Frank Minirth, Paul Meier, *Love Hunger* (Nashville: Thomas Nelson, 1990).

Melody Beattie, *Codependent No More* (San Francisco: Harper & Row Publishers, 1987).

Gary Smalley, John Trent, *The Blessing* (Nashville: Thomas Nelson, 1987).

William Backus, Marie Chapian, *Telling Yourself the Truth* (Minneapolis: Bethany House Publishers, 1980).

Ross Campbell, *How to Really Love Your Teenager* (Wheaton, Ill.: Victor Books, 1981).

Ross Campbell, *How to Really Love Your Child* (Wheaton, Ill.: Victor Books, 1977).

Zig Ziglar, *Raising Positive Kids in a Negative World* (Nashville: Oliver-Nelson, 1985).

John Rosemond, *Six-Point Plan for Raising Happy, Healthy Children* (Kansas City, Mo.: Andrews and McMeel, 1989).

Notes

Chapter 1

1. Robert Hemfelt, Frank Minirth, and Paul Meier, *Love Is a Choice* (Nashville: Thomas Nelson, 1989), p. 11.
2. Ibid., p. 12.
3. Art Levine, "Lifestyle: Having It All," *U.S. News & World Report*, December 25, 1989/January 1, 1990, p. 113.
4. Quoted by Barry Bearak, "Searching for the Soul of a Decade," *The Los Angeles Times*, December 18, 1989, p. A15.
5. Urie Bronfenbrenner, "The Calamitous Decline of the American Family," *The Washington Post*, January 2, 1977.
6. Quoted in *Ethology*, publication of resources for members of the Washington Evolutionary Systems Society.
7. Ann Landers, "A Tough Time for All Teens," *The Los Angeles Times*, December 15, 1989, p. E29. Permission granted by Ann Landers and Creators Syndicate.
8. "Kids Who Kill," *U.S. News & World Report*, April 8, 1991, p. 26.
9. "On the Home Front," *U.S. News & World Report*, December 25, 1989/January 1, 1990, p. 80.
10. Scott Peck, *The Road Less Traveled* (New York: Simon and Schuster, 1978), p. 16.

Chapter 2

1. Kevin Leman, *Making Children Mind Without Losing Yours* (New York: Dell Publishing, 1987), p. 9.
2. Rudolph Dreikurs did a great deal of pioneer work on the effects of logical consequences on human behavior, particularly in rearing children. See, for example, Rudolph Dreikurs, *Coping with Children's Misbehavior* (New York: Hawthorn Books, 1972).
3. Galatians 6:7.

Chapter 3

1. Charles Hummel, *The Tyranny of the Urgent* (Downers Grove, Ill.: InterVarsity Press, 1971), p. 4.
2. Kevin Leman, *Bonkers: Why Women Get Stressed Out and What They Can Do About It* (New York: Dell Publishing, 1990).
3. Mary Ellen Schoonmaker, "The New Decade: What's in Your Future?" *Family Circle*, January 9, 1990, p. 42.
4. *The Gallup Poll News Service*, vol. 54, no. 37, February 5, 1990. Used by permission.
5. Sarah Rimer, "Sequencers: Putting Careers on Hold," *The New York Times*, September 23, 1988, p. A21.
6. Felice Schwartz, "Management Women and the New Facts of Life," *Harvard Business Review*, January-February 1989, p. 65.

7. Paul J. Rosch, M.D., president, American Institute of Stress, in a letter to *The New York Times*, December 12, 1986.
8. Jim Schachter, "The Daddy Track," *The Los Angeles Times Magazine*, October 1, 1989, p. 16.
9. Ibid.

Chapter 4
1. See, for example, the work of Dr. Irenaus Eibl-Eibesfeldt, *Love and Hate: The Natural History of Behavior Patterns* (New York: Holt, Rinehart and Winston, 1972). According to Dr. Eibl-Eibesfeldt, the human child first acquires the capacity to love another through love from its mother.
2. William A. Westley and Nathan B. Epstein, *The Silent Majority* (San Francisco: Jossey-Bass, 1969).
3. John Bradshaw, *Bradshaw On: The Family* (Deerfield Beach, Fla.: Health Communications, 1988), p. 1.
4. H. Norman Wright, *Always Daddy's Girl* (Ventura, Calif.: Regal Books, 1989), p. 10.

Chapter 5
1. "A Time to Seek," *Newsweek*, December 17, 1990, p. 51. Source of statistics: Wade Clark Roof, David A. Roozen.
2. Ibid.
3. David Augsburger, *Caring Enough to Confront* (Ventura, Calif.: Regal Books, 1973), p. 8.

Chapter 6
1. Willard F. Harley, Jr., *His Needs, Her Needs* (Old Tappan, N.J.: Fleming H. Revell Company, 1986), p. 31.
2. Ibid., p. 29.
3. Kevin Leman, *Sex Begins in the Kitchen* (New York: Dell Publishing, 1992), p. 9.

Chapter 7
1. Author unknown.
2. Willard F. Harley, Jr., *His Needs, Her Needs* (Old Tappan, N.J.: Fleming H. Revell Company, 1986), chapter 2.
3. Trish Hall, "Breaking Up Is Becoming Harder to Do," *The New York Times*, March 14, 1991, p. C1.
4. Quoted in Victoria Sackett, "Couples Discovering Marriages Can Be Saved," *USA Today*, April 2, 1991, p. A13.
5. Harley, *His Needs, Her Needs*, p. 70.

Chapter 8
1. U.S. Senate Judiciary Committee, Subcommittee on Juvenile Justice, "Effect of Pornography on Women and Children," 98th cong., 2nd sess., 1984, p. 227.
2. Victor B. Cline, "Correlating Adolescent and Adult Exposure to Sexually Explicit Material and Sexual Behavior," University of Utah, Department of Psychology, National Conference on HIV: Human Immunodeficiency Virus.
3. "Scientific Evidence Shows Pornography Is Harmful," *Focus on the Family Citizen*, June 1989.
4. National Coalition on Television Violence, "Rapes by Young Males Increase," reported in *A.F.A. Journal*, February 1990, p. 9.
5. *The Chronicle of Higher Education*, 35 (September 1, 1988).
6. Deirdre Carmody, "Increasing Rapes on Campus Spur Colleges to Fight Back," *The New York Times*, January 1, 1989, p. 1.
7. *Parade Magazine*, September 27, 1987, p. 4. Also, "Scientific Evidence Shows Pornography Is Harmful," *Focus on the Family Citizen*, June 1989.
8. "Your Jacket or Your Life," *U.S. News & World Report*, February 26, 1990, p. 14.

9. Ron Harris, "Children Who Dress for Excess," *The Los Angeles Times*, November 12, 1989, p. A1.
10. James Calano and Jeff Salzman, *Real World 101* (New York: Warner Books, 1982), p. 57.
11. J. Neusner, quoted in Malcolm Stevenson Forbes, Jr., "As Undergraduates Recommence Their Efforts," *Forbes Magazine*, October 26, 1981.
12. Ephesians 6:4.

Chapter 9
1. Proverbs 22:6.

Chapter 10
1. Quoted in Charles Colson, "The Secularization of America," *Discipleship Journal* 38 (1987), p. 41.
2. David G. Savage, "High School Test Cheating: 75% Admit It, Cite Pressure," *The Los Angeles Times*, April 17, 1986, p. 3; and "Cheating: Just Part of the Game," *San Diego Tribune*, November 24, 1987, p. 1 of "The Scene" section.
3. Steven Muller in *U.S. News & World Report*, November 10, 1980, pp. 57-58.
4. Douglas Kreutz, "A Giant Step: Pacheco Rises to UA Challenge," *The Arizona Daily Star*, April 7, 1991, p. B1.
5. Josh McDowell, *How to Be a Hero to Your Kids* (Dallas: Word Books, 1991), especially chapter 13.
6. Nicky Marone, *How to Father a Successful Daughter* (New York: Fawcett Crest Books, 1988), p. 6.
7. Ibid.
8. Ibid., p. 7.
9. "American Teens Speak: Sex, Myth, TV, and Birth Control," The Planned Parenthood Poll, Louis Harris and Associates, September/October 1986, p. E15.
10. Warren E. Leary, *The New York Times*, February 9, 1989.
11. David Elkind, *The Hurried Child*, rev. ed. (Reading, Mass.: Addison-Wesley, 1988), p. xi.
12. Ibid., p. xiii.
13. Ibid., p. 33.
14. Ibid., p. 36.

Chapter 11
1. Josh McDowell, *Research Almanac and Statistical Digest*, 1990, p. 118.
2. *USA Today*, October 18, 1989, p. D5.
3. Cited in *AFA Journal* (October 1989).
4. David Elkind, *The Hurried Child*, rev. ed. (Reading, Mass.: Addison-Wesley, 1988), p. 157.
5. Carol J. Castaneda, "Facing a Teen Fact of Life," *USA Today*, November 9, 1990, p. A3.
6. Elkind, *The Hurried Child*, p. 137.
7. James Dobson, *The Strong-Willed Child* (Wheaton, Ill.: Tyndale House Publishers, 1978), p. 204.
8. Marilyn Elias, "Bridging the Teen Communication Gap," *USA Today*, March 13, 1991, p. 40.
9. Kevin Leman and Randy Carlson, *Unlocking the Secrets of Your Childhood Memories* (Nashville: Thomas Nelson, 1989), p. 11.

Chapter 12
1. Susan Figliulo, "The Many Reasons Children Turn to Drugs," *The Buffalo News*, September 4, 1990.
2. "Worth Imitating. . .," *Dads Only Newsletter* 92, Paul Lewis, ed., 1992, p.1.
3. Vicki Torres, "Documents Tell Details of Murders," *Los Angeles Times*, March 27, 1991, p. B1.

Chapter 13
1. David Elkind, *The Hurried Child*, rev. ed. (Reading, Mass.: Addison-Wesley, 1988), p. 42.
2. Ibid.
3. Kevin Leman, *Bonkers: Why Women Get Stressed Out and What They Can Do About It* (New York: Dell Publishing, 1990).

4. Elkind, *The Hurried Child*, p. 143.
5. Hans Selye, *The Stress of Life* (New York: McGraw-Hill, 1956).
6. Selye coined *stressor* to explain what he called the "causative agent" of stress. See Selye, *The Stress of Life*, p. 51.
7. Selye, *The Stress of Life*, chapters 3 and 8.
8. These are Jesus' words in Acts 20:35.
9. See Keith Sehnert, *Stress/Unstress* (Minneapolis: Augsburg Publishing House, 1981), pp. 28-30.
10. Luke 6:31.
11. Kevin Leman, *The Pleasers: Women Who Can't Say No and the Men Who Control Them* (New York: Dell, 1988).
12. Elkind, *The Hurried Child*, p. 152.
13. Ibid., p. 155.

For information on Dr. Leman's books, tapes, seminars, or radio program, you can contact his office at the following address and phone numbers:

7355 N. Oracle Road
Suite 205
Tucson, AZ 85704

(602) 797-3830
(602) 797-3809 (fax)